PRAISE FOR

POSITIVE DISCIPLINE FOR TODAY'S BUSY
(AND OVERWHELMED) PARENT

"As a parent of a toddler, as a business owner, as a woman-on-the-go—this book provides the necessary blueprint for raising a well-rounded child and creating a more peaceful home."

—Rachel Paige Goldstein, founder of Agent of Change events

"Every parent needs to own *Positive Discipline for Today's Busy (and Overwhelmed) Parent.* An honest read that will make you feel like you are not alone. This book will give you the tools you need to parent better in the modern world and will build your confidence as a parent."

—Lyss Stern, CEO of Divamoms.com, bestselling author, and mom of three

"I'm so grateful to Positive Discipline for reminding everyone how important it is to be kind AND firm when parenting. These practices help me raise self-reliant problem solvers—and I know they will help you too. Joy is one of Positive Discipline's leading disciples, and this book is an invaluable parenting and coaching tool."

—Kristen Glosserman, Life Coach and mother of four

"Now, more than ever, it is critical that parents impart in their children an intrinsic and upbeat tool kit for self-discipline, empathy, and developing character. *Positive Discipline for Today's Busy (and Overwhelmed) Parent* is a compassionate, practical, and psychologically grounded guide for parents who are eager to stay connected to their children in real life, helping them face life challenges with self-control and optimism."

—Dr. Catherine Steiner-Adair, author of *The Big Disconnect: Protecting Childhood and Family Relationships in the Digital Age*

"As a progressive educator, school leader, and parent of twin boys, I find Nelsen, Bill, and Marchese's advice to be as timeless as it is timely, as profound as it is simple, and as inspiring as it is instructive. The authors give us permission to humanize both ourselves and our children, and they remind us that effective parenting involves being with rather than doing to our kids."

—Jed Lippard, EDD, dean of Children's Programs and head of the School for Children at Bank Street College of Education

POSITIVE DISCIPLINE FOR TODAY'S BUSY (AND OVERWHELMED) PARENT

...TIVE DISCIPLINE FOR TODAY'S BUSY (AND OVERWHELMED) PARENT

HOW TO BALANCE WORK, PARENTING, AND SELF FOR LASTING WELL-BEING

JANE NELSEN, EdD, KRISTINA BILL, AND JOY MARCHESE

HARMONY

BOOKS · NEW YORK

Published in the United States by Harmony Books, an imprint of the Crown
Publishing Group, a division of Penguin Random House LLC, New York.
harmonybooks.com

Harmony Books is a registered trademark, and the Circle colophon is a trademark
of Penguin Random House LLC.

Library of Congress Cataloging-in-Publication Data
Names: Nelsen, Jane, author. | Bill, Kristina, author. | Marchese, Joy, author.
Title: Positive discipline for today's busy (and overwhelmed) parent :
how to balance work, parenting, and self for lasting well-being /
Jane Nelsen, Ed.D., Kristina Bill, Joy Marchese.
Description: New York : Harmony, 2018.
Identifiers: LCCN 2018021057 | ISBN 9780525574897 (paperback) |
ISBN 9780525574903 (ebook)
Subjects: LCSH: Parenting. | Child rearing. | Self-reliance in children. | Families.
| BISAC: FAMILY & RELATIONSHIPS / Parenting / General. | FAMILY &
RELATIONSHIPS / Reference. | FAMILY & RELATIONSHIPS /
Conflict Resolution.
Classification: LCC HQ755.8 .N4524 2018 | DDC 649/.1—dc23
LC record available at https://lccn.loc.gov/2018021057

ISBN 978-0-525-57489-7
Ebook ISBN 978-0-525-57490-3

Printed in the United States of America

Cover design by Jessie Sayward Bright

10 9 8 7 6 5 4 3 2 1

First Edition

To the many parents all over the world who have told me how much the Positive Discipline books have changed your life. You keep gratitude flowing in my heart. (Jane Nelsen)

To my beautiful baby girl, Chloe Eloise Skye, who was born alongside this book. You are and will always be my greatest teacher. (Joy Marchese)

To Matthew, you are the love of my life. (Kristina Bill)

CONTENTS

CONTENTS

POSITIVE DISCIPLINE FOR TODAY'S BUSY (AND OVERWHELMED) PARENT

INTRODUCTION

IS POSITIVE DISCIPLINE FOR YOU, OR FOR YOUR CHILD?

This is not a trick question, and the answer is crucial to your understanding and success with Positive Discipline. The answer is both. However, you will be more successful if you understand that it is for *you first*.

Many parents have discovered this truth on their own. We can't count the number of times we have heard, "I thought Positive Discipline would help me change my child, and it did; but I learned that it is more about me first. This philosophy has changed my life as I learned that I needed to make some changes myself. I now find more joy in parenting because of the skills I have learned."

So, exactly what does it mean to say "you first"?

Positive Discipline is based on universal principles of living that include connection and encouragement to increase belonging and significance (the primary goal of all people); social interest that includes contribution in the family, classroom, workplace, and community; the development of compassion through understanding the beliefs behind behaviors; motivation through kindness and firmness; skill development (not just for children, but also for adults); self-regulation (learning to control your own behavior before expecting children to control theirs); focusing on solutions; and last but not least the joy of seeing mistakes as opportunities to learn.

All Positive Discipline tools are based on these principles, and principles can be used in many different ways. When you understand and live the principles behind each tool, take them into your heart, and add the words and actions that come from your wisdom, they will be sincere and unique. If you don't understand and live the principles, the tools often sound like empty techniques— and children are not impressed. If you are not developing these attributes in your own life, how can you expect to teach them to children?

If you choose "children first," what does this mean? You might use Positive Discipline tools to try to change children without incorporating the same tools in your own life. You will not model what you are trying to teach, and will then wonder why it isn't effective. If this is the case, you are unlikely to understand the importance of making a connection before correction. You may fall into the trap of wanting to make kids "pay" for what they have done in the past, instead of valuing mistakes and helping them learn and focus on solutions. You may try to disguise punishments (which are not part of Positive Discipline) by calling them "logical consequences." You may continue to use praise and rewards because children like them and they "work"—in the short term. We know that at times the short-term option seems the most doable, especially when you're overworked, overtired, and overstressed. But in this book we'll give you the Positive Discipline tools (backed by the latest research in neuroscience) to help you motivate yourself and your children to make wiser choices with proven long-term benefits.

Let's now widen the lens and take a look at dynamics impacting our ability to balance work, parenting, and self-care.

THE CULTURE WE'RE IN

Family dynamics have changed considerably in the last few decades, especially in relation to women working professionally outside the home and men participating more in child-rearing. This is a big shift from historical and more traditional families with a stay-at-home mother (most of the time) who did the majority of the child-rearing and housework, while the father worked outside the home. Additionally, extended family was often close by to help and participate, which may not be the case for today's global nomads. This dynamic shift has considerable impact on effective parenting and work choices. Most parents today need to juggle professional obligations and parenting, often to the detriment of their own well-being. Many believe they have to reach perfection in every endeavor. Since this is impossible, too many are suffering from anxiety or exhaustion, feel overwhelmed, and/or are experiencing depression. Finding a way to manage it all is essential to our overall well-being.

There are three major parenting-related stressors that are on the rise in our society:

- *Lack of time.* The number of external demands and obligations placed on both parents and children that eat up the time available for parenting, family time, and self-care.

- *Increasing competition.* The pressure and battle to be the best (almost perfect) in both the educational and professional fields as well as in personal achievement and the home.

- *Confusing advice.* The sheer amount of parenting sources, offering (often conflicting) guidance for parents who want to help their children develop into healthy and successful human beings.

Where is all this pressure coming from? How can we navigate through it in order to help both ourselves and our families thrive?

Let's start by looking at the environment we are currently in. The landscape of the working parent, for women in particular, is rapidly changing. In 2011 the scales were tipped, and women officially outnumbered men in the workforce in the United States, with similar statistics across Europe. Increasing numbers of women in the workplace isn't just a Western phenomenon either. China, for example, has a large proportion of working mothers: 72 percent of mothers between the ages of twenty-five and thirty-four with young children are in the workforce. In total, 64 percent of all women work in China. One of the pressures added in the three-generation household common to this culture is differing ideas about child-rearing and male-female roles. In China it is common for three generations to live together, with parents and grandparents having differing ideas on child-rearing.

The second important trend is the growth of flexible working and self-employment, which has doubled as a percentage of the workforce since the 1970s (currently at 16 percent in the United Kingdom) and accounts for the majority of new jobs being created. This isn't a coincidence. Many women find ingenious ways to further their careers and fulfill their professional ambitions while also having children. Others, however, fall into the trap of thinking they can juggle both full-time parenting and full-time work without help. Women who choose to work from home because they cannot afford childcare (or choose not to use childcare) may be especially vulnerable.

As more women work, more men are becoming actively involved in parenting, and so they too need greater professional flexibility. The idea that we have to choose one or the other feels increasingly outdated as women (and men) start their own businesses, join professional networks, work remotely, and take sabbaticals to explore life while also raising families. We are seeing a new generation of parents, the millennials, who are disrupting the outdated idea of a "career for life," instead focusing on personal fulfillment, leading to multiple careers and a merging of hobbies and professional work. Technology further enables us to find any number of new ways and places from which to work.

However, challenges remain. Increased flexibility often comes at a price in the form of reduced job security. Both women and men who parent and continue to work are, as we've just seen, increasingly pressured in all areas to perform at maximum levels, leading to increased levels of anxiety and stress. Balancing competing priorities between work and home without compromising standards and hopes in either area is a recurring issue for many. Despite greater professional elasticity, research continues to confirm that valuable employees (mostly women) leave the workforce because they are unable to balance work and family commitments. This comes at a high cost for employers and society, because organizations thrive on diversity. In response, in the last five years we've seen increased interest by employers to invest in work-life balance initiatives, albeit from a low starting level.

This is the environment that we live and work in today. How do we personally manage all of these factors and know what tools to apply in our homes and at work to give ourselves, our families, and our colleagues the best chance for success and well-being? We need to start by addressing our own feelings about our life choices, and to be realistic about how to manage it all.

The Dilemma Many Parents Face

The question that haunts many parents is "Will my not being there because of my work negatively affect my children?" There is no right answer to this question. The critical factor is whether you feel guilty or confident about the choice you have made.

One of the most significant factors affecting children is the feelings of the parents and how the parents behave because of those feelings. Unhappy parents create unhappy children. Children absorb the stress and unhappiness of their parents and express it in many kinds of misbehaviors, including fussiness, defiance, temper tantrums, and outright rebellion. Too many parents do not accept accountability for their part in the misbehavior—mostly because they don't understand the relational dynamics between parent and child. If parents believe pursuing their professional goals by working and not being with their children all the time makes their children suffer, chances are they will feel guilty. That guilt will make them feel stretched to the limit as they try to compensate for being absent. They may consequently choose ineffective parenting strategies such as overdoing things, giving too much, pampering, rescuing, and rendering their children incapable by robbing them of opportunities to contribute and to solve some of their own problems. We sometimes refer to this as your "guilt button." Parents with a guilt button are probably pretty unhappy or discontented too. So yes, like a self-fulfilling prophecy, it is true that with this belief system, working will invite children to suffer! If, on the other hand, parents feel happy about their decision to work and provide for their families, and provide guilt-free love when they are with their children, chances are they will be operating out of that happiness, and consequently will apply more constructive parenting choices. These children will feel their parents' contentment and benefit from the positive parenting.

Many people have deep convictions about parents who work, and mothers in particular. But where did these beliefs come from? There still exists a misconception that having a full-time stay-at-home parent is the only variable that accounts for success or failure in a child's development. There are many full-time moms (and dads) who are depressed, feel isolated, and don't fully engage with their children. There are full-time parents who overprotect their children, give them everything they want, and keep them from developing into capable people. There are also parents who are perfectly capable and fall somewhere in the middle of the spectrum. The point is that the act of being a full-time parent in itself does not equate to great parenting skills.

The same is true for working parents. Some are guilt-ridden, stressed, and tired, and do not have any energy left for their children. This leads to reactive parenting choices such as yelling, punishment, and pampering. Other working parents know how to balance work and family and are delighted to be with their children after a long day at work. They get their children involved in creating routines and problem-solving sessions. They establish healthy priorities, find ways to attend important functions most of the time, and help their children deal with disappointment when everything doesn't work out perfectly. They see that family and work can be a beneficial partnership rather than a conflict, and that it works both ways. Not only will content working parents experience a happier home life and feel good about what they are doing with their children, but they will also have less anxiety and a greater ability to contribute more to their work.

The good news is that perfection isn't necessary, as long as wise priorities and effective parenting skills are in place. Being a parent means having to forgive yourself often, because you're going to make a lot of mistakes. It will help to remember that there is now ample evidence to suggest that children (and adults) flourish in diversity. This supports the idea that a child thrives when several people are involved in the rearing—mothers, fathers, siblings, child minders, grandparents, teachers, and so on. This evidence invites you to question to what extent you may buy into the outdated idea of the full-time parent as the best and only real choice. Once you can reevaluate your belief system, you'll be a more confident and assured parent.

Life and Leadership Skills Development Begins in the Home

Most parents have many different roles and responsibilities to manage. The more closely these are aligned, the more energy and time are available for personal growth and well-being, for supporting others, and for positively impacting the wider community. There are huge synergies to be achieved when we realize that the leadership and communication skills we use and develop outside the home are just as effective at home, and vice versa. This way, instead of creating conflict, work becomes a resource for home, and home a resource for work.

Children learn by observing and copying. In your role as a working parent, what behaviors are you modeling to your children? As with all behaviors, these can be both challenging and positive. On the challenging side, you may be modeling stress, a sense that external events are more important than family, or an overemphasis on "doing" and lack of time to just "be." Undoubtedly, we need to address these less positive behaviors, and the strategies and tools in this book will help you with that.

On the plus side, by pursuing your professional goals, you may be modeling to your children that personal dreams matter, that it's important to contribute to society and develop a sense of individualism at the same time. Hopefully how to maintain healthy finances comes in here somewhere as well.

Children can learn resilience, problem-solving, and self-motivation from their working parents, whether "work" is writing a blog from home or clocking in at an office every day. These are also the very qualities that consistently appear in studies of effective leadership, and they are markers of emotional intelligence. Social-emotional intelligence is now recognized as possibly a greater barometer of success than a high IQ and even academic achievements.[1] Increasing competition in our society makes it hard for many parents to accept that academic excellence is not the golden ticket to future success. They find it challenging to take time to train "softer" skills such as seeing mistakes as opportunities to learn, focusing on solutions, and developing a sense of capability and significance through contribution at home, at school, and in their community. Recognizing how their working lives can provide excellent examples to their children provides parents with valuable opportunities for positive skills training.

The truth is that whether we work or not, our children are most likely going to have to work in their future adult lives. They will also be faced with a working life very different from ours. A report from the U.S. Department of Labor in 2013 suggests that 65 percent of all jobs for current schoolchildren have not yet been created.[2] How can we help train our children for such an uncertain and changing world? By accepting old ideas and the status quo, or by teaching them how to question and learn, to be curious and brave?

Providing your children with the confidence and interest to go out into the world and explore it is possibly one of the most important gifts you can give them. Being a happy and fulfilled parent models those very behaviors. That is also what we mean by leadership. By being a leader in your own life and staying true to yourself, you will be modeling healthy behaviors to your child and embodying true personal leadership.

Nobody Said It Would Be Easy

Is it easy? Oh no! Working requires juggling numerous competing priorities at work and at home, and finding a brief moment for yourself means actively making the choice to drop something that you "should" be doing. School and childcare challenges only contribute to the stress. Parents wonder how to find good childcare, and then worry about how to handle illness. Even with all those issues put aside, what happens when parents must miss their children's special events?

Raising children is a complicated task, whether one parent is full-time or not, and we see no evidence that it's going to get simpler anytime soon. Regardless of whether you are a full-time parent or are working in or out of the home, balancing personal and family commitments is one of the greatest challenges you will face as a parent. But when you feel good about what you are doing with your children, you will be a happier person—which will benefit your working life as well.

Perhaps we are at a crucial turning point where the boundaries between work and life are becoming increasingly blurred. We question the helpfulness of compartmentalizing yourself into a "professional self" and a "personal self," and we make a case for a healthier approach. We will show you how comprehensive Positive Discipline is, and how it can indeed support this integration for yourself, your family, your colleagues, and your friends.

PART 1

POSITIVE DISCIPLINE EXPLAINED

CHAPTER 1

HISTORY AND RESEARCH

UNDERSTANDING OUR PROBLEMS BETTER HELPS US FIND SOLUTIONS

As we found out earlier, the top parenting challenges for the professional parent are lack of time, performance pressures, and an overwhelming amount of advice and strategies. Unfortunately, we cannot give you more time—we all have twenty-four hours per day. What we can and will give you are tools that will help you wisely prioritize how to invest the time you have to make your parenting as effective as possible. We can't take away the pressure to compete that exists in our society, but we can and will provide you with a deeper, more enlightened viewpoint on personal wellness, parenting, and life choices. To help you choose the right path, we can also provide you with a guiding light through all the advice and suggestions that are out there. We will start by looking at research, the history of psychiatry, and brain development, thereby increasing our understanding of what important factors influence effective parenting.

Supporting Evidence for Positive Discipline

Parenting research for several decades has focused on identifying which parenting practices are most effective. Numerous studies show a direct correlation between parenting style and the child's levels of self-regulation, overall life satisfaction, academic achievement, alcohol use, aggression, and oppositional behavior.[3]

One of the most rigorous studies in this field was conducted by Diane Baumrind, whose longitudinal parenting style research at Berkeley spanned several decades.[4] Baumrind systematically examined how parenting impacts the social and psychological adjustment, academic success, and general well-being of children and adolescents. She summarized her own research this way: "Adolescents from authoritative (but not authoritarian) families showed by far the most social competence, maturity and optimism." Authoritative parenting is what we call Positive Discipline parenting—kind and firm, not controlling or permissive. Children who were raised in an authoritative atmosphere also scored the highest on verbal and mathematical achievement tests.[5]

Baumrind's research and the research of others show that punishment and reward are not effective long-term, and in fact negatively impact the development of self-regulation, intrinsic motivation, and the quality of family relationships.[6] A number of faulty and destructive beliefs and behaviors are created by punished children. We call them the 5 R's of Punishment: resentment ("This is unfair, I can't trust adults"), rebellion ("I'll do just the opposite to prove I don't have to do it their way"), revenge ("They are winning now, but I'll get even"), retreat ("I won't get caught next time"), and reduced self-esteem ("I am a worthless person"). Authoritarian (domineering) parents who are highly directive because they value immediate obedience are ineffective in the long term.

Baumrind's findings further illustrate how a permissive parenting style is just as damaging as punishment. Few demands are made on children, and the lack of structure and routine coupled with overindulgence (even in the name of love) leaves children with ineffective life skills. Permissiveness invites children to develop beliefs and behaviors such as selfishness ("Love means I should be able to do whatever I want"), helplessness ("I need you to take care of me because I'm not capable of responsibility"), and low resilience ("I'm depressed because you don't cater to my every demand").

Baumrind's work supports Positive Discipline's (kind and firm) parenting model, which focuses on the practical application of the same methods Baumrind and others identify as influential in positive child and adolescent development. Each of the Positive Discipline tools in this book is designed to help you practically apply what is well identified in the research and, therefore, most beneficial for family relationships and child development.

Alfred Adler

Alfred Adler was a Viennese doctor, and one of the original creators of the field of psychiatry in the late 1800s, along with Freud, Jung, and others. By observation and experimentation, Adler came to the conclusion that humans are fundamentally social beings, and that our primary goal is therefore to belong (connection) and to feel significant through a sense of purpose and contribution. When people don't feel a sense of belonging and significance they feel inferior. In their efforts to overcome this feeling of inferiority, they make all kinds of mistakes. Those mistakes often are identified as misbehavior. Adler believed misbehavior was based on faulty beliefs such as "I will feel good enough *only if* I get lots of attention," or "*only if* I am the boss," or "*only if* I hurt others as I feel hurt," or "*only if* I give up and assume that I am inadequate" (we call this "only if" thinking). These beliefs form what Adler called the private logic of each individual, which is a subconscious process that starts in early childhood.

Children (and adults) are always making decisions: about themselves (am I good or bad, adequate or inadequate, capable or incapable?), about others (are they encouraging or discouraging?), about the world (is it a safe or threatening place?), and consequently about what they need to do (can I thrive through encouragement or merely survive [misbehave] in discouragement?). Seen another way,

Adler taught that events invite thoughts, which often turn into a belief, which in turn invites a feeling that, finally, inspires behavior. We often refer to this cycle as "think, feel, do," and we invite participants in our workshops to engage in this process when working on uncovering mistaken beliefs.

Repetition of socially unacceptable behavior subsequently comes out of this mistaken private belief system. It is therefore not sufficient to address the behavior. Instead, the only way to change behavior permanently is to help an individual change his or her (mistaken) underlying beliefs. Adler believed the best way to do this is through encouragement that helps people experience the deep need to belong as social beings, and to feel capable through contribution. This way, the negative subconscious beliefs are replaced by positive beliefs, leading to fruitful behavior. His was a philosophy of treating everyone (including children) with dignity and respect. (This in many ways makes him a man well ahead of his time and more current than ever.) His thinking was in opposition to another trend in behavioral psychology that some may be familiar with, behaviorism, which advocated achieving change by affecting the observable behaviors through punishments and rewards.

Rudolf Dreikurs was a psychiatrist and colleague of Adler. He continued practicing the Adlerian philosophy after the death of Adler in 1937, and continued his work in America. Instead of confining it to the psychiatric office, however, he took this philosophy of equality, dignity, and respect for all to parents and teachers through open forum demonstrations, where he counseled parents and teachers in front of an audience. Dreikurs referred to his and Adler's philosophy as "democratic" (freedom with order), as opposed to "authoritarian" (order without freedom) or "anarchistic" (freedom without order). In his practice, he used this three-dimensional model to examine how parents influence their children. Dreikurs identified the democratic parenting style as most beneficial (which, as we saw earlier, has been confirmed in Baumrind's work). Dreikurs advocated a responsive yet firm approach to leadership at home as well as in schools in order to help children feel a sense of belonging and contribution. Adler and Dreikurs both recognized the need for respectful discipline designed to teach problem-solving and other important life skills, thereby addressing any mistaken underlying beliefs. In 1972, Dreikurs published a book about his model called *Children: The Challenge*.

The Development of Positive Discipline

In 1981, Dr. Jane Nelsen, a student of Adlerian psychology, self-published the book *Positive Discipline*, based on her experiences of using the philosophy of Adler and Dreikurs and teaching it to parents and teachers as an elementary school counselor. In the beginning, many thought Positive Discipline meant they could learn to punish in a positive way. It took them a while to get used to the idea of eliminating all punishment and reward in favor of encouragement and joint problem-solving to address the basic needs of children to belong and feel significant through contribution. Her book provided a workable model for how to apply Adler's and Dreikurs's principles to parenting and teaching. It taught that although punishment and rewards work in the short term with obedience and compliance as a result, the concern is with the long-term consequences, which can be damaging.

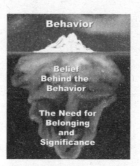

A child's behavior, like the tip of the iceberg, is what we see. However, the hidden base of the iceberg (much larger than the tip) represents both the belief behind the behavior and the child's deepest need for belonging and significance. Positive Discipline addresses both the *behavior* and the *belief behind the behavior*. Our task as parents and educators is to help children find belonging and significance in socially useful ways. We begin by (1) understanding and addressing mistaken beliefs about how to achieve belonging and significance and (2) teaching skills that meet this need in socially useful ways.

Adler and Dreikurs taught, "A misbehaving child is a discouraged child." When children misbehave they usually have a *mistaken belief* about how to gain a sense of belonging. Most parents *react* to the behavior with some kind of punishment (blame, shame, or pain). This only confirms a child's belief that he or she doesn't belong, creating a vicious cycle of discouragement. In most cases, the child's belief that he or she doesn't belong in the family is shocking to parents. They wonder, "How can my child believe she doesn't belong? How could she not know how much I love her? This doesn't make sense." How and why do children create their beliefs, especially when they don't make sense to us? As we've seen, according to Adlerian psychology, we know that humans have a fundamental need for belonging and significance, and when we perceive (realistically or not) that this need is not being met, we misbehave. The reason this need is unmet is that our faulty belief system makes us misinterpret events and actions of others. For children, whose belief system is being formed, this is significant, and the clue to this misinterpretation can be found in the development of the human brain.

Brain Development

Brain development happens in stages. Our instinctual and emotional centers (the amygdala and the limbic brain) develop first, and the thinking, logical brain (the neocortex) later. Children may therefore be able to experience and perceive the world through their senses, but their thinking and logical ability are not yet fully developed. This comes later, in adolescence and early adulthood. Children, therefore, are good perceivers but poor interpreters of the world around them.

Further research shows that children's brains work on a different wavelength than the brains of adults: delta waves up until age two, and theta waves from ages two to six.[7] This enables children (1) to absorb a huge amount of data very quickly, which is essential because they need to learn how to survive in their environment, and (2) to be more suggestible, so they can quickly alter their behavior to adapt to changes in their environment and growing cognitive ability. However, the ability to critically assess the data comes at a later developmental stage and another brain wave pattern. In other words, children are simply not yet able to see the big picture and engage in higher-level thinking, such as figuring out complex cause-and-effect patterns. Parents unaware of brain development may think of the child as a mini adult. This often leads to them asking their children to engage in behavior that is not yet age appropriate. When children don't, it is seen as misbehavior. This is why it is so important to get into the child's world to understand the child's "private logic."

Many parents may understand *what* they are supposed to do but lack the tools and insight to know *how* to do it. Understanding the history and theory of parenting and child development helps you grasp the importance of the underlying principles of Positive Discipline. In this book, you will learn to understand the beliefs your children form as they interact with the world, and the tools, the "how," you can use to empower your children to adopt more encouraging beliefs.

CHAPTER 2

THE ENCOURAGEMENT MODEL

A little boy finds a lovely cocoon in his garden. He watches it intently every day since he knows there is a butterfly inside. One day he can see little cracks in the surface of the cocoon as the butterfly is starting to emerge. Excited and wanting to be helpful, the little boy gently peels off the layers of the cocoon to reveal the butterfly inside. The butterfly tries to open its wings but has no strength, as it did not have an opportunity to build its muscles by breaking out of the cocoon. The little butterfly dies in the boy's hands.

POSITIVE DISCIPLINE PROVIDES THE SOLUTION

Time and time again we see how parents' misguided love leads to overprotection and the stymieing of children's ability to develop the resilience and intrinsic motivation they need to be happy, contributing, well-adjusted members of their communities. "So," you ask, "am I to allow my child to suffer when I can help ease her struggles?" Well, actually, true suffering occurs when children grow up without developing a sense of capability, confidence, and the joy of contribution. Alfred Adler taught, "Every human being strives for significance, but people always make mistakes if they do not recognize that their significance lies in their contribution to the lives of others."

You'll find many tools in this book that foster capability, and you will also hear over and over how important it is to avoid lecturing, punishing, and displaying affection inconsistently. Our job as parents is to gently let our children experience both the ups and the downs and to be there with love and support to help them make sense of the world. There is of course no way we can be there always and forever to protect them and sort things out for them. What we can do is help them cope and thrive and provide them with the life skills they need to handle life's ups and downs. It is not your job to *make* your children suffer, but it is your job to *allow* them to suffer in a supportive atmosphere where you teach skills so they can build their resiliency muscles.

Positive Discipline is an encouragement model. Since a misbehaving child is also a discouraged child, Dreikurs taught that "a child needs encouragement like a plant needs water." All of the tools we share with you are encouraging to children (and to parents). They are designed to increase a sense of belonging and significance, and thus address the belief behind the behavior. To be more specific, they meet all five of the criteria for Positive Discipline that have been developed over decades of experience. Even though all Positive Discipline tools are designed to meet these criteria, it is essential to understand that they are based on Adlerian principles. They are not effective if used as "techniques" based on a script. When you understand the principles upon which a tool is based, and add your own wisdom and experience, you will find your own unique way to apply these tools.

Five Criteria for Positive Discipline

You can think of these criteria as core skills or mindsets that are essential to be an effective Positive Discipline parent. Your parenting choices should, as fair as possible, meet these five criteria, and it is worth checking in from time to time to make sure they do. In this section, we will refer briefly to many Positive Discipline tools to illustrate the underlying principles. Don't worry, all these tools will be described again in more detail.

1. Is it respectful (kind and firm at the same time)?

2. Does it help children feel belonging (connection) and significance (contribution)?

3. Is it effective in the long term?

4. Does it teach valuable social and life skills for good character?

5. Does it invite children to discover how capable they are and to use their power constructively?

1. Is It Respectful (Kind and Firm at the Same Time)?

Many people believe that "no punishment" equals "permissiveness." Not so. Children need the firmness of limits and guidance, and they need the kindness of how the limits are imposed. One of our favorite examples is "Honey, I love you and the answer is no." Kindness usually involves some kind of connection before correction. It is respectful to the child and the situation. "I love you" makes a kind connection. Firmness involves respecting yourself and your boundaries, and "no" is a firm correction.

You can also validate a child's feelings before being firm: "I know you are upset that you can't have the latest smartphone, and I'm sure you can save enough to purchase one soon." You can kindly show understanding first: "I know you think this homework is meaningless, and I know you would rather do it anyway so you don't experience the consequences of not doing it." You can kindly share what you aren't willing to do and follow up with what you will do: "I can't spend time with you now, and I'm looking forward to our special time in an hour." You can show kindness and firmness by redirection with a choice: "Would you two like to solve your fight by going to the Wheel of Choice to find a solution, or would you like to put the problem on our family meeting agenda and get the help of the whole family?"

Another way to be kind and firm is to consistently decide and communicate what you will do, and then stick to it. Countless power struggles could be avoided if parents would decide what *they* need to do under certain circumstances rather than trying to control what their children do. A very good way to illustrate these criteria is in the fruitless act of demanding respect from a child. You can't control another person. You can control only yourself. Let your children know in advance that you will treat them respectfully, and that you will treat yourself respectfully. Since you can't make them treat you respectfully, you will take care of yourself and, for example, leave the room if they choose to be disrespectful. Many parents instead talk disrespectfully to the child by saying, "Don't talk to me that way, young lady." In other words, they model the very thing they want their children to stop doing. It is much more effective to demonstrate your refusal to stay in a situation where you are being treated disrespectfully. Here are some other ways to apply "deciding what you will do":

"I will serve dinner after the table is set."
"I would love to talk with you when no phones are in sight."
"I will read two bedtime stories."
"I will help with homework at the times we agree to in advance."
"I will drive you to your game as soon as you have taken care of your
   stuff in the living room."

The key is to follow through—silently—with what you say you will do.

ONE OF THE hardest and most important scenarios for practicing being kind and firm at the same time is around spending. Too many parents feel guilty when they aren't willing to spend more than they can afford, and guilty when they say no if they can afford it. In either case, they make the mistake of overindulgence. If you decide buying a certain toy isn't in your child's best interests, follow through with dignity and respect minus the guilt. It is often helpful to have a conversation with your child explaining your decision in a kind but unapologetic way: "Honey, I know you really want this toy. I'm not willing to buy it. I am willing to help you figure out how to save for it, or to choose something else."

Undoubtedly you are sometimes thinking, as do we, "But it's just easier to give in!" And that's probably true in the short term. However, giving in means you guarantee yourself many ugly scenes and manipulations from your child in the future, so while you've escaped this one hassle, you've just guaranteed several more power struggles. And the longer you spend training your child that you'll give in, the longer it will take to untrain him or her so the child learns that "no" means no. When you consider the negative long-term results, both the harm in overindulging and the benefit of being kind and firm become apparent.

2. Does It Help Children Feel Belonging (Connection) and Significance (Contribution)?

Effective parenting requires that you recognize that your children need to belong as well as have the opportunity to learn skills, make mistakes, and survive them. They need to stretch and grow, to learn that they are capable of acquiring new abilities and taking risks. Children need to learn the sound judgment that comes from facing problems, exploring solutions, and learning from the results. Effective parenting means equipping children to succeed in a challenging and difficult world. Offering emotional support and helping them brainstorm for solutions is much different from overprotecting and/or rescuing.

Many loving parents believe that effective parenting is about knowing where your children are, what they're doing, whom they're with, and when. We believe that it is more important to know *who* your children are. Knowing who your children are gives you the security and the faith to let them learn, let them try new things (and make mistakes) in a supportive environment, and let them become the people they truly are. Ultimately, a parent's job is to teach, guide, and encourage, and then to let go in loving, appropriate ways. The letting go is always a little scary, but it becomes less so when you know who your children are and what they are capable of. You will know that far better when you take time to get into their world, stay awhile, and truly connect with the interesting, capable people they are becoming. The more quality time you spend with your children, the less time you will spend dealing with the misbehaviors that result from discouragement. Being invited into a child's world is a fascinating and truly educational experience, and you can't force your way in. Like it or not, children determine whom they will trust, when they will speak, and what they will say. Wise parents learn to offer a little space, some understanding and encouragement, and the time to listen.

3. Is It Effective in the Long Term?

If you ask yourself the question "Is this in the best interest of my child in the long term?" and the answer is yes, you know you are doing the right thing. One of the biggest mistakes parents make is their failure to consider the long-range results of what they do. So how do you know?

We have already talked about the belief behind the behavior (remember the iceberg). Punishment will usually stop the behavior for the moment. But what is your child thinking, feeling, and deciding about himself, about you, and about what to do in the future? What behavior will these thoughts, feelings, and decisions produce in your child's future? One of the most important messages of this book is the importance of parenting for the long term. Understanding this will help you avoid a great deal of stress and feelings of being overwhelmed as your children grow older.

In one exercise coming up, we will ask you to identify a list of qualities you hope your children will have as adults. The goal of parenting and its greatest challenge is handling each day's problems and crises in ways that promote those qualities we want our children to have in the long run. Parents are more effective when they consider, "What will my child decide if I do this?"; "What will she learn about herself, about me, about what works?"; "What are the long-term consequences of giving too much or controlling too much because I feel guilty about my professional work, or am simply too frazzled because I haven't learned to balance work and life?"

In a world where parents feel torn between family and professional goals, where they often feel they have too little time and too little energy, this sort of thinking is hard to do. Yet it is crucial that we do it! When parents are indulgent and satisfy every demand, what are they teaching their children? Here are some possibilities: "If you want it, you should have it now"; "Material goods are the most important things in life"; and "You can't deal with disappointment in life, so I'll make sure you don't have to." When parents overindulge, children get the toy and short-term happiness, but they are deprived of an opportunity to learn valuable life lessons. Avoiding overindulgence helps children learn that they are capable of solving their own problems and handling disappointment without needing someone to "rescue" them. Solid life skills!

4. Does It Teach Valuable Social and Life Skills for Good Character?

You may already be convinced that punishment and/or permissiveness are not effective methods to use for consistent and lasting positive results. We know, however, that it is almost impossible to give up old habits without new ones to take their place, which is why it is so important to take time for training—both for you and for your child. One of the most encouraging things you can do as a parent is to teach, to give your children opportunities to learn the skills they will need to be successful in life. The problem is that teaching takes time and patience, and as a result, many parents find it easier "just for now" to do things for children or to punish them for their mistakes. When children learn that hassling and whining will make their parents give in and do the work for them, or that punishment is a small price to pay for irresponsibility, they will have zero motivation to take responsibility. Teach your child how to problem-solve and he or she will be able to find ways to teach him- or herself other social and life skills. To become good problem-solvers, children need to learn how to explore consequences and focus on solutions.

Exploring consequences is an extremely important part of teaching effective life skills. But it mustn't be confused with imposing consequences, which is effectively a form of punishment—making the child "pay" for her mistakes. Consequences (both good and bad) happen as the natural and/or logical result of behavior. Imposing a consequence might mean "No more phone privileges until you do your homework." Exploring consequences happens when you wait for a friendly moment and ask questions that help your child think for herself: "What do you think caused you to get that lower grade? How do you feel about it? What are your goals for yourself? What ideas do you have to achieve your goals?" A friendly tone of voice is essential. A threatening tone of voice invites children to give the standard response: "I don't know." (Sound familiar?) Children can always tell the difference between when you are truly interested in what they think and when your real goal is to get them to do or say what you want. Children are much more likely to choose to apologize or make things right if you ask them to think of solutions. When you tell them what to do, they feel resentful and will most likely resist or do it grudgingly. (Wouldn't you, even as an adult?)

Problem-solving teaches so many of the life skills and characteristics you want for your children in the long run that it should be your first-line offense in parenting. Most parents are programmed to think, "What is the problem? What is the punishment?" Those who have made the paradigm shift to focusing on solutions ask, "What is the problem? What is the solution?" They rave about how much more effective they and their children become when focusing on the latter formula. We have talked to many parents who have told us that most of their power struggles ended when they stopped imposing consequences and started focusing on solutions. Learn to think in terms of problem/solution instead of problem/blame/punishment. It can be effective and empowering to help children explore the consequences of their choices by empathetically asking, "What do you think caused that to happen, and what ideas do you have to solve the problem?" This teaches them many valuable life skills: problem-solving, respectful communication, decision-making, conflict resolution, and negotiating. It also keeps their self-esteem intact and teaches them how to voice their feelings and needs.

Of course, solutions don't always have to involve your children. As stated above, sometimes the most respectful thing you can do is stop trying to make your child do something and simply decide what *you* will do. For example, instead of trying to make your kids buckle their seatbelts, let them know you will sit quietly and read your book until they are all buckled up. Of course, it might take them a while to believe you, so it is important to follow through on what you say. During training time, leave early and bring a good book.

Involving children in solutions is always the best whenever possible. Teach children the valuable skill of brainstorming for ideas to solve a problem. Brainstorming is effective only when the child is actively involved in the process and then chooses the suggestion that would work best for him or her. It always amazes us what solutions children come up with when given the opportunity.

We know a young boy who was dealing with the fact that his dad had said no to his request for a coveted game that was about to be released. Dad thought the game was both too expensive and hard to acquire, as it would require waiting in line during work hours. The boy concluded, "Dad won't buy me the game, but I still want it." His father then engaged his son in a brainstorming session to help him figure out what he needed to do to get one. After brainstorming several possibilities, they agreed that Dad would provide a bridge loan so the imminent release would not be missed. The boy would then do some extra jobs around the house to earn the money to repay his dad. Finally, he would ask his aunt, who was available during the daytime, to stand in line with him for the release. What a wonderful life lesson in self-reliance and ingenuity!

5. Does It Invite Children to Discover How Capable They Are and to Use Their Power Constructively?

To truly grasp the significance of this criterion, let us give you two examples of a child's innate desire to contribute. You may have experienced it when your two-year-old demanded, "Me do it!" However, child development researchers have observed the desire to contribute in children even younger than two. They called it altruism, but as we describe the experiment you'll see that it could also be called contribution. Tomasello and Warneken conducted a series of experiments with eighteen-month-old toddlers that is adorable to watch.[8] The child is brought into a room with his mother (who is purposely passive) where the child can observe a researcher trying to put books into a bookcase with the door closed. The researcher keeps bumping the books into the closed door. After watching for a few seconds, the child walks over to the bookcase and opens the door and looks expectantly at the researcher to see if he understands that he can now put the books in the bookcase. In another experiment, the child observes the researcher pinning towels on a clothesline. The researcher drops the clothespin and attempts to reach for it, unsuccessfully. The child crawls over to the clothespin, picks it up, and struggles to stand up so he can hand it to the researcher, and then displays satisfaction that he was able to help.

Just as language is an innate ability that requires development, contribution requires development. When we pamper children, we rob them of their innate desire to contribute. When we understand this, we understand the importance of allowing the development of contribution in our children and helping them expand it. How do we do this? All Positive Discipline tools are designed to help children develop their capability and feel empowered, but we will start with the tool of having faith in our children to be capable. We love using the following example shared by Jane's daughter, Mary Nelsen Tamborski:

One day Mary noticed her two-year-old son, Parker, struggling to put on his big brother's T-shirt. As Mary watched him try to find the holes for his head and his arms, she was so tempted to rush in and help him. Instead, she remembered the importance of allowing children to struggle and instead rushed to get her camera. It is such fun to share these pictures with others at our workshops. As we share the first one, where his head and arms are lost in the T-shirt, we ask, "How many of you would want to rush in and help?" Everyone in the audience raises their hand. We show the next picture, where one arm is protruding from the head hole, but his other arm and his head are still covered by the T-shirt. We ask, "Okay, how many of you are feeling very uncomfortable just seeing these pictures of this struggle?" Every hand goes up. The third picture shows a tiny hand showing through one armhole and the other arm still in the head hole. The fourth picture shows Parker's face appearing in the head hole, and he has a big grin on his face. It is impossible to describe in words the proud smile of accomplishment on Parker's face when he managed to get his head and arms in the proper holes of his brother's T-shirt. It provides a clear picture of the pride we rob our children of when we jump in and rescue them from what we perceive as a struggle but is really the essential empowering development of capability and contribution.

EMPOWER YOUR CHILD

It has been said that children need both roots and wings to be prepared for successful living in today's world. Positive Discipline provides your children with the ability to develop the roots they need for stability and the wings they need to soar. Take a moment to think about your hopes and dreams for your children, about the qualities you want them to develop and the people you hope they will become. Let your love for them—that overwhelming, heart-melting feeling you get at unexpected moments when they catch your eye, hug you, or simply lie dreaming on their pillows—empower you to choose resilience, ingenuity, and competence for them. Love them enough to make the tough decisions: to teach, to guide, to let them wrestle a bit with life, and in so doing, to learn how to live it well.

PART 2

ANSWERING THE FUNDAMENTAL QUESTIONS

CHAPTER 3

DEALING WITH GUILT

Karen was late getting home—again! Her executive job at the bank was thrilling and ticked all her boxes professionally, but it meant many late nights and worries that five-year-old Laurence was spending too much time with his nanny. Laurence ran out to the front door as soon as he heard Mommy arriving. "Mommy, Mommy, come, I need to show you what Sue and I got in the park today!" Sue, the nanny, was at the door already putting her boots on. She had evening plans, so Karen had promised Sue an early night. Sue started telling Karen about Laurence's meals and homework all the while Laurence was tugging at Karen's coat. Karen snapped, "Laurence, can't you see I am talking? Go to your room and wait for me there!" Laurence's lips started to quiver and he ran to his room. Karen felt heartbroken and furious at herself for snapping at her little boy.

SOURCES OF GUILT

For many of us, work is not a choice but a necessity. However, some choice is hopefully within your control, and our aim with this book is to guide you in that process; to be the most contented parent, partner, and colleague you can be, no matter what your circumstance. We discussed in the Introduction how your underlying beliefs about your choices impact behavior. If you feel guilty about working and following your professional dreams, or about choosing to be a full-time parent, chances are it will affect your behavior and might lead to overcompensation and stress. Children copy our behaviors, so stressed parents lead to stressed children. So where is the guilt coming from?

Work-Family Conflict

We live in a fast-paced world, one that seems to accelerate every year. Forty years ago, mothers who also pursued a career were in the minority. Today, there are few mothers who don't have a professional life, and few fathers who aren't actively involved in the rearing of their children. As a consequence, new opportunities and challenges are surfacing. People are now required to fulfill multiple and sometimes conflicting commitments at home and at work. This demands a lot of time and energy, more than is available to most working parents, few of whom have been trained in time management, home management, and effective parenting. The guilt from never feeling sufficient in any area builds and takes a massive toll on parents and children.

It is well known that the number one cause of employee absenteeism is family-related issues. These work-family conflicts create stressors that result in physical and psychological challenges to the health of parents and children, which contribute to more absenteeism. Issues such as equal pay and childcare costs arose as women entered the workforce, and fathers have encountered their own struggles with guilt around work and family. Many men have stepped off the fast track at work because of the overwhelming stress inherent in trying to meet the unending demands at home and at work. With divorce rates holding steady at about 50 percent, single parents and stepparents juggle multiple family issues. More and more single moms and dads are working and raising their children. No matter what your family situation is, it may seem to you that there is never enough time and energy to get everything done.

Others' Expectations

Many working parents, perhaps particularly women, also feel guilt around carrying their weight in their place of work. Once they decide to have a family, they often need to make adjustments at work: parental leave, flextime, time off to care for sick children, and so on. Women can feel like they are letting their colleagues down, and might worry about being passed over for a promotion in favor of someone who doesn't have as many commitments. Negotiated part-time work can also be seen as "days off" by colleagues who aren't parents, when anyone who's a parent knows that looking after a little one is full-on and hardly a day off! And if you don't take time off to care for your child—surely you are a bad mother.

If you work for yourself, you may find yourself justifying to your partner, friends, and family that you may be at home, but you are still working. People around you who don't have children might not understand why you can't finish a proposal while running after a toddler who's just learned how to walk! What do you need childcare for? And surely looking after your child is more important than "whatever it is that you do."

There are also many men who would love to take more parental leave and have greater involvement with their children, but feel the pressure of old stereotypes that say they should support their family financially, or "not let the team down" at work. The ensuing guilt can have just as detrimental an effect as the guilt parents may feel toward their children for being absent due to work.

Guilt Caused by Poor Parenting Choices

Many parents are aware that they are at times operating on autopilot while at home. They may even see that their children aren't thriving. Yet they are so overwhelmed by all the pressures that they continue using short-term strategies such as punishment and rewards, often getting stuck in the negative guilt-anger-remorse cycle, leading to more ineffective parenting choices. This state is not healthy for anyone, parent or child.

Let us offer some clarification around what you are actually feeling. There is a difference between a healthy longing to be part of your child's life and feeling worried or guilty that your child is somehow not cared for while you are prioritizing yourself. Chances are you will always want to be there to share your child's growth and experiences and always have a slight pang at missing out on certain things, whether you work or not. That is not guilt. That is love and it is healthy, although at times it may conflict with your other life goals. If you use wise parenting strategies and know that your child is well looked after in expert care, don't add guilt on top of those pangs. It is easy to get the two confused, especially when you are tired and stressed and stuck in reactive behavior. We will shortly look at a story that illustrates how to break the guilt-anger-remorse cycle and use healthy strategies for both you and your child. Before we get there, let's look at some guilt-busting strategies.

FACTORS HELPING PARENTS TO FEEL LESS GUILTY AND CHILDREN TO THRIVE

Apart from your own feelings, there are a number of other factors impacting your child's well-being. Understanding those better can help ease your guilt. Let's start by looking at how children actually feel about their working parents.

How Our Children Feel About Us Working

Research by Ellen Galinsky in *Ask the Children* shows that the majority of children, when asked how they felt about their working mothers, were proud.[9] (Although the study does not cover how children felt about their working fathers, we can perhaps assume they also felt proud about their dads.) A study published in *Psychology of Women Quarterly* in 2015 further confirmed how children's attitudes toward their working mothers are improving across generations. Also in 2015, Harvard Business School published a study confirming that daughters of working mothers were generally more successful and higher earning as they grew up, and boys were more likely to be involved in caring for the home and children. Anecdotal evidence from numerous respondents to the survey confirmed how the "working mother effect" had positively benefited their drive, confidence, and compassion. Children, then, do not have a problem with us working—provided, of course, it does not lead to neglect and stress in the home.

One would assume that working means spending less time with your children, but a groundbreaking study in 2012 showed that working mothers spend as much time with their children today as at-home mothers spent in the early 1970s.[10] If it is not the quantity that is lacking, is it the quality? In many cases, this is the true challenge. In our modern lives, where work is only ever a click away, meaningful interaction requires greater focus and intention on your part to set boundaries around family time.

So it would seem that parental guilt is largely misplaced. Children feel fine about their parents not being with them all the time, provided they get some consistent quality time.

External Childcare

Finding excellent care is paramount to ease working parents' guilt. We have an entire chapter dedicated to this important topic, coming next. To help reduce guilt, let's look at the supporting evidence.

In 2005, the U.S. National Institute of Child Health and Human Development (NICHD) completed one of the most comprehensive studies ever conducted. It tracked 1,364 children over fifteen years and concluded that children with 100 percent maternal care did *no better* than children who had spent time in external childcare. Children in external care also showed marginally *higher* numeracy and literacy scores in preparation for grade school transition than children who had only home care. It further concluded that external care did not have any adverse effects on the mother-child bond, which will be reassuring to some concerned mothers.

Benefits to children in childcare are numerous: Children learn to accept and interact with other adults and authority figures. They spend time with peers, which helps them to develop interpersonal skills such as teamwork, sharing, and communication. They get exposed to wider diversity, and they often get to experience more pedagogical and formalized learning than that which takes place in the home. All this prepares them well for both education and their future adult lives.

Another aspect of the same study showed that the impact of parenting on the child is at least twice as significant as the experiences the child has while in childcare. So you can breathe a sigh of relief and worry less about the "risks" of leaving your children in care (provided, of course, you have done your research and found excellent care). Hopefully this will help you change your own beliefs, and thus your behavior. When you are firm in your choices, you are much less likely to give in to your children when they push your buttons.

Dual-Income Families Provide Greater Security

As a working parent, you can model independence, resilience, care for others, community, and much more. Two incomes tend to provide greater financial stability, and a further benefit is your contribution to the home unit. If the home unit consists of two parents who are both working and sharing home responsibilities, research shows that the more equally home-related tasks are shared, the healthier the relationship is as measured by decreased divorce risks. Why might that be? You are sharing a more similar life experience if you are both in and out of the home. You have a wider frame of reference to share experiences from, you can share the stresses of conflicting priorities, and you can agree more democratically about who does what, hopefully leading to greater understanding. This may also help couples feel equal ownership of the home and children, positively affecting their desire to contribute time and effort.

None of this is easy, of course. Chances are that one person's career is more demanding or higher-paying than the other's, at least at times, and that leads to differences in needs and approaches. However, dual working parenthood at least provides more of an even playing field.

Active Fatherhood

Active fatherhood invites greater equality in the home. It empowers men as carers and women as providers. This models equality, openness, and choice to children, and prepares them well for the world in which they will grow up. An influential book in 2000 by child psychiatrist Kyle D. Pruett confirms that lower levels of problem behaviors such as lying, sadness, and acting out were associated with children who had experienced active father care.[11] Children experiencing active fatherhood also display increased empathy as adults, higher academic scores, greater reported happiness, and lower delinquency.

A study published in the April 2015 *Journal of Marriage and Family* showed that the average number of hours fathers spent with their children each week has risen steadily since 1985; however, most important was the finding that it is the quality, and not the quantity, that counts. Due to the pressure that many mothers feel to "do it all," mothers may on a daily basis spend more actual hours with their children than fathers. However, much of that time is spent managing daily schedules, enforcing routines, transporting, and supervising. The time that fathers spend may be more focused on quality activities, such as reading, talking, playing games, and homework. Both parents being actively engaged in activities with children will thus contribute to positive behavioral, emotional, and academic outcomes.

Although quality is key, according to a study published by the Fatherhood Institute in 2005, just being around can still have a positive effect on both children and fathers. Children who spend more time with their fathers will gain a greater sense of trust and feel that they can depend on their fathers. In addition, the study concludes that the more time fathers spend parenting, the better they will get at it, resulting in parenting that is more sensitive and intuitive. The institute's research further shows that the greater the paternal involvement at an early stage, the better the outcome for everyone. For instance, paternal involvement before and at birth—such as participation in prenatal classes and being present at the birth— further strengthens the father's role as caregiver. Many fathers worry about becoming second to their children in their partner's eyes once the children are born. Establishing an equal responsibility and care from the beginning, together with ongoing communica- tion and couple care, can help combat this issue too.

What about those traditional gender stereotypes of the woman as the main carer and the man as the main provider? There are no quick fixes here—societal and gender views take time to shift. But younger generations are slowly but surely disrupting these outdated norms. Certain countries, such as Sweden and Norway, have come further by far-reaching legislation around both parental leave and childcare, and 90 percent of fathers in those countries now take paternity leave. While the rest of the world is catching up, we can help ourselves by being aware of our sources of pressure and guilt. Clearly communicating your intentions with your employer and other stakeholders will certainly help, as we will see in Chapter 14.

Some inspiring men lead the way already. A senior recruiter at a global professional services firm shares this story: "A couple of years ago, I cold-called a candidate about a new opportunity. It was a big step up from his current role, and he had all the right skills and qualifications. 'Sorry, but I'm not interested,' he politely said. I pressed him on it until he said something that really confused me. He told me that he had 'already made it to the top.' I was famil- iar with his current company and looked at his résumé again. He wasn't even a manager yet. He explained to me that 'making it to the top' for him meant he loved the exact work he did each day, he loved his company, he was treated fairly and with respect, he made enough money to be comfortable, he had excellent benefits, he had flexibility, and, most importantly to him, he's never missed a single Little League game, dance recital, parent-teacher conference, anniversary, birthday, or any family event. He knew what taking the next step in his career meant: more time, travel, and sacrifice. 'Not worth it,' he said."

Helping Children Feel Special

There are many little things that busy parents can do to help their kids feel special and assuage their own guilt in the process. Some will involve extra time, but some will just take a little bit of additional thought and planning. One small but powerful thing can be to create nonverbal signals that you can use with each other to share love—for example, a quick thumbs-up when you pass in the hall, or patting your heart to send a message of love across the room.

One of the most powerful ways to build strong bonds with your child is to spend special time with him or her. You may already spend lots of time with your children. However, there is a difference between obligatory time, casual time, and scheduled special time. Special time is something fun that you schedule with your child, uninterrupted and just for the two of you—real quality time! There are several reasons special time is so encouraging: Children feel a sense of connection when they can count on special time with you. They feel that they are important to you. This decreases their need to misbehave as a mistaken way to find belonging and significance. Scheduled special time is a reminder to you about why you had children in the first place—to enjoy them. When you are busy and your children want your attention, it is easier for them to accept that you don't have time when you say, "Honey, I can't right now, but I sure am looking forward to our special time at four-thirty." Imagine how much better Karen, in our opening story, could have handled the situation with Laurence if she had had special time already planned.

A few important notes about special time: Do not allow special time to be screen time. Special time is interpersonal and interactive. Special time is *doing* something together, not *watching* something together. This does not mean you should never watch a screen together. Just make sure to take time to discuss what you have watched. Find out what your children are thinking about what they have seen. If moral issues are involved, discuss them. Otherwise, turn off your phones or leave them somewhere else entirely while you and your child are enjoying special time. Children must know that they are your main priority for that time. Neither is special time a time to talk about a child's behavior challenges or bring up problems. Instead, let kids lead the conversation with whatever might be on their minds. This is a time to listen reflectively. Parents can apply the concept of special time as part of the bedtime routine (although the bedtime routine should not replace daytime special time).

Another great way to bond and help children feel special is to share the day's happy and sad moments. When tucking your child into bed at night, take a few minutes to let her share the saddest thing that happened to her that day. Just listen respectfully without trying to solve the problem. Then share your saddest time of the day. Follow this by taking turns sharing your happiest event of the day. You may be surprised at the things you hear when your children have your undivided attention to evaluate their day and hear about yours.

A working dad told us he decided to try sharing sad and happy times while tucking his children in bed at night. At first, four-year-old Jesse really got into the sad times and went on and on. Soon she was crying for sympathy, and Dad wondered if this was such a good idea. However, he listened patiently without trying to solve the problem (though he did ask Jesse if she would like to put the problem on the family meeting agenda). Jesse finally stopped crying. When Dad asked Jesse to share her happy time, she pouted and said, "I didn't have a happy time today." Dad knew this wasn't true. He had seen his daughter laughing earlier. He was wise enough to say, "Okay, I'll tell you mine. Actually, my happiest time is about to happen. I can't wait for my butterfly kisses." Soon Jesse was laughing as they exchanged butterfly kisses.

Even though sharing sad and happy times with his other two children had been successful, Dad wondered if he should skip it with Jesse. He decided to give it another try. The second night Jesse tried again to get more sympathy from her sad story. When it didn't work any better than it had the night before, she went ahead and shared her happiest time. It wasn't long before Jesse often wanted to skip her saddest thing and share two happy things.

"Tell me another story," whined four-year-old Angela. Mom was getting angry. She had already given in to the plea for three stories. But she felt guilty for leaving Angela at the daycare center while she worked all day. Mom felt she had to make it up to Angela, even though she felt angry because she also wanted some time to herself. So she gave in and told Angela a fourth story.

When Angela whined for one more story, after that, Mom was at the end of her rope. She scolded, "Angela, you are never satisfied. I'm not going to tell you another story because you just want more, more, more. You can just do without until you learn to appreciate what you get!"

Angela burst into sobs. Mom ran to the bathroom, locked the door, and burst into tears herself. Then she remorsefully scolded herself: "She is only a child who wants to spend some time with me. If I'm going to leave her alone all day, the least I can do is read her as many stories as she wants." Then the guilt started again. "It isn't her fault that I'm tired. I don't want my poor daughter to suffer because she has a working mom. How will I ever manage?"

What is truth and what is fiction regarding this scene? It is true that Angela needs time with her mom. It is fiction that she needs to hear four stories. When Mom allows Angela to push her guilt button, she is teaching Angela the skill of manipulation.

When Mom learns to allot a reasonable amount of time, she can avoid the anger stage. After one or two stories (in the amount of time Mom can give with enjoyment), Mom can say, kindly and firmly, "Story time is over. Time for our hug and kiss."

43

Angela will know if Mom means what she says, just as she will know if Mom's guilt button can be pushed. However, when Mom is just learning to give up her guilt, it would be only natural for Angela to up the ante in an attempt to keep the old game going. She may scream, "I want another story!"

Again, kindly and firmly, Mom can say, "Do you want to go to sleep without a hug and kiss or with a hug and kiss?" This may be enough to distract Angela from the power struggle by giving her an opportunity to use her power to make a choice. If Angela keeps whining or screaming, however, Mom can say, "I'll just sit here for five minutes to see if that is enough time for you to get ready for a hug and kiss." (After all, Mom helped Angela perfect her manipulation skills. It may take patience for her to learn mutual respect.) If Angela continues the manipulation pattern, Mom can say, "I can see you are not ready for a hug and kiss now. We'll try again tomorrow night," and then leave.

POSITIVE DISCIPLINE TOOLS

Along with special time, there are several parenting skills that can prevent and eliminate negative cycles such as guilt-caving-pampering and guilt-anger-remorse, and help you to build a stronger connection with your child. Let's look at them in turn.

Work on Your Guilt Buttons

Children know when you have guilt buttons that can be pushed, and they know when you don't. Guilt sends out a certain kind of energy that speaks louder than words! The first step to giving up guilt is to work on your belief system about your choices, as discussed in the Introduction. Awareness is the first step; then behavioral change can follow. It may take some time for the guilt to subside, and some may never fully go away. However, with awareness and self-reflection you are better able to correct your behavior and ensure you model healthy choices to your children.

Decide What You Will Do and Follow Through

"I will read two stories." Again, confidence, kindness, and firmness are the keys. Deciding what you are willing to do is a demonstration of self-respect. The willingness to spend reasonable time and perform reasonable tasks for and with your children demonstrates respect for them. However, if you state your intentions in a threatening way instead of a respectful way, the effectiveness is diminished. It is far more effective to act than to use words. Children respond to actions but become "hearing impaired" with too many words. Let your kind and firm actions speak loud and clear. If you say you will read two stories, stick to your decision. At the end of the stories, give a hug and a kiss and leave the room with confidence.

Limit Choices

Giving the child a limited choice makes her feel engaged, as she is using her power, but it also enables the parent to stay in control of the situation by offering only two choices. (For example, "Do you want to go to sleep without a hug and kiss or with a hug and kiss?")

Plan Ahead

Another way to avoid the "tell me another story" scene is to talk about it in advance. Engage your child in planning for the future. When you decide to make a change, it is respectful to let your child know and to work on a plan together (e.g., "What should happen after I finish reading the second story?").

EXERCISE

Plan Special Time with Your Child

Brainstorm a list of things you would like to do together during your special time. When first brainstorming your list, don't evaluate or eliminate. Later you can look at your list together and categorize. If some things cost too much money, put them on a list of things to save up for. If the list contains things that take longer than the ten to thirty minutes you have scheduled for the special time, put these items on a list of longer family fun times that you can turn to when you do have more time. Write down what you and each of your children have decided to do for your special time this week. Make sure to include the exact day and time this will happen, and commit to it.

SPECIAL TIME   DAY   TIME

_____   _____   _____

CHAPTER 4

WORK-LIFE INTEGRATION

Anne remembers when she had her wake-up call: "Anne, can you step into my office please?" She didn't like the tone she could detect in the senior partner's voice. She didn't need another earful! She had just gotten off the phone with her husband, Richard, who had said in no uncertain terms that he needed her to pick up six-year-old Cindy from school on Thursdays and Fridays from now on. Richard's boss was coming down hard on him, and he wasn't prepared to put his career on the back burner any longer. Anne had been working eighty-hour weeks and had just delivered another successful case for her law firm. Okay, so Richard wasn't happy, but surely the senior partners should be pleased, Anne thought.

"Anne, we know you are doing a fantastic job delivering success for the firm," Penelope began. "But we've had repeated complaints about your treatment of the junior staff, with two resigning as a result. Hiring and training juniors is very costly, and the firm simply can't afford to lose its reputation in the market place. Retaining top talent at all levels is a priority, Anne, but you are making this very hard for us. Success can't come at any price!" Anne remembers feeling stunned. Instead of being appreciated for all her hard work, she was being scolded. Then it dawned on her that she was also being too demanding of her husband. And how was her hard work affecting their child? Was she willing to pay the price of her family for success at work?

REDEFINING SUCCESS

Pursuing personal and professional goals doesn't have to mean trade-offs. They can be mutually beneficial and provide a positive way of living. This is called work-life integration. Our professional lives today are increasingly seen as part of our personal fulfillment and self-actualization, not just somewhere we go to clock in and out. Is that most people's experience of their work? Maybe not all the time. Sometimes work has to take a backseat. Certain things can't be moved around—your children will be children only once, and for a very short time. Having firm priorities may mean being willing to take a less demanding job to have the flexibility to work part-time or, at the very least, be home on time. Most of us work because we have to. Developing a mature attitude and accepting that work isn't always incredibly exciting and inspiring may be a sensible investment.

Other times you may want to be able to prioritize whatever opportunities come your way to experience growth and development. If home life is stressful, it can impact every aspect of your life, including affecting your performance at work. An absence of clear priorities can feel like you are compromising your professional goals and lead to resentment toward your children and partner. Accepting that, at times, one area of life will have to make way for another is fine as long as we search for balance over time. This is not always easy. It can help to understand where the underlying conflicting feelings come from, and what you can do to set yourself up for success rather than failure.

Having a Clear Vision for Your Life

According to Plato, Socrates is credited with saying, "An unexamined life is not worth living." In this instance, that can mean thinking about what success really is and what it looks like in your world. Typically, we all have a sense of who we are and what we do, but how does the job of parent fit in? There may be some conflicts between this new role as parent and our previously existing sense of self. How can we give adequate time and attention to both our children and our career? It can easily feel like we are being unsuccessful when one area falls behind.

A lot of us suffer from the "grass is always greener" effect—"If I'd stayed at my job I would be there now, making that kind of money"; "If I'd chosen that partner and moved to that city, I'd be happier." What if, what if, what if? The truth is that we don't know for sure how anything could have panned out—there are too many unknown variables outside of our control. Truly examining your life means redefining success not as something that has to be externally achieved but instead as a sense of well-being that can be internally reached. Here's a game-changer: "Success for me means that I strive to be the best version of myself, and to reduce any negative impact my behavior might have on others." To be the best version of yourself means being honest about all your needs, including accepting that some of these needs may be in conflict in the short term but important in the long term, as they lead to wholeness for you as a person. Acting with integrity toward yourself, your family, and your colleagues reduces any negative and harmful effects and leads to greater closeness.

To create this internal motivation, it can help to develop a life vision. We start by asking a profound question: What do you want your life's purpose to be? When you have greater clarity around your life's vision and you are living true to that vision, you will find greater peace and contentment. If you betray yourself by violating that vision, you will have stress, anxiety, and unhappiness. If you don't even know what that vision is, you may be traveling aimlessly through life with the risk of regrets and missed opportunities. If you are like most people, you have a deep desire for a meaningful, close relationship with your children and mate, and at the end of your life you want your children to say that they felt connected to and loved by you. Achieving your family dreams, as well as a measure of happiness and fulfillment in your career, will require introspection and conscious decisions to support that vision. It is fine to be driven by professional and financial success, but when you enlarge your definition of success to include accomplishments in your intimate relationship, your relationship with your children, and your ability to stay physically and emotionally healthy, you will find yourself living a more balanced and fulfilling life.

Making Conscious Parenting Choices

With a clear vision, you can take a step back and look at all the aspects of your life that may be causing personal and professional conflict. Let's start with your expectations around parenting. In the past, being a successful professional often meant working long hours whenever required, while being a good parent meant being available at home 24/7. Today's parents want (and often need) to achieve success in both areas. If the standard is 24/7 in both areas, however, then you are setting yourself up to fail. Your expectations around parenting will be instrumental in shaping how you manage your home and work-life balance. If the parenting dynamics you observed growing up are harmful or incongruous with life today, it's important to unlearn what you learned from your parents (this book provides you with tools for how to do that).

It will take time for you to achieve a deep connection with your children, and time to teach them the life skills they need to become responsible and well-adjusted adults. If you want to be successful with your family, it will require a firm commitment to protect family time. Without this commitment, the urgent demands from work and the incessant beckoning of household tasks will steal precious relationship-building time. Equally, to be successful and content at work you need to protect that time too and not feel guilty about it. Communication is key so that your family never feels deprioritized. Often all that is required is a shift in mindset and a little bit of planning. Honoring fixtures such as special time and family meetings will help greatly (more on family meetings later in the book). Plan your time so that errands and personal needs can be taken care of at lunchtime or when the children have evening/weekend dates away from home. Try not to multitask during family time. Check in with your focus—where is your mind? If you're spending time with your child but your mind is elsewhere, chances are he or she will feel it and possibly act out.

To help you stay focused when at work, you will want to make sure that your kids are fine when you are not around. We clarified earlier that a natural yearning to be with your children is normal and healthy, and it is only when we are unsuccessful in our parenting choices and arrangements that guilt is the more accurate emotion. Kids aren't nearly as materialistic as we tend to think. They'll take quality time and genuine signs of affection any day over "bad conscience" presents from guilty-feeling, absent parents. As a busy working parent, you'll be wise to devise a strategy with your children for how to stay in touch—how and when they can contact you when you're at work. They want to hear the message "You are important to me and your needs count." As long as that message comes through, you don't need to be with them all the time for them to feel belonging and significance. Use the digital world to your advantage—Skype or FaceTime when you're traveling, and send cute texts and emojis to your kids once they're old enough to have phones. Let them know in advance when you're out of reach (on a flight, for example) so they don't worry if they can't get hold of you.

It is not just parents who are busy—children are too! Your mind will be more at ease if you have good communication around plans and schedules. You will want to keep track of your busy children, so have a plan in place for communicating schedule changes and/or conflicts. Setting up agreements in advance is important in case of last-minute changes.

Making conscious parenting choices means that it's a good idea to check in with your partner to discuss your parenting expectations and what your ambitions are, both personally and professionally. You have probably heard the saying that opposites attract. One difference that doesn't show up until after children arrive is that one parent is often a little too permissive and the other is a little too strict. A small bit of difference is of course normal and unavoidable. Trouble starts when parents fight over who is right and who is wrong, which is ineffective. Try to meet in the middle and practice new skills that are both kind and firm at the same time, as described in Chapter 2 when we discussed the five criteria for Positive Discipline, the first of which is being kind and firm.

Making Conscious Professional Choices

Achieving successful work-life integration requires understanding what you truly want to achieve professionally. It can therefore be worth investigating whether you're in the right job for the right reasons. Ask yourself: "Is work providing me with what I need, or do I feel stuck in an understimulating position in order to make room for other competing priorities from my partner and/or family?" Since half of your waking life is spent on the job (if you work full-time), it is critical that you find fulfillment in what you do. Is it enough to have a high level of satisfaction in the financial arena if you hate what you do, day after day? *Forbes* reports that almost 2.5 million Americans a month—or about 30 million a year—are willing to quit their jobs.[12] It is doubtful that these workers have careers that are meaningful or fulfilling to them.

If you know intuitively that you are in the wrong field, or if you've been thinking about taking the plunge and becoming your own boss but are worried, take a risk on your own behalf (and on behalf of your family) and do something that uniquely suits you. If you don't know what that would be, do some research or see a career coach. Think about what you like doing and what you are good at; give yourself some leeway to figure out what that might be. It is also helpful to ask yourself what you would be willing to do for free. One woman turned her love of gardening into a full-time business by creating beautiful flower displays for the storefront businesses in her small town. A gourmet cook quit a job he found tedious to cater parties and weddings. Find out what career would be fun and meaningful to you. The effort will be well worth it. It will breathe new passion into your life and make you a more enjoyable person to be around. It's important to consider whether your work offers you the flexibility to not only spend quality time with your family but also do other things you personally enjoy.

Addressing Overwork

Parkinson's Law states that "work expands to fill the time available for its completion." What does that really mean? It means that no matter how much we work, there is always more to do. It never stops! Most of us feel the pressure to work long hours to succeed and climb the ladder in our chosen professions. The effects of overwork include overwhelming stress, loss of intimacy with children, marital tension, increased physical illnesses, sleep disorders, anxiety, and depression. In spite of the harm caused by long hours on the job, there is tremendous resistance among employees to ask to work fewer hours. While you may know that you need to work fewer hours to have the time and energy necessary for your family's well-being, you may be reluctant to seek the necessary changes. Some of this resistance is grounded in the practical realities of our work culture. Even the most family-friendly organizations often expect you to perform as if you have no other life. You may fear reprisals or loss of respect from your employer if you are forthright about your need to spend more time at home and less time at the office. It can be dangerous to behave in a way that suggests work is not far and away the top priority. Then there is the issue of over-consumption and materialism forcing us to work long hours to keep up with our "needs."

Part of living a balanced life is addressing your beliefs about how you are valued as a human being. If you need to climb to the top of the career or financial ladder to feel valuable, and you feel your work defines you as a human being, you may struggle to set the boundaries necessary around personal and family time. You may be addicted to work. Until you realize that you have worth outside of your professional accomplishments, you will not be able to scale back at work when needed, and any pressure (from yourself or others) to do so will likely lead to guilt and anxiety.

Let's revisit Anne in our opening story. Under the pressure from both her senior partner and her husband, she had to reevaluate what success really meant to her. When she was faced with losing her job because of her lack of compassion and respect toward her support staff, she realized her parents had taught her at a very young age that her worth was contingent on financial success and prestigious work. This had turned her into a workaholic. She realized that personal success was so much bigger than money or prestige. She began to expand her definition of worth to include how she treated others, her relationship with her husband and daughter, her quality of life, and her friendships. As she began to base her value on more than just money and career, she found herself able to detach from work in a healthy way. She no longer needed the praise from overwork to feel worthy as a person.

Workaholics, unlike other addicts, are socially and culturally sanctioned in our society. When you work long hours, you receive praise and material rewards. This reinforces the need to continue the destructive addiction to work. A workaholic is very different from someone with a solid work ethic. A person with a good work ethic is in control of his or her schedule and has balance in life. A workaholic receives a fix from the work itself; the work meets an intrinsic need that is so powerful it spirals beyond the person's control. This makes balance impossible. And if you work for yourself, it can be even harder to separate work from the rest of your life.

It's hard to break free of the "all work, no play" mindset, but a good starting point is to remember that you are able to make changes. You have chosen your life at work and at home and you can choose to change it, one step at a time. Begin with the end in mind. Think about how you would like to be remembered by your children, and think hard about how much time you are giving to work. Then set healthy boundaries around your personal and family time. Set goals for all areas of life and begin to take your partner and children on dates, find a new hobby, and make some friends (more on this in Chapter 13).

If the culture inherent in your organization is workaholic, consider telling your employer about your other priorities. If there is a total unwillingness to allow you a private life away from work, make a plan to get out. You and your family deserve better. Think long and hard about promotions and the impact they will have on your family. Be cautious about accepting a job with a lot of travel, which can take a real toll on family life. Unhook from the electronic leash to work. Let your supervisor and colleagues know you will be unavailable during certain hours. Look at flexible working or freelancing from home to cut down on commuting.

If you are self-employed, you may have more control over your work hours and habits. Set yourself a specific work schedule and stick to it. If you have to do more work, wait until after you have eaten dinner and enjoyed some quality evening time with your children. Of course, some self-employment means you always have to take the work when it's there, so you might actually have less control over your work hours. This lack of control and uncertainty can be harder to cope with when also caring for small children. If you find that the arrangement is not working for your family, consider taking a part-time job for the time being until you have more energy to go it alone again.

Addressing Financial Pressures

Taking an honest look at your expectations around finances is an important step toward reaching work-life integration. Many people overwork for one simple reason—they overspend. If you, like most Americans, consume 110 percent or more of what you make, you will have little choice when it comes to changing to a less stressful profession or cutting back your hours, even if it is in your family's best interest. Personal indebtedness is the antithesis of freedom and can be a factor in determining people's unwillingness to reduce hours. Many of you would love to scale back at work and spend more time with your family, but high debt service makes it impossible. Interest payments are a cruel taskmaster.

There are plenty of strategies for putting your financial house in order. The first one is to only use debit cards, so you spend only what you have—credit is a killer! Seek debt consolidation advice from your bank or other institutions in your area if you are seriously in debt. They will help you consolidate and lower your debt payments so you can avoid bankruptcy. Attend Debtors Anonymous if your spending is out of control. Then think long and hard about large purchases and consult with your partner. Set goals as a family and budget together. Your children will learn how to manage money by watching what you do, not what you say. Consider if your attitude toward money accurately reflects your values and priorities.

Once we become adults, sooner or later most of us realize that we will not "have it all" all the time. Life is about choices and compromises. Decide what you will do and where you are willing to compromise. You are modeling maturity and integrity to both your children and colleagues by being clear and consistent in your choices. What makes work-life integration possible is having clarity around what you want to achieve in all areas, and courage to let go of outdated ideals that no longer serve a purpose. Later in the book you will learn tools and strategies for personal and professional goal-setting. To continue to solve the work-life conundrum, we now want to look at some attitudes and strategies worth adopting both at home and at work.

SMART HOME MANAGEMENT HELPS TO MANAGE EXPECTATIONS

In the last section, we discussed defining success in a much deeper context—as personal inner well-being and integrity rather than external achievement. Applying this thinking to your home and lifestyle as a whole will help you manage expectations and reach better balance.

Outsource

If you can afford a cleaner, get one. Even if the cleaner comes only once a month to do a thorough cleaning, it will free up a lot of valuable time you can spend with your family. Getting help from a local handyman for odd jobs and having a gardening service once or twice a year will probably not break the bank, but it can eliminate a lot of stress around those niggling jobs that need doing but for which we never seem to find the time.

Shopping with the kids can be great fun, but it can take a lot of time too. If you work long hours and have precious little time for your family, perhaps you'd rather take your kids to the library or to the park than have to focus on shopping. Having your groceries delivered, if at all possible, can be a huge help. Several services offer organic and healthy foods if that is important to you, and most services can be set up as a regular delivery. There are plenty of healthy ready-to-heat meals available these days, and keeping a few of those in the freezer at all times can help free up an evening from cooking.

Get help from your children. Teaching independence and life skills from an early age takes a lot of pressure off you to do everything for them. Asking them for help makes them feel valued and special. At the end of this chapter, we provide tips on how to win cooperation by working with your children to divide up jobs and create chore charts to make contributing to the home a fun activity. It takes time in the short term, but the rewards are huge in the long run.

Any other help that is available in your area, get it: carpooling, dog walking, nanny sharing, and babysitting. Perhaps there is a local parent network? In the United Kingdom, they offer National Child Trust classes during pregnancy to prepare for the baby's arrival. Participants in these groups often stay in touch later and become a network for one another. Other parenting classes may be available in your area where you can meet likeminded parents you can share duties with. Don't forget the virtual world: there may be local parent groups on social media that can help with creative solutions.

Design Your Space to Suit Your Family

Is your home practical and well suited to children? Perhaps you have a garden or yard outside that requires a lot of attention and no one has the time. If so, consider AstroTurf! It won't look quite like real grass, but it is oh-so practical as a play area for little ones. You can always turn it back into a lovely lawn once they're grown up. Same thing goes for indoors. Take a look at your space and see if the dining area can perhaps become a play area instead. Maybe some practical flat-packed organizers and shelves won't look like something out of a home décor magazine, but on the other hand, you won't have to worry too much if the kids get fingerpaint on them. If you have little ones, put any expensive furniture in storage and use throws, beanbags, and rugs to create a cozy, child-friendly space. Having affordable items in the home means parents can relax and not worry if something gets broken or spoiled; this can also free up playfulness and creativity. If you have a smaller space that is crowded with too much stuff, evaluate what absolutely needs to stay and what can be donated or thrown out. You'll feel better about having an uncluttered space, especially if you work from home.

Protect Family Downtime

It is so important for both children and adults to have some downtime. Many parents and educators report concern at how busy their children are with scheduled activities, sports clubs, playdates, and tutoring. It is of course wonderful to invest time and funds in educating and training your kids and helping them discover their unique talents. It just needs to be balanced with quiet time, calm, and reflection, which are equally important life skills to develop. Periodically prune activities that may be taking more from your family than they give. Try to have some evenings every week that are free from meetings and carpooling to extracurricular activities. Your family will benefit from some scheduled, unhurried time to play board games, watch a movie together, or just talk.

A good idea is to have one screen-free evening each week: no TV, phones, tablets, laptops, or video games. Key here is to communicate the benefits to the kids and help them discover other ways to interact and have fun; otherwise, it might feel like punishment. If the baby hasn't arrived yet, you may want to start practicing screen-free evenings with your partner so that it becomes natural for the child from the beginning (and it might help with your or your partner's digital addiction).

Protect the family meal as often as you can. The family dinner hour has been one of the casualties of our fast-paced world. Some families eat in front of the television, connecting with the TV but not with one another. Other families eat on the go and at different times as a result of busy and conflicting schedules. The family meal is an important tradition that has served to keep families connected for centuries. Several American studies conclude that regular family mealtimes lead to better academic achievement and lower rates of negative behaviors in teens, such as delinquency, drug and alcohol abuse, and early sexual behavior.

Use your calendar to schedule non-negotiable family time. Schedule specific blocks of time for family meetings (Chapter 10), evening family time, special one-on-one dates with your children, and couple time. Don't be afraid to say no when your boss or coworker asks you to stay late or do extra work. You can say, "I'm sorry, I already have a very important meeting scheduled." They don't have to know it is a family meeting or an appointment to take your nine-year-old miniature golfing.

Celebrate Differences

A great way to let go of perfectionism, overachievement issues, and futile attempts at control is to celebrate differences. The home is an ideal place to do this, as the family is a naturally diverse collective of different genders (most of the time) and ages. In Positive Discipline, we talk a lot about creating belonging and significance by helping our children feel part of a family unit by means of family activities, mottoes, and values. Celebrating our differences helps with modeling autonomy and personal power as individuals. You are also valuing diversity, a hugely important life skill for adulthood. This is why it is key to let even the little ones (after age four) chair family meetings. Regardless of age, everyone has a voice and it matters. Model to your children the importance of putting effort into getting into someone else's world, and show that you care.

As we've seen, some of the qualities required for effective home management are flexibility, discipline, and acceptance. These are fantastic life skills that you will do well to model to your children. They are also essential for success in the professional space.

GREAT PARENTING SKILLS *AND* GREAT PROFESSIONAL SUCCESS

The modern workplace is an increasingly changing, time-pressed, and unpredictable place. Jobs, roles, companies, and functions are forever shifting. To retain security and success it is therefore becoming increasingly important to develop transferable skills and a strong sense of self. One of the greatest factors that will help parents achieve greater work-life balance is to recognize that some of these transferable skills are the very same ones that make them effective parents.

Make a list off the top of your head of what you feel are the top skills and abilities you are developing as a parent. We can think of a few: patience (oh yes!), organizational skills, punctuality, communication skills, emotional regulation, selflessness, sense of humor, resilience, lightheartedness, adventurousness, creativity, playfulness, courageousness, leadership, and self-awareness. There is nothing like parenting to force us to take a look within.

Let's look at some common workplace requirements. Empowering and motivating colleagues, managers, clients, collaborators, and staff is an essential part of most people's professional life. Coaching and delegating are common workplace practices that are regularly taught in leadership training. What are the key skills required to be a good coach and delegator? Patience, communication skills, selflessness, and leadership. Coaching your kids' playdates at the museum or imparting the joy of learning during homework time need not be so different from delegating part of your project with passion and enthusiasm to a junior member of your team.

As another example, a lack of innovative thinking, risk-taking, and flexibility is a huge problem for many organizations. What are the key skills required to help your organization be more creative? Perhaps adventurousness, playfulness, resilience, and creativity. Do you see the parallels yet? Roles may vary, but a skill is transferable from area to area. If you value playfulness with your children, you can transfer that to a creative brainstorm in your field. It does not matter if you are a banker, nurse, or entrepreneur—a bit of playfulness releases endorphins and enables you to think outside the box. One of the fundamental cornerstones of Positive Discipline is to value mistakes as opportunities to learn. Pioneering this policy in your everyday life will help you to relax those exacting standards you hold for yourself, and help you become a little more flexible and forgiving at home and at work.

It might take a while to see the parallels. Working your way through this book will hopefully help you feel more confident in your parenting abilities. Then start talking about it—start sharing the parallels between your parenting life and your professional life. Start looking for the transferable skills and communicate their applicability during performance reviews, interviews, and discussions of deliverables. Experiment. Start small, as always when trying new behaviors. Try a new approach with your team, something that worked at home. Imagine how great it will be when being a parent is seen as a plus in the workplace!

EMBRACE MODERN WORKING METHODS

New players in tech industries have understood the value of letting their workforce have autonomy and flexibility to work where and when they want and still be productive. If this is not yet the policy in your workplace, can you get involved in influencing that policy? This may be easier in smaller organizations, but perhaps you can influence your team. Starting small is always a good idea. Your employer needs to trust that you can deliver although you have other responsibilities as well. Showing that you do so when given more flexibility will impress them and perhaps help other colleagues in a similar situation. Not all industries can offer similar amounts of flexibility, of course. If you are a physiotherapist, you need to physically go and see your patients. In most industries, however, innovative thinking can still tease out a lot more flexibility than what is currently there.

Making flexibility happen at work requires discipline and letting go. It often requires setting boundaries around family time and work time, and finding creative ways of delivering even if you can't physically be at work all the time. It may require speaking up and making demands at your place of work. When you focus on all the benefits a flexible work situation brings to your family in terms of income, personal fulfillment, and security, it will feel easier to do. This of course isn't always doable, and sometimes we just need to keep our heads down and get on with it.

In conclusion, we made a point earlier about the wholeness that parenting brings. What are the benefits of that to our working lives? More and more hierarchies and structures are breaking down and individual autonomy and initiative are required. Freelance engagements, short-term contracts, and individual entrepreneurship are becoming more commonplace. By living a full and whole life, you are well placed to provide that initiative to your industry. You are, after all, the leader in your own life!

POSITIVE DISCIPLINE IN ACTION

Monica had been a successful sales manager at a software company for ten years. She had an excellent salary, received hefty commissions and bonuses, drove a company car, had outstanding benefits, and got a bonus of an annual luxury vacation for herself and her husband. She also enjoyed a fairly flexible work schedule, so she could be home by 4:00 p.m. and care for the home and their two kids. But there was one fundamental problem. Monica hated what she did. She hated the constant cold calls to potential customers, the infighting among her sales staff, the detailed proposals she had to write, and the endless number crunching. She had wanted to be a psychologist for as long as she could remember. But she had lacked the support for her dreams growing up, and believed money was the only true measure of success. So the financial perks in sales kept her from following the desires of her heart year after year. She dreaded work every day, but her husband, Don, was an entrepreneur with less job security, so they had all become accustomed to her high income. She felt trapped, resentful, and unfulfilled.

Monica became increasingly unhappy with her work and life as a whole. She came home grouchy and was depressed Sunday evenings in anticipation of going back on Monday to a grind she despised. Desperate, she and her husband came up with a plan for Monica to realize her dream of becoming a psychologist. They found a master's program that offered courses one evening a week and one Saturday a month for two years. They agreed she would stay with her current job while she completed her advanced degree. Don took on a part-time consulting job that still enabled him to spend some time on his entrepreneurial activities. They significantly reduced their monthly budget so they could save for the time when Monica would quit her job and work at a reduced rate of pay.

Initially, having less income put a strain on the family. They had to cancel their yearly family skiing holiday, much to the kids' disappointment. With Monica now combining work and studies, she also had a lot less time to care for the home. It took a lot of family discussions and some trial and error, but eventually Monica and Don were able to communicate to their children the importance of being happy and fulfilled at work. Once the kids understood that, they were happier to cooperate and help out more at home, and they created routines and job charts that everyone followed. They could also see how their mom was excited every day because of her new reality, rather than being grumpy and difficult—a change they enjoyed tremendously! Once Monica had a plan in place to move into her preferred career, she stopped resenting her current position, and instead viewed her job as a means to a much-desired end.

POSITIVE DISCIPLINE TOOLS

Your children are a large part of your home life, so we've equipped you with some hands-on tools that will make that time enjoyable rather than stressful.

Winning Cooperation

Rudolf Dreikurs taught the importance of "winning children over" instead of "winning over children." Winning over children invites rebellion or giving up. Winning children over invites cooperation. Winning your children over does not mean giving them what they want so that they like you and are more likely to do what you want them to do. Winning your child over means you created a desire for cooperation based on a feeling of mutual respect. One of the best ways to win children over is to do things *with* them instead of *to* or *for* them. Doing things with them means respectfully involving them in finding solutions that work for everyone. In the process your children will learn thinking skills, problem-solving skills, respect for self and others, self-discipline, responsibility, listening skills, and motivation to follow through on the solutions they have helped create. Imagine how successful we can be both in the home and in our professional lives when we let go of a bit of control and empower others.

Jobs and Chores

Harmony and respect are maintained when family responsibilities are discussed and shared together. Avoid stereotyped role expectations such as Mom cooks, Dad does DIY, the youngest sibling never takes responsibility, and so on. At a family meeting, make a list of all jobs and chores that need doing. Find a way to creatively rotate who does what. For example, create a chores chart that spins around like a roulette wheel, or come up with another creative way to display what needs doing when. Make sure the system includes a way of taking note of who does what and when. This also helps teach valuable life skills around home management and teamwork. Regularly reevaluate progress at family meetings.

Routines

Most everyone responds well to clear expectations and routines, and younger children in particular need them. At family meetings discuss all areas that need routines, such as mornings, evenings, and mealtimes. Decide as a family where you need to have fixed routines and look for creative ways to capture them. Try taking pictures of your children doing each aspect of their bedtime routine and timing them. Then create a chart with all the process pictures attached to a large clock showing how long it takes to complete each task. Then when the child gets stuck and whines, you can refer her to the chart and to your agreement ("What's next on your routine chart?"). Children are more likely to follow the routine if they had a hand in its creation. Regularly reevaluate progress at family meetings.

Scheduling

This is very similar to jobs and routines. The key is to have fun. Create a clearly visible chart of everyone's schedules, and then sit down as a family to discuss what everyone's priorities are and figure out how to make that work in a balanced way. Write down a list of everyone's commitments. Detail any requirements such as driving, chaperoning, fees, and so on. Ensure that there is an even distribution of time, effort, and funds for each child. Create a fun schedule that everyone can refer to.

EXERCISE

Hopefully you've now taken a closer look at how to integrate your work and home life by setting healthy boundaries and redefining what success means. Remember, balance doesn't happen overnight, and it doesn't happen all the time. There is an ebb and flow to life that is helpful to accept. Certain things have a "best before" date—your children will be children only once and for a very short time. Career opportunities come and go, but if ever there is a once-in-a-lifetime opportunity, by having a healthy partnership with your mate, well-functioning problem-solving strategies at home, and great communication with your children, you shouldn't have to pass it up because you're a parent. It is possible to do both!

A Personal Vision Statement Helps Redefine Success

This is a simple but very powerful exercise. You may want to make sure you have some quiet time around you before settling down to do it. To help redefine success, it is helpful to start with the end in mind:

1. What is your vision for your life? Write it down. Write several versions if you need to and then try to pick the one that feels the most truthful. Try not to let your ego take over; really listen to your deeper, inner voice.

2. How would you like to be remembered and by whom? After you've answered that question, go back to your vision in point 1 and ask yourself if you want to redefine it.

3. What specific actions, activities, and relationships are helping you achieve this vision? Divide a page in half and write them down on one side of the page.

4. What specific actions, activities, and relationships are blocking you from achieving this vision? Write them down on the other half of the page.

5. Pledge right now to take action to increase what you wrote under point 3 and decrease point 4. Write down specific, measurable targets and how you will achieve them.

6. Pat yourself on the back! You've just done a great thing for yourself and your family.

Then, as part of your routine and to check progress, ask yourself every week:

• How well did I take care of myself?

• What did I do to connect with my mate?

• What did I do to connect with my kids?

• How did I do at work?

Let the answers guide you so you don't lose sight of that long-term inner balance.

CHAPTER 5

THE AGONY AND ECSTASY OF CHILDCARE

Camilla tells us the story of the first time she left her daughter in childcare: " 'Bye, Mommy!' My lips were quivering. This was her third day at the childcare center and I felt extremely grateful that I had had the presence of mind to take a whole week off work to help Sophia get used to her new surroundings. My gorgeous little three-year-old had already run off with a beaming smile to make new friends. Clearly, I had a greater problem than her at handling the end of our full days together, and accepting the new reality of back to work and childcare."

FINDING QUALITY CHILDCARE

To avoid guilt, getting good childcare is essential for busy parents. Availability and cost will vary greatly depending on which country or community you live in. However, there are some universal questions to answer during your research process, which will provide greater clarity around your choices.

Childcare options fall under two main categories: in your home and outside your home. If you choose childcare outside your home, you may prefer the structure and child-centeredness of a quality childcare facility, or you may find yourself drawn to the family atmosphere of a private home. In either situation, there is a huge difference between quality childcare and poor childcare. Think outside the box. Some families combine professional childcare on some days with time at grandparents' or other relatives' homes on other days. Finally, if you are employed, check with your employer—there may be parenting support systems in place. Whatever you decide, start early, so you have plenty of time to do your research and feel comfortable with your choice.

Researching Your Options

As we discussed, there is now ample and compelling evidence that children in high-quality childcare do just as well as children in parental care, which is great news for busy parents. To help you in your search, a study by the National Institute of Child Health and Human Development offers a framework of standards for exceptional childcare.

The study states that the quality of the childcare is essential in determining the effect on the behavior and well-being of the child. For these purposes, quality is broken down into two relevant parameters—regulable features and process features. This valuable information provides a framework you can apply to your own research to make this experience easier, faster, and, hopefully, less anxiety-inducing.

Regulable Features

Despite the slightly awkward title, this is actually pretty straightforward: measuring the adult-to-child ratio and assessing the care provider's education level. How many children is each adult taking care of? In general, the lower the number of children an adult is caring for, the better the observed quality of that care, and the better the children's developmental outcomes. It also takes into account

69

the group size. How many children are in the child's classroom or group? Smaller groups are associated with better observed quality of care. Then it considers the caregiver's education level. Did the caregiver complete high school? College? Graduate school? Higher caregiver education predicts higher quality of observed care and better developmental outcomes in children.

Education isn't everything and some people are naturally good with children. Still, we suggest at least two years of education in an early childhood education program that includes the basics of child development, brain development, and age-appropriate behavior. However, many of these programs do not cover enough tools for responding to behavior challenges. If you find a childcare situation that feels right to you in every other area, you might ask if the caregiver would be willing to read a Positive Discipline book that includes many tools for encouraging children to develop capability and contribution skills through self-discipline, responsibility, and problem-solving.

The NICHD study provides the following guidelines for the above parameters:

AGE	ADULT-TO-CHILD RATIOS	GROUP SIZE	TRAINING AND EDUCATION OF STAFF
6 months–1.5 years	3 children to 1 staff person	Maximum of 6 children	Staff should have formal post-high school training, including certification or college degree in child development, early childhood education, or a related field.
1.5–2 years:	4 children to 1 staff person	Maximum of 8 children	
2–3 years:	7 children to 1 staff person	Maximum of 14 children	

In the United States, state and local governments set minimum standards for regulable features, like those listed above, that childcare providers must meet in order to get licensed. In the United

Kingdom, OFSTED (the Office for Standards in Education) has this same responsibility and regulatory role. In addition, there can be other bodies that set standards, such as the National Association of Family Child Care (in the United States) and the Professional Association for Childcare and Early Years (in the United Kingdom). The first action on your list is therefore to contact your relevant local body and ask for a list of accredited childcare providers in your area, as well as research if any other official authorities or organizations provide similar standards and/or accreditations.

Once you have your list of accredited providers, you can contact them and ask about the parameters set out above. You will be able to get a general view of a childcare provider by the quality of the answers and by comparing a few different providers. This will help you select a handful that you can then investigate further. We suggest that you ask if you can visit the provider in question and spend several hours observing to see if the staff follows the policies they advertise. This is where the process features come in.

Process Features

Process features focus more on children's actual day-to-day experiences in the childcare setting. Here we're looking at the outcomes of observable behaviors such as interaction with other children and adults as well as with toys and games. One of the strongest and most consistent predictors of children's development, according to the NICHD study, is positive caregiving! The following table compares process features set out by the study with the equivalent Positive Discipline tools. You would, of course, be extremely lucky to find a caregiver who delivered on all these things all of the time. Just as there are no perfect parents, there are no perfect caregivers. However, by applying this checklist to your research, you are increasing your chances of finding a caregiver who follows a positive approach, one that will chime with the Positive Discipline you practice in your home. This consistent approach will surely lead to a contented and secure child, and consequently a more guilt-free busy parent!

71

PROCESS FEATURES	POSITIVE DISCIPLINE PHILOSOPHY/TOOL
Showing a positive attitude. Is the caregiver generally in good spirits and encouraging when interacting with the child? Is he or she helpful? Does the caregiver smile often at the child?	*Kind and firm.* Rudolf Dreikurs taught that kindness shows respect for the child. Firmness shows respect for ourselves and the needs of the situation. Authoritative methods are kind and firm. As a result, this method will lead to higher self-esteem, greater social competence, and overall greater life satisfaction.
Having positive physical contact. Does the caregiver hug the child, pat the child on the back, or hold the child's hand? Does the caregiver comfort the child?	*Connection before correction.* We cannot influence children in a positive way until we create a connection with them. Create closeness and trust instead of distance and hostility by communicating a message of love. This can be done with a hand on the shoulder, getting down to the child's level and looking into his eyes, validating her feelings, or by giving a hug.
Responding to vocalizations. Does the caregiver repeat the child's words, comment on what the child says or tries to say, and answer the child's questions?	*Validate feelings.* Don't we all feel connected when we feel understood? Try to validate a child's feelings through a question or a statement, such as "How are you feeling about that?" or "I can see that makes you very angry."
Asking questions. Does the caregiver encourage the child to talk/communicate by asking questions that the child can answer easily, such as yes-or-no questions or asking about a family member or toy?	*Curiosity questions.* Designed to invite your children to share their perceptions of what happened, what caused it to happen, how they feel about it, how others may feel, what they learned from it, and what ideas they have to solve the problem. The true meaning of education is "to draw forth," which comes from the Latin word *educare.* Too often adults try to stuff in instead of draw forth.
Talking in other ways. For example, praising or encouraging (in Positive Discipline we prefer encouraging; for detailed discussion, see Chapter 7). Does the caregiver respond to the child's positive actions with positive words such as "You did it!" or "Well done!"? Does the caregiver encourage the child to learn or have the child repeat learning phrases or items, such as saying the alphabet out loud, counting to 10, and naming shapes or objects? For older children, does the caregiver explain what words or names mean? Does the caregiver tell stories, describe objects or events, or sing songs?	*Encouragement.* Every Positive Discipline tool is designed to help children feel encouraged and to develop valuable social and life skills that will help them feel capable. Use the kind of praise that invites self-evaluation rather than external validation. (More on this in Chapter 7.)

PROCESS FEATURES	POSITIVE DISCIPLINE PHILOSOPHY/TOOL
Encouraging development. Does the caregiver help the child to stand up and walk? For infants, does the caregiver encourage "tummy time"—activities the child does when placed on his or her stomach while awake—to help neck and shoulder muscles get stronger and to encourage crawling? (We have known of childcare situations where babies spend hours in an infant seat and toddlers spend hours in front of a TV watching cartoons.) For older children, does the caregiver help finish puzzles, stack blocks, or zip zippers?	*Take time for training:* Training is an important part of teaching children life skills based on their developmental readiness. Don't expect children to know what to do without step-by-step training. Parents often don't take time for training because life is hectic or because they don't fully understand how essential it is for children to contribute.
Advancing behavior. Does the caregiver encourage the child to smile, laugh, and play with other children? Does the caregiver support sharing between the child and other children? Does the caregiver give examples of good behaviors? Expecting children to share before it is developmentally appropriate is typical. It is important to teach skills such as sharing without expecting children to master this skill until much later.	*Modeling.* Model what you want. Be the person you want your children to be. Responsibly control your own behavior before expecting your children to control theirs. Encourage sharing without expecting children to share all the time. Understand developmental appropriateness. And know that you will sometimes make mistakes—and can learn from them. Don't expect perfection from yourself or your children. Enjoy the process.
Reading. Does the caregiver read books and stories to the child? Does the caregiver let the child touch the book and turn the page? For older children, does the caregiver point to pictures and words on the page?	*Character and life skills.* Think about how children learn to talk. First they hear you talk for a year. Then they say a word, but you don't expect them to talk in sentences. When they learn to speak in short sentences, you don't expect a college vocabulary. Children learn responsibility the same way—one step at a time.
Eliminating negative interactions. Does the caregiver make sure to be positive, not negative, in interactions with the child? Does the caregiver take a positive approach to interacting with the child, even in times of trouble? Does the caregiver make it a point to interact with the child and not ignore him or her? In addition to these questions, the implication is how the caregiver deals with misbehavior. Most caregivers do not have enough education (specific tools) for responding to the misbehavior in positive ways. In fact, they may cling to old ideas that avoiding punishment allows children to "get away" with misbehavior.	*Mistaken goals.* Positive Discipline teaches that "a misbehaving child is a discouraged child," and punishment only adds to the discouragement. Positive Discipline methods help children improve their behavior through tools that are encouraging instead of punishing. Most good childcare providers will welcome learning about Positive Discipline tools if you share a Positive Discipline book and/or deck of Positive Discipline tool cards with them (for a detailed discussion on Mistaken Goals, see Chapter 8).

Childcare Inside or Out of the Home

Childcare Inside Your Home

You may choose the services of a live-in or live-out nanny. Many people have found qualified caregivers who provided such quality childcare that they were almost like a family member.

Finding well-qualified people is a challenge for any kind of employer, whether you are hiring for your business or for your childcare. However, much more is at stake when employing a childcare provider for your children. It is essential to require a background check, check employment references, and be very clear (in writing) about your expectations (such as other housekeeping duties) as well as your discipline philosophy. We would recommend that you have the carer sign a contract and that you check employment law in your city/country of residence to make sure you adhere to the legal requirements (i.e., taxes, holidays, and sick days). In addition, it is a good idea to require your carer to have infant and child first aid and CPR training (and you should have this training too). Once you have found someone you like, we suggest having the nanny start during a vacation period or a weekend, so you can be in the home with your new childcare provider for several days before leaving that person alone with your children. You can learn a lot in a few days about a nanny's attitude, skills, and relationship with your children.

Jane had a live-in nanny, Joanne, for eleven years. Joanne was willing to read several Positive Discipline books and to implement the discipline theories. She understood the importance of not becoming a slave to the children, but instead supervising their involvement in chores and following the other routines they helped create. Joanne was part of every family meeting where the whole family worked on finding solutions to challenges on a weekly basis.

Childcare Outside Your Home

Childcare outside the home is either in a designated childcare facility or in a private home. If you are one of the many parents who have decided that childcare outside your home meets the needs of your family, there are several additional factors you should consider.

Childcare Facilities

A childcare facility is a center that is dedicated solely to the care of young children (as contrasted to a childcare provider's home). The advantage is that childcare is the sole occupation of the staff and a quality facility will be filled with age-appropriate equipment and toys. However, not all childcare facilities can claim the "quality" label. On top of the parameters suggested in the NICHD study, we would suggest you also check the following:

- Apart from the educational level of staff, what kind of training do they get and how often? Does the staff receive training to detect learning disabilities or physical and cognitive problems?

- Does the center do a background check on their employees? (This may be automatically done in order to achieve accreditation, but do check.) How is this background check performed? *No matter what form of childcare you select, be sure you take the time to do background checks.* Personal references are nice, but a background check of the individual or facility may turn up information that will help you decide whether or not this is the provider for you.

- What is the turnover rate for the staff at the facility? Very young children need consistency, not only with curriculum and daily routines but also with those who care for them. Will your child consistently interact with the same provider?

- Is there a discipline policy? How are problems handled? In Chapter 7 we will discuss in detail the problems with punitive and permissive care. The best childcare is void of any kind of punishment (shaming and blaming) and uses discipline based on kindness and firmness at the same time. All Positive Discipline tools promote capability, contribution, and, whenever possible, the involvement of children in solving problems. You will want to ensure that the facility you choose has a similar policy.

- Does the provider prepare meals and/or snacks, and if so, what do they consist of? When and how are meals and snacks prepared and served? Childcare facilities that appreciate the importance of involving children to enhance their sense of belonging and capability will allow children to take turns with meal preparations and will allow children to serve themselves as often as possible.

- How does the center handle toilet training? What is your responsibility regarding providing extra clothing, diapers, and so on? What are the sanitary conditions in the toileting area? Many childcare facilities are willing to toilet-train young children. This works very well because the childcare staff are not emotionally invested in your child's toileting. It is especially effective when the facility has small toilets and a regular schedule for toileting. Your child will see other children using the toilet and usually want to follow their example. "Accidents" are handled with a minimum of fuss, simply allowing a child to change into clean, dry clothes, helping only as much as necessary without any sense of blame or shame.

- Does the center have an open-door policy? Can you drop by unexpectedly to visit with your child during your lunch hour? Can you volunteer in the classroom for special events? This is a very important point to consider. Some centers may tell you it is disturbing to the child to have you visit, and this could be true. However, don't consider leaving your child anywhere that doesn't have an open-door policy. If your visits disturb your child, consider finding a way to peek around corners once in a while to observe without being seen.

- Consider opening hours and logistics of getting to and from the facility to ensure it works with your (and your partner's) travel routes and times.

- Check the options offered by each facility to see if they suit your needs. For instance, do they offer both part-time and full-time care? School-year-only care or full-year care? Do they offer care during school holidays?

A Private Home

Some parents prefer childcare in a private home because of the family atmosphere. Some are lucky enough to find a close friend or relative to take care of their children. The same considerations as for a childcare center, as well as the process features, apply to a private home. If you choose childcare in a home, we strongly suggest that you spend a full day with your child in the private home. Spend this time whether you know the provider well or not. If that is not allowed, do not consider this home. You cannot make a better investment of time to be certain your child is receiving quality childcare.

Just as you hear horror stories about nannies and daycare facilities, there are horror stories about childcare in private homes. Some are literally parking places for children who spend their day sitting in front of a television, are subjected to physical punishment, and are lacking in the kind of equipment that enhances child development. On the other hand, many daycare providers have a solid background in child development and/or other training for quality childcare. They create an environment filled with developmentally appropriate equipment, flexible routines, and positive discipline.

After you have decided on the type of care you want and have completed your detailed research looking at both regulable and process features (including spending time with the provider on your own), spend several hours watching the carer together with your child. Below is a handy checklist you can use while quietly sitting on the sidelines and observing what goes on. Give a rating from 1 to 10 (with 10 being the best) on each item to help you establish whether this really is the right place for your child.

OBSERVATION CHECKLIST

1. Staff/carer seems to love and enjoy children.

2. Staff/carer does not expect things of children that are not age appropriate, such as expecting a two-year-old to sit quietly during story time.

3. Staff/carer uses kind and firm discipline and avoids all punishment.

4. There are no televisions in sight (in a private home there might be one, but it is turned off or used only for educational purposes).

5. The facility is clean and safe.

6. There are routines without rigidity. For example, do they have a "reading time" but allow children to wander and play with other toys if they are not interested? Do they serve nutritious food but allow children to eat only as much or as little as they want? Do they have naptime but allow children who aren't sleepy to quietly read a book?

7. Are there toys that are just plain fun as well as plenty of developmentally appropriate educational toys?

8. Do they avoid pushing academics for children under six, who learn best from play and socialization?

9. Do they treat parents as partners rather than as intruders?

After-School Care

Once your children enter school, other childcare options become available. Some schools have on-site care so your children never have to leave the school's grounds. Other schools will bus your children to a childcare center. The same licensing, safety, discipline, and parent involvement guidelines listed above apply to those caring for your school-age child.

Communication Is Key

Regardless of what option you choose, it is important to stay connected to your child and his or her childcare provider. Take the time to keep your childcare provider updated about your child's development and anything happening at home; for example, the birth of a new baby or illness in the family can have an effect on your child's behavior, and your childcare provider will deal with it best when the situation is understood. In addition, ask your provider to keep you updated, and make sure you formalize the process—weekly emails, monthly phone catch-up, et cetera. It is not always possible to chat for any length of time at drop-off or pickup.

A mother shared, "I learned the importance of regular communication with my husband and our nanny after discovering Julianne got peas and spaghetti for lunch *and* dinner two days in a row. The nanny gave her the same lunch twice in a row, and my husband fed her the same dinner twice in a row." That led to the creation of daily journals and regular family meetings that included the nanny. The parents completed the daily journal while they were with Julianne to convey key information to the nanny, and the nanny completed the other parts of the journal while she watched Julianne so the parents were informed. Part of the family meeting included menu planning that involved everyone.

JULIANNE'S DAILY JOURNAL	DATE: _____	
WOKE UP:	NAPPED:	WENT TO BED:

MEALS/ SNACKS/BEVERAGE	TIME	COMMENTS
Breakfast:		
Morning snack:		
Lunch:		
Afternoon snack:		
Dinner:		

MEALS/ SNACKS/BEVERAGE	TIME	COMMENTS
Activities:		
Health and general disposition:		
New accomplishments:		
Medicine:		

Creative Solutions

Many men and women have opted for more flexible working lives, as we discussed in the Introduction. Perhaps it involves a combination of working from home, at freelance hubs, in cafes, and on client sites. Or perhaps you work only from home. How can you solve the childcare dilemma when that is your reality? Some of you may feel this is no different from working full-time away from home. You would still consider full-time care. How well does the option of having childcare within the home work if you or your partner is there in the home too, but engaged in professional activities? Undoubtedly, new mothers in particular will find it extremely hard to get any work done when the new baby is nearby. And that is as it should be—after all, we are hardwired to nurture our young.

If you have decided to continue to pursue your career when having children and you work from home, you may have to make some changes to your home office setup. For some the only solution is to leave the house and work somewhere else. If you have chosen a caregiver to be at your home, he or she can then get on with caring for your child without you hovering over them—and you can get on with being productive. Depending on how big your home is, you may be able to be sufficiently secluded from the area of the house where the children are, so it may work that way. Or if you need to work from home but do not have sufficient space, childcare outside the home may be the best option.

Many areas these days offer flexible services such as part-time nannies—for example, you have a nanny on Tuesdays and Thursdays. That can be another great alternative if you decide you want to work part-time while also caring for your child. There are also nanny shares, in which you share a nanny with another family (i.e., two babies with one nanny in your home or the other family's). All this will of course also depend on your flexibility and which sector you are in. For example, is your work seasonal? Do you have to be available at fixed times every day, or can you set your own hours? Thinking through these factors will make it easier to decide on the best option for you and your family.

Whatever solution you choose and however confident you are in your research, we know few parents who haven't suffered some separation anxiety when the time comes to leave the little one for the first time, just like Camilla in our opening story. Even if it goes well in the beginning, something can shift for your child and he or she can go from loving childcare to hating it, with ensuing misbehaviors. Either way, being prepared for some emotional times is key.

USING POSITIVE DISCIPLINE TO DEAL WITH SEPARATION ANXIETY

Allow children to have their feelings. It is never a good idea to tell a child to stop crying—or, even worse, to tell a child, "Big girls [or boys] don't cry." We know adults mean well when they say "Don't cry," but it is the same as saying "Don't communicate. It makes me uncomfortable." You may feel differently about crying when you understand it is a language. You will be more effective when you learn to understand (not speak) the language. You might say, "It is okay to cry. I hope you feel better soon." Use your intuition (and/ or the Mistaken Goal Chart, explained in Chapter 8) to give you clues about why your child is crying. He or she may be using "water power" as a misguided way to seek belonging. Crying doesn't always mean anxiety. Sometimes it is an expression of genuine need, and sometimes it is an expression of a preference. (Needs should be satisfied, but it is not always healthy to have every preference granted.) Sometimes crying represents frustration, lack of communication skills, or simply a transition method. For nonverbal children, separation anxiety is very real. (Children raised in extended families seldom experience separation anxiety because they get used to having many people around them. Of course, their anxiety may kick in when they meet a stranger.) However, you can feel confident that when you follow all the precautions for finding quality childcare and when you model faith and confidence, your child will be fine.

Be sure your childcare provider is willing to rock and comfort your child if needed. Then, if your child is still having difficulty separating, leave as soon as possible so your child doesn't have to deal with the energy of your guilt and anxiety as well as making his own adjustments. The same goes if you are struggling. Don't linger, as that may unsettle your child. Leave and deal with your feelings in private. Who hasn't had a good cry in the car on the way to work? As soon as your children are old enough, take time to teach skills that will help them learn other ways to behave and communicate instead of acting up, such as "Use your words." Provided there are no allergy considerations, spray some of your perfume or aftershave on your child's shirt. Tell her, "You can smell this when you miss me and remember that I'll be back to pick you up at the end of the day." You probably already have mementos of your child with you at all times! Screensaver pics, anyone?

POSITIVE DISCIPLINE IN ACTION

Linda, a single mother of three young children, found in her church a part-time student with excellent references to come to her home forty hours a week. Linda had the added benefit of knowing this person and her family. She found it was more cost-effective and less stressful to have someone in her home. As she put it, "I needed someone wonderful to watch my kids, and I also needed a helper to do some of the housekeeping duties. After long days selling advertising I was able to come home to a tidy house, with the laundry done and dinner on the table (expectations that had been agreed to in advance).

"My kids loved her, and they loved having someone in their home because they could have their little friends over. My nanny would also do errands like grocery shopping, buying birthday presents, or picking up the dry cleaning. That way I was able to relax and really enjoy my kids when I came home at night. I can't imagine how stressful it would have been to pick up my kids from daycare and go home to a messy house and an empty refrigerator. This arrangement worked beautifully for me for seven years. My kids never had to miss out on anything because I worked, and I was able to attend most of their events because I didn't have to take time to do all the other chores and errands."

POSITIVE DISCIPLINE TOOLS

"It breaks my heart when my child cries and clings when I drop him off at the childcare center. It is enough to make me want to stop working." Ever had that thought? Even if you aren't sharing your anxiety with your child, you might still feel it, like Camilla in our opening story, who suffered terrible separation anxiety at the thought of leaving her daughter even though Sophia seemed to adjust well to her new surroundings. Let's look at some specific Positive Discipline tools that can help.

Show Faith

The process of coping with separation is part of every child's normal developmental challenges. Children do survive (and thrive) in separation so long as they are provided with love and support, both at home and in the childcare environment. It can help to know that some children will adjust sooner than others. Encouraging dependence is counterproductive to the development of self-trust and leads to excessive dependence on others. Yes, babies must depend on others, but the goal of parents and caregivers is to help children develop a sense of trust in themselves—including the confidence that they can handle disappointment and anxiety. Remember, research has shown that children can thrive when they receive love at home and love in a quality childcare situation. This will help with your own separation anxiety as well.

Letting Go

Letting go does not mean abandoning your child. It means allowing your child to learn responsibility and to feel capable. It is difficult to watch your child suffer, even when you know the lessons learned will provide strength in the long term. Often it is harder on you than on your child. Hang in there. Remember letting go allows your child to gain strength by building his or her "disappointment muscles" and problem-solving skills.

Take Time for Hugs

No matter how busy you are, there is always time for a three-second hug. A substantial hug can lift spirits and change attitudes, yours and your children's. Sometimes a hug can be the most effective method to stop misbehavior. Try it the next time you are feeling frazzled and your child is whining, and see for yourself how well it works. A mother shared, "I remember the time I was so angry at my three-year-old son that I felt like hitting him. Instead, I stooped down and gave him a hug. His whining stopped immediately and so did my anger. Later I realized that he was whining because he could feel the energy of my stress. Hugging him was enough to calm me down, even though I thought I was doing it to calm him down. Well, it takes two for a good hug, and both people benefit."

Don't wait until you are angry or your child is misbehaving. Give hugs in the morning, right after work, several during the evening, a longer one just before bed. When you offer that hug, you may also want to whisper a loving word to your child about how much you love her and how much she means to you.

One father shared how he once stopped his four-year-old during a tantrum by asking if he could have a hug from his son. It totally confused the boy, who completely forgot that he was in the middle of a tantrum. Instead he got a chance to, in his mind, help his dad, who needed a hug, and that made the boy feel needed and special. You may want to try that one next time!

Write Love Notes to Your Children

It doesn't take much time to write a note for your child's lunch bag, pillow, or mirror. One very busy working mom decided to put a note in her daughter's lunch bag every day for a year. She took time on airplanes or while waiting for an appointment to write several notes or silly rhymes in advance, such as "Roses are red / Violets are blue / Every day / I think about you." When she traveled, she gave her childcare provider notes to tuck into the lunch bag for each day she was gone. Her daughter's friends gathered around her at lunch in eager anticipation to hear the note of the day. Her daughter felt very loved.

EXERCISE

Review the childcare checklists from earlier in this chapter to map out what your needs and ideas are. Review your existing provider(s) to see if any improvements need to be made. To help you decide, write down what you'd like the ideal care to be: What does it look like, what feelings are you expecting both for you and your child, and what activities are important to you—say, time in nature, or maybe excursions? This ideal picture can serve as a guide once you start researching and interviewing caregivers. Remember, whether you choose care in your home or in another family home or facility, it is worth having a backup plan in case of illness and during holiday periods.

PART 3

PARENTING AND CHILD DEVELOPMENT

CHAPTER 6

GENERATIONAL DYNAMICS AND HOW TECHNOLOGY AFFECTS PARENTING

"Just five more minutes!" Janine shouts from the other side of her locked bedroom door. Mom is annoyed. This is the third time she has asked Janine to turn off her laptop and settle in for the night. "I'm still doing my homework, Mom, promise." Mom has heard that one before. Janine is a sophomore in high school and an average student. She participates on numerous after-school sports teams and has a busy social life. Because of all her commitments she needs to work hard to keep up with her schoolwork, and Mom is concerned that she struggles to get enough sleep during the week. Recently Mom has noticed that Janine is staying up later and later. Janine says she is busy doing homework, but when Mom checks in, she finds Janine surfing the Internet, chatting with friends online, and watching YouTube videos. "I don't understand her obsession with being online. It seems like such a waste of time!" Mom complains to her best friend, who can only agree. It certainly wasn't like that when they were growing up.

WHAT HISTORY CAN TEACH US ABOUT PARENTING

We often hear that children are different today, and therefore we have to adapt our parenting to meet the needs of this new generation. That is undoubtedly so. However, there is also considerable evidence to suggest that over the past few decades parents too have changed. So we have a chicken-or-egg situation—is it the kids or the parenting that is the cause? Probably a bit of both.

Alfred Adler taught the importance of belonging and significance for healthy child development, and emphasized that significance is achieved through a healthy sense of contribution. The goal of Positive Discipline is thus to help children develop feelings of belonging and significance through contribution that leaves them with a strong sense of both self and others. Our ability as parents to do that will be greatly influenced by how our own needs were met growing up and the belief systems that were instilled within us. How does this play out across generations?

GENERATION	PRE-BOOMERS (SILENT GENERATION)	BABY BOOMERS	GEN X	MILLENNIALS (GEN Y)	GEN Z (iGEN)
Birthdate Range (approximate— there are no agreed-upon dates)	Before 1945	1946–1955 (sometimes called the old boomers) 1956–1965 (late boomers)	1966– 1980	1981– 1995	1996– 2010
Whom do they parent?	Baby boomers and Gen X	Gen X and Millennials	Millennials and Gen Z	Gen Z and ?	?

Before we answer that question, let's get some clarity on what the generations are called and who parents whom. It is interesting to note that there is no generally agreed-upon view of exactly when a generation starts and finishes, so the years given here are approximate. Since behavioral changes are gradual, perhaps that doesn't matter so much. At the time of this writing we do not as yet have a name for the generation after Generation Z. It will be interesting to see how society views the development of these young children and what will be the defining characteristics of that generation.

Key Trends Shaping Generations

According to the Center for Generational Kinetics, there are three key trends that shape a generation: parenting, technology, and economics (keeping in mind, of course, that at an individual level everyone is different). The center also confirms that how we parent is shaped by how we were parented. We do certain things because we see them as wise or because that's the only way we know how. There are also things that we deliberately do differently because we didn't like when they were done to us (for example, spanking) or because times have changed and our children have different needs (such as around technology).

Let's look at some examples of how parenting shapes a generation. Many believe the parenting philosophy of late baby boomers and Gen Xers is "We want it to be easier for our kids than it was for us, and we want to be able to give them everything that we didn't have." This helped create the millennials' perceived sense of entitlement (a fiercely debated topic). This trend is still strong in parenting today (mainly through the influence of Generation X), and it revolves around the idea that children are the center of the universe, are vulnerable, and are in need of constant protection and nurturing: "If my child is in any way not happy/successful/engaged, it reflects badly on me and I must be a failure as a parent; therefore, I must check all the time that they are okay." These parents have made the mistake of thinking significance is enhanced by more belonging (pampering, rescuing, spoiling), rather than by letting their children build resilience through trial and error, thereby creating a "me, me, me" generation. Many children and young adults today therefore have a strong sense of belonging because of the unconditional love they receive, but lack a sense of significance through contribution.

Previous generations, on the other hand—those from before the baby boom and those from the very first years of the baby boom—emphasized achievement and loyalty (to the family, profession, academics, etc.). They made the mistake of thinking these characteristics could be developed by "obedience" to authority—government, parents, and teachers—rather than through love and acceptance. Their great quest is to find intrinsic value apart from achievement and to feel a sense of being "good enough." Many children of this generation (late boomers, Gen X) therefore grew up with significance through skills (and often make great contributions to society) but without a sense of belonging (unconditional love). They in turn wanted to parent differently and give their children "everything they didn't have," hence the dynamic described earlier.

Pre-Boomers, Baby Boomers, and Generation X

Many of our readers may not be of the baby boom generation but may have been parented by boomers. As such, it is interesting to understand how these older parenting styles and beliefs have shaped today's parents. Pre-boomers and early baby boomers raised late boomers and Gen Xers quite differently from the way they were raised. There were many changes in family dynamics caused by socioeconomic changes that came during and after World War II. Many women started working outside the home, both parents worked longer hours, and divorce rates increased, leading to many late boomers and Gen X children becoming latchkey children. This meant that children often came back to an empty home after school, completed their homework on their own, knew how to entertain themselves, and at times may have even cooked for themselves and their families. This has led late boomers and Gen Xers to function with independence and self-directed behavior—basically a strong sense of significance and contribution. Many, however, suffer from a poor sense of belonging (feelings of abandonment). To compensate for that, these generations often display an unhealthy emphasis on achievement and competition—a dynamic of doing more and more in an effort to try to make up for an intrinsic sense of lacking.

Perhaps as a reaction to this dynamic, the millennials who were raised by these late boomers and early Gen Xers had a completely different experience of parenting. These families were much more child-focused, and the boomer or Gen X parents were actively involved in their children's lives (too involved at times, hence the terms "helicopter parent" and "tiger mom"). Many millennials grew up being overscheduled, overprotected, and overpraised (it's important to remember that this was all done in the name of love). Therefore, this generation is seen neither as independent nor as self-directed, and is in need of lots of praise and validation (hence strong belonging plus weak significance or contribution).

We do not as yet know how Gen Z (and the next generation) will turn out, although in the following sections we will make some predictions. What we can see is that a lot of their parents, late Gen X/early millennials, the majority of whom are professionally active, continue to feel stretched to the limit trying to achieve perfection in all areas, with detrimental consequences for both themselves and their families. Two of us writing this book have personal experience of this struggle; in addition, several friends have suffered anxiety and depression as a result of trying to juggle everything without compromising on standards. Remember, Gen X is conditioned to "do," to take care of the practicalities of life, but may not have felt so nurtured due to parental absence; hence they may find it hard to feel emotionally secure and to let go of the need for perfection and achievement.

THE MILLENNIALS

There has been much talk about this generation as being entitled and self-interested; sometimes they're even called Generation Me or the selfie generation. Where did this feeling of entitlement come from? As we've just seen with this generation, children were the center of the family, told that they were special (as a reaction to their parents' upbringing) and that they could have and achieve anything they wanted. They received awards for just showing up (even if they came in last place), and if their parents had enough leverage, they may have even been placed in higher-level classes because teachers and administrators just didn't want to take the heat.

We know that when children receive rewards and awards without really earning them, it both devalues the awards given to children who actually earned them and leads to a sense of shame and embarrassment for those who didn't. There is no hiding it, since there is no corresponding improvement in skill to back up the award. In her book *Mindset*, Carol Dweck explains that this process leads to a fixed mindset in which the child will be afraid to take risks and will always seek external motivation through praise and rewards from others.[13] In addition, if parents swoop in and do everything for them, these children do not grow up either with the belief that they are capable or with the understanding that lasting reward and life satisfaction take time and effort.

A further complicating dynamic is that millennials are challenged socioeconomically. They are the first generation in the Western world that is unlikely to achieve a higher standard of living than their parents. Education and housing have become more expensive, and the job market is more competitive than ever. Job security and a job for life are things of the past. Couple that with the dynamics of growing up in a world of technology, which has taught us that we can have anything almost instantaneously—except, as it turns out, job satisfaction and deep, meaningful relationships. At the same time, due to developments in healthcare, nutrition, and education, millennials are smarter and better educated than any generation before them. Many argue that societal structures are in fact what is holding them back. For example, there is currently a net financial flow going from young to old in many Western countries. Why? Perhaps because older people are richer, more influential, and tend to vote, and so are favored politically.

Millennials as Parents

Ninety percent of all babies being born today are born to millennials, and of the 40 million U.S. millennials ages twenty-five to thirty-four, 22.9 million already have children.[14] With 10,000 millennial women giving birth each day in the United States alone, what will their parenting be like?

A recent study from the popular parenting web portal Baby Center reveals that millennial parents show more relaxed parenting styles than the generation of parents preceding them. "Millennial moms are clearly reacting to the way they were raised," says Mike Fogarty, at BabyCenter. "They reject the pressure they grew up with."[15] Sixty-three percent of millennial moms describe their own parents' parenting style as "protective" and consequently want to provide their children with a greater sense of freedom, hopefully leading to greater resilience and self-direction. Millennial dads are the most domesticated yet of any generation, and will more naturally accept shared home and child-rearing duties. This will potentially make it easier for millennial couples to reach greater equality and work-life balance as well as allowing millennial women to be more assertive in their careers.

Some millennials may be putting off parenthood due to economic pressures around education, housing, and job market. Many of them will also have memories of their own, perhaps first-generation, working mothers suffering from a lot less equal opportunity and work/life balance. But for those who do become parents, raising their child well is a top priority. According to a 2010 Pew Research survey, some 52 percent said parenthood was one of the most important goals of their lives. In the 2015 survey, half of millennial parents said that they felt they were doing a good job as a parent. They certainly have the most information available to them—there are a multitude of parenting blogs and websites where parents can learn and commiserate like never before.

MILLENNIALS IN THE WORKPLACE

Millennials want to make an impact on the world—they want to have a purpose. Perhaps because of all the uncertainties facing them, they, more than any generation before, are demanding to know the *why* of what they are asked to do. They have a much higher demand for work-life integration, and value activities outside work for their personal satisfaction just as highly. While there may be a gap between their expectations and the realities of the workplace, they're also extremely adaptive—changing jobs often because they have to, and working online and out of the office. They are much more likely to have "slasher" careers (such as IT consultant/yoga instructor/astral photographer), and they do not view interests and hobbies as something separate from professional endeavors. This is putting added pressures on organizations to shape up and become clearer in purpose. Millennials are ingenious, creative, and flexible. They are also much more egalitarian, well suited to the more horizontal structures that are emerging across society.

GENERATION Z, BEING SHAPED BY TECHNOLOGY

This generation is referred to as the on-demand generation. They have never known a world without technology. They've abandoned TV and the desktop PC for laptops and mobile devices. And it's no wonder—technology has been a part of their lives since toddlerhood. This generation's parents didn't give them a coloring book and crayons or even put them in front of a TV for distraction. Instead they gave them a tablet or smartphone, so they learned to swipe before they learned to speak (go to any restaurant and you'll see dozens of smartphones propped up so that toddlers can watch their favorite characters or play their favorite games while the adults enjoy their meals and adult conversation). More than one-third of Generation Z say they use technology as much as possible, compared to 27 percent of millennials. In addition, they have an eight-second attention span (shorter than a goldfish's!), sparking the increasing popularity of ten-second (or less) video advertising and apps like Snapchat.[16] A striking statistic says that 100 percent of Gen Z are connected for at least one hour each day.

Today's technology is allowing children to quickly learn and assimilate certain skills that earlier generations never had, or have had to work hard to develop, and that are essential in the digital world we now live in. But with the increasing presence of screened media in kids' lives, as parents we have to ask what are they missing out on? What is happening to their personal relationship skills, delayed-gratification skills, and ability to plan for solutions that may take more than three minutes or even three days to accomplish? Technology is also proving to be highly addictive, and since Generation Z is the first generation to be born without any memory of an analog world, they are very vulnerable to this addiction (even most millennials will remember a childhood less dominated by screens, and can therefore have some perspective). We are seeing some Generation Z kids struggling to form deep, meaningful relationships because of their addiction to technology. This is because they have less opportunity to practice interpersonal skills face-to-face with their peers, and they don't have the coping mechanisms to deal with stress because they are turning to devices instead of to people.

Electronics and technology are here to stay, and they present what is possibly the most challenging change to our parenting to date. We want to make the most of it while also teaching our kids the value of interpersonal connections. Especially with the introduction of new technology, we are going to see more opportunities for screen time (positive and negative), not less. As parents of Generation Z (and beyond)—Generation X and millennials—we have to take this dynamic very seriously. Since our children have no memory of the analog world, it is up to us to ensure we provide plenty of opportunities for them to experience screen-free activities centered on interpersonal relationships, creativity, and problem-solving. Since many of us are pretty addicted to screens ourselves, this can be a real challenge. Remember that children's interpersonal connections take priority over their virtual ones any day; they need time with you more than they need time with their devices. What is most important is to discover what works best for your family, and to find that balance of embracing technology and embracing one another.

POSITIVE DISCIPLINE FOR ALL GENERATIONS

Understanding the particular dynamic that may shape your parenting, as well as the socioeconomic pressure the current generation of children is under, can help you adjust your parenting style. It is worth checking your own balance between belonging and significance. If you are a Gen X parent, are you suffering from a poor sense of belonging? Or do you believe that your belonging depends on your achievements and perfectionism? If so, chances are you overcompensate by doing too much for your child, which may render your child less able to develop a strong sense of contribution. You may therefore want to ensure you don't swoop in and rescue, but rather learn to let your child discover, fail, and learn resilience.

Catherine Steiner-Adair makes the point in her book, *The Big Disconnect*, that when it comes to technology replacing face time there is no longer any real generational divide. "Digital natives or immigrants, we all love our screens and digital devices." That's why it is essential for parents to manage their own technology use in order to model the self-regulation needed to survive and thrive in this rapidly changing digital world. In addition, you'll want to schedule many screen-free times, such as outside activities, mealtimes, and board games or other family activities, and weekly family meetings (where screens are not allowed). During family meetings, children practice face-to-face giving and receiving of compliments as well as face-to-face brainstorming for solutions to family challenges. And don't forget to schedule "special time" (without screens or work) with each of your children and your partner.

POSITIVE DISCIPLINE IN ACTION

Let's look at a real-life example of how limiting screen time can help strengthen children's (and parents') sense of belonging and significance. Here single dad Brad tells his story.[17]

"When my children are not doing their homework or practicing their instruments, they are in front of a screen: TV, computer, Wii, or iPad. Even when we leave the house, they watch a DVD on the drop-down screen in the car. I'm not proud of this fact. But when my kids aren't staring at a screen, they are staring at each other, arguing, bugging each other, and yelling, 'Daaaaaaad!' Then I have to come referee the current squabble. Adding difficulty to the situation, my job requires that I spend a fair amount of time in front of my computer screen. So it's hard for me to set a good example for my children. But I am committed to improving my parenting skills, so I was going to make every effort to limit screen time.

"During a family meeting, my kids decided that during the school week, they would watch one hour of TV each day and only after homework and music practice was complete. We also agreed on half an hour of recreational computer time and half an hour of video game time each day. Using the computer for homework didn't count.

"We immediately hit a snag. Because my kids get home from school at three and I work until five, there was no way for me to monitor the amount of time the kids spend watching television or playing video games. I realized that it was nearly impossible to limit screen time to any specific amount of time. The only really effective method would have been to turn off the power switch.

"So instead we were going to try to have a time of day when everything is off. From six to eight p.m. each day, we would be screen-free. My teenage son was skeptical at first—he was convinced that keeping track of screen time worked great—but soon realized that we were way over the limits we had previously set.

"That evening, the clock struck six and I turned off all the screens in the house. After a moment of uncomfortable silence, we looked at each other and my son said, "So now what do we do?" I said, "Well, what are some of the things on our list? How about if we take the dog for a walk?" My daughter hadn't felt well that day, so she stayed home and read a book while my son and I took the dog for a walk. We both really enjoyed the time together and the chance to get out of the house for some fresh air.

"When we returned, we decided to play a card game, and then my son showed my daughter and me a couple of card tricks. Then we sat down and played a game of Pictionary with much laughter and enjoyment. By now it was seven-thirty, and I told my daughter it was time for a bath. While she was taking a bath, I sat down and played my guitar, something I hadn't done for months. When eight o'clock rolled around, we all sat down together and watched *American Idol*. And we were able to watch it without commercials because my son had recorded the program during our screen-free time. (Another bonus!)

"All in all, the plan worked quite well. I hadn't anticipated how much I would enjoy turning everything off for two hours. One thing I needed to remember was that perfection in parenting is unattainable. I had found myself expecting perfection from my children, which strained our relationship. And in my focus to limit screen time, I ended up replacing that time with relationship-building activities. It was a good reminder for me to focus on the long-term goal of improving my relationship with my children."

—*Brad Ainge, "Single Dad Brad," www.singledadbrad.com*

POSITIVE DISCIPLINE TOOLS

We want to emphasize Positive Discipline tools that will help you ensure a healthy sense of belonging and significance in your children. We also want to look specifically at managing screen time. As you go through these tools, think back to Janine and her parents in the opening story and imagine how the effective use of these tools can help their situation. It's important to keep in mind that even the best solutions may not work forever and will need revisiting and revising from time to time.

Spend Regularly Scheduled Special Time

You've seen this tool pop up a few times now, for good reason—having time set aside for regularly scheduled "special time" is a very powerful way to help children feel a strong sense of belonging. Very young children need special time daily for at least ten to fifteen minutes.

After the age of six, thirty to sixty minutes a week works well. Take a few minutes at the end of each special time to decide what you will do during your next special time by brainstorming a list of fun things to do together. Your child's contribution here is key to helping him or her feel significant. It could be a bike ride, a ball game, a board game, a trip to the library, or whatever you and your child like to do together. And remember that special time is never a time for correcting behavior; it is a time of pure bonding and enjoyment.

Sadly, teenagers often lose interest in spending time with you, preferring their friends. They may feel especially embarrassed to be seen with you in a public place. However, you may be able to talk them into a date night for just the two of you, once a week. Or take them skiing or on some other trip long enough to spend time traveling together. If you're driving, make an agreement in advance that you will listen to your teen's music half the time if he or she will talk with you about important things the other half.

Children interact differently when they are one on one with you than they do when they are competing with their siblings or others for your attention. These special times will help you get to know your child better and forge a strong connection.

Make Agreements

Sometimes parents interpret an agreement with their children as "I will tell you what to do and you will agree to do it." Many moms and dads will think they have come to an agreement with their kids about screen time when really it's a rule that they have dictated to their kids—a rule to which kids "agree" only in order to get their parents off their backs. Parents are then surprised and frustrated when kids don't keep their end of the agreement and the problem escalates.

The key to creating successful agreements is involvement. Involvement equals cooperation. Children will usually keep their agreements when they have been respectfully involved in creating those agreements. Sit down together during a calm time when all screens are off and have a respectful discussion about healthy screen use. It is important to wait until you are not currently engaged in an argument about screen time and everyone has calmed down so that a rational discussion can be achieved. (Use the exercise at the end of this chapter as a guide to creating this agreement.)

Share equally. During the discussion time, be sure that everyone has an opportunity to share his or her thoughts and feelings about the issue. Interruptions are not allowed when someone is sharing. Some families use a three-minute sand-flow timer. The person who is sharing can have the whole three minutes, or can stop before his or her time is up by saying so. The person or people listening are not allowed to defend, explain, or give their opinion until it is their turn. Brainstorm solutions.

Children, being children, may not keep their agreements, even when they have been respectfully involved. Even when they really do intend to do so, they don't have the same priorities as adults. They may intend to turn off the TV after one show, but since limiting their TV time is not high on their priority list, it may be forgotten. How many times do you get caught up in an activity you enjoy and want to keep doing it "just a little longer"? Since limiting your kids' time watching TV is high on your priority list (not theirs), and since you have involved your child in creating an agreement surrounding screen time, it is okay to respectfully remind your child, "What was our agreement?"

If these steps don't promote successful agreements regarding electronic media use in your household, start again from the top. During the discussion, you may discover the reasons—and you will be giving everyone an opportunity to keep learning from mistakes.

Follow Through

Many parents have great intentions to set limits around and manage their children's screen time, but for one reason or another, the limits are never held. Or they're not held consistently. Sometimes a lack of follow-through on screen-time limits is due to losing track of time—you tell your kids they can watch a half hour of television, and before you know it, an hour or more has gone by because you were absorbed in other tasks. Or as Brad admitted in his story, maybe you don't really want screen time to end because it will mean the kids will go back to their arguing, bickering, or fighting; the screen is a welcome distraction and you're not ready to handle the problems that come when it gets turned off. Or perhaps you just don't want to be the "bad guy" and have to tell your kids that screen time is over, or that they have to put the phone away and stop texting their friends. They're enjoying the time, and it's tough to be the one who brings it to an end.

Whatever the reason, not following through on a limit you have set about your child's time in front of a screen sends a few negative messages: that limits on screens are not important; that you don't care what they do with their time; that you don't really mean what you say; that it's okay to keep playing or watching even when you've said stop; that you don't prioritize family engagement; and that you lack confidence as a parent.

Children know when you mean what you say and when you don't. It is really that simple. If you say it, mean it, and if you mean it, follow through. Parents who say what they mean and mean what they say do not have to use a lot of words. In fact, the fewer words used, the better. When you use a lot of words, you are lecturing, and children tune out lectures. One reason you may use a lot of words is that you are trying to convince yourself, as well as your child, that what you want is okay. If what you are asking is reasonable, have confidence in your request.

When it is time for TV or video games or computer play to be over, ensure that it does indeed end in a timely manner. You may need to help your children stick to the media limits by following through with kind and firm action. It may take a while for kids to get used to your decisiveness about the limits, but when you are able to follow through each time, they will understand that you mean what you say when it comes to limits on electronics. Say it, mean it, and follow through.

Modeling

What you model to your children is key, as we've already found out. What are your own habits around screens? Do you think it's okay to say to adolescents "Do as I say, not as I do"? For instance, if you make an agreement that there will be no phones at the dinner table, then it's not okay for you to use your phone at the dinner table. Even if you have an important work call to take, you can model respectfully excusing yourself from the dinner table to take the call and not disrupt mealtime for everyone. Even better, you can let the family know in advance that you are expecting an important work call and you may have to step away for a few minutes during dinnertime.

The same goes for having technology in the bedroom. Research shows us that using screens an hour before bedtime reduces the release of melatonin (the sleep hormone) in the brain and stimulates the brain to switch on instead of switching off. So it's not good for any of us (including adults) to use technology in our beds. Many families have a docking station for all electronics in a central location where they can charge everything during the night and not be tempted to switch it on during rest time.

Screen time is truly addictive to parents and children alike, so if possible, discuss as a couple what your expectations are before your children are old enough to copy your behavior. If you wait until they have phones and have not limited your own screen time until then, it will be more difficult, as they have already been observing you for several years. You will then have to unlearn your own behavior at the same time as you clarify your expectations with your children. Limiting screen time often means we also switch off from work, an equally important benefit that helps us be more focused during family time.

Create a Positive Discipline Technology Agreement
as a Family

Here is a sample of some points you may want to include in your family's technology agreement. This is meant to be a guide, not a substitute for following the steps described in the "Positive Discipline Tools" section of this chapter. Remember to periodically review the agreement, decide as a family what is working and what is not, and revise as needed.

1. We don't expect you to know everything about using technology. We will take time to teach you about responsible phone, tablet, and laptop ownership.

2. We will start off knowing your password. If we feel it necessary to access your phone or check your emails, we will do so. We are not trying to invade your privacy and this won't be forever. It is to help us keep you safe and help you develop sound habits around technology.

3. When we call you, answer the phone. We aren't calling just to chit-chat; we don't want to be screened.

4. Use the same respectful manners on your phone and computer you've always used in person. Say "hello," "goodbye," "please," and "thank you." Be kind, courteous, and understanding. If you wouldn't say it to someone in person, or if you are wondering if it's okay to say, refrain from saying it on your phone or computer.

5. You can take your phone and laptop to school with you, but they need to be turned off during school hours and remain in your backpack or locker (unless needed for schoolwork). You must agree to adhere to your school's device-use policy.

6. Docking your phone will become part of the after-school and evening routines. You can check your phone for fifteen minutes after school while you have a snack, and then it must be docked. After

homework and sports, you may have access to it again, but it will need to be in the charging station by eight o'clock on weeknights and ten o'clock on weekends.

7. Put the phone away in public places such as theaters or restaurants, and especially when you are engaged with another person. This may be difficult sometimes. We will use the silent signal we came up with to remind you to use phone etiquette.

8. Remember that the number of "likes" you get on your social media posts has nothing to do with how many true friends you have. To have a friend, be a friend.

9. Social media breeds insecurity. Stay away from naming any "besties" publicly and don't post photos that will hurt someone else's feelings.

10. Be aware of the photos you post of yourself on social media. Limit the number of selfies posted. Does that photo really need to go up for the world to see?

11. There will be times that we insist you leave your phone at home. Family time is important.

12. You are human and will make mistakes, and that's okay! We make them too! Mistakes are opportunities for learning; we will help you figure out how to fix them when they happen. We are on your team.

13. We will review and revise this technology agreement periodically in our family meetings.

14. We have faith in you to handle the responsibility of using technology and to make good choices. We will step back and allow you to learn as you go, being there to support and encourage you along the way.

15. We will agree to adhere to the same guidelines. There may be times that we have to deal with work or an emergency and we will communicate this to you.[18]

CHAPTER 7

EFFECTIVE VS. INEFFECTIVE PARENTING

During a parenting group meeting, Stan shared a story from his childhood, when he'd cheated on a fifth-grade test: "I was stupid enough to write some answers on the palm of my hand. The teacher saw me open my fist to find an answer. She grabbed my paper and, in front of everyone in the class, tore it up. I received an F on the test and was publicly called a cheater. The teacher told my parents and my dad gave me a whipping and grounded me for a month. I never cheated again, and I certainly deserved the F. So yeah, I was punished as a kid, but I think I turned out just fine." Is "fine" what we want for our kids, or can we do better?

PARENTING STYLES

How do you learn to be a better parent? After all, the baby comes without a training manual. In Chapter 6, we learned that most of us do one of two things: (1) we parent the way we were parented, or (2) we parent the opposite of how we were parented because we don't feel good about how we were brought up. In this section, we will review the four types of parenting styles most commonly used (most parents are made up of some combination of the four types). They are:

- Authoritarian (dictator)

- Permissive (laissez-faire)

- Neglectful (absent)

- Authoritative (Positive Discipline = kind *and* firm at the same time)

Authoritarian Parenting Style (Dictator): Order Without Freedom

Parents with an authoritarian parenting style use control as a basis for their parenting, such as imposing rules and using threats, punishment, and rewards to get children to "conform." Often parents use this method because they believe that the only alternative is permissiveness. They want to avoid being taken advantage of, and fear the chaos and lack of control that come with permissive parenting.

Unfortunately, the implied message to the child is "It's obvious you are not able to do it well enough on your own, so I will make you do it my way and in my time." This type of parenting style usually invites power struggles, revenge, and feelings of inadequacy. As a result, parents usually get the opposite behavior from what they want (irresponsibility, rebellion, risky behaviors, etc.). The irony is that in the parents' effort to control their children's behavior, they often lose all control.

When parents feel stressed and overwhelmed, it is easy to fall into the trap of authoritarian parenting. "Because I said so" is just so much easier. Lecturing and directing seem to come naturally: "Do this," "Don't do that," "Don't forget this," "Why can't you just . . ." The sad thing about falling into these traps is that we are expecting our children to control their behavior when we don't control our own. Sometimes the best we can do is make these mistakes, recognize the mistake, apologize, and work with our children for solutions.

Permissive Parenting Style (Laissez-Faire): Freedom Without Order

Parents who focus on permissive parenting (pampering) usually become overinvolved, overprotective, and overindulgent. Are you trying to do everything? Do you think it's your job to get your children out of bed, get them dressed, make sure they have breakfast, fix their school lunches, find their homework, settle their fights, and get them out the door on time—all while trying to get yourself ready and to work on time? If so, you are generating unnecessary stress for yourself, and creating pampered children who will become more demanding and less cooperative as they progress in their manipulative skills.

Let's face it. When we are feeling stressed and overwhelmed, it can be as easy to be permissive as it can to be authoritarian. We often make the mistake of feeling sorry for our children. It may seem easier just to rescue them. Again, we forget the long-term results. Children hassle, hassle, hassle. Parents say no, no, no. Children hassle, hassle, hassle. Parents say no, no, no. Children hassle, hassle, hassle. Parents run out of time or patience and give in, which stops the behavior (in the short term). This scene is repeated over and over in stores, during bedtime, in the morning. Just as excessive control invites children to think and act "against" their parents, permissiveness invites children to think and act "for" themselves in selfish ways. Permissiveness invites children to adopt the belief "The world owes me a living" or "Love means getting other people to give me everything I want." When children hassle and parents eventually give in, they teach their children that "no" doesn't mean no. It teaches them that "no" means "keep hassling until I give in." In essence, they train their children that the temper tantrums or other forms of misbehavior work. We have a saying: "Don't do anything for children that they can do for themselves."

Neglectful Parenting Style (Absenteeism/ Abandonment): No Freedom, No Order

Parents who follow a neglectful parenting style probably won't be reading this book. A parent may be absent due to sickness, addiction, death, or abandonment. For whatever reason, the parent may feel incapable of doing his or her job as a parent. Sometimes this is a person who just does not like being a parent and would rather be doing something else instead. He or she may leave childcare up to a nanny, or just leave the children to fend for themselves. This invites the child to feel unimportant, unloved, and unworthy, and certainly would not help the child to feel any sense of belonging or significance.

Authoritative Parenting Style (Positive Discipline): Freedom with Order

The authoritative parenting style embodies the Positive Discipline principle of kind *and* firm at the same time. It means respect for self and others in equal measure. It means including children in decision-making as soon as they are old enough. The principles of Positive Discipline are based on an authoritative parenting style.

Even if you feel you are a mix of styles (or vacillate between two), you can most likely identify a dominant trait. In Chapter 12 we will discuss the notion of "top card," which is a way of understanding your behavioral tendencies. The top card concept will give you further clues to what type of parenting style you are most drawn to. By being aware of your own tendencies, it will be easier to identify which particular behaviors you need to work on in yourself. Keep this in mind as you work your way through this book.

How does it work when parents have different styles? Many couples struggle because one may be permissive while the other is authoritarian. How might this influence your children and the family dynamics? Children learn very early on who is the "good cop" and who is the "bad cop," and very quickly they will figure out how to manipulate the situation. They often create a wedge in the couple relationship by playing one parent against the other. When one says no, they run to the other parent, who is likely to say yes. To be fair, children don't consciously want to cause problems between their parents. They aren't thinking about the long-term consequences of their behavior. They just want what they want, and are very clever about working the "system" that their parents create by the differences in parenting styles. It is best to respect your partner's parenting style while quietly modeling your own. As long as there is respect for both your partner's style and yours, and the children feel loved, they will be just fine.

No matter what your parenting style, will you be perfect and never make mistakes? No, of course not. This can, however, be a blessing for your children. Embrace your own misbehaviors and teach the Positive Discipline concept of seeing mistakes as wonderful opportunities to learn.

THE PROBLEMS WITH PUNITIVE (AUTHORITARIAN) PARENTING

Wherever did we get the idea that to make children do better, we must first make them feel worse? This describes the philosophy upon which punishment is based. Does this work as a motivational theory for us adults? No! Yet we think it should work for children, usually because of two things: (1) we ourselves were punished as children and we "turned out fine," and (2) it works as a way to discipline children. Yes, the last statement is true—punishment does work, but only in the *short term*. It will not help your children develop effective character traits, at least not to their very utmost level. Children will learn to cope and manage, but how about excelling with their sense of self-worth intact? How does punishment leave you feeling as a parent? Would you still want to punish if you could motivate improved behavior in ways that were both kind and firm? In the punisher, punishment usually invites feelings of guilt and regret and a sinking feeling of not doing the right thing in the long run.

Sadly, most parents who punish children do so because they truly love their children. They believe punishment will help their children learn better behavior. Alfie Kohn eloquently states what we know to be true: "The unsettling news is that rewards and punishments are worthless at best, and destructive at worst, for helping children develop such values and skills. What rewards and punishment do produce is temporary compliance. They buy us obedience. If that's what we mean when we say they 'work,' then yes, they work wonders. But if we are ultimately concerned with the kind of people our children will become . . . no behavioral manipulation ever helped a child develop a commitment to becoming a caring and responsible person."[19] Physical punishment also communicates to children that it is okay to use violence against those weaker than us.

Punishment is designed to make children *pay* for their mistakes. Discipline that *teaches* (the definition we prefer) is designed to help children *learn* from their mistakes in an atmosphere of encouragement and support. This learning will help them grow and develop positive belief systems built around being capable and loved, which will make them thrive—not merely cope and be "fine." Let's illustrate this crucial concept by revisiting our opening story. Stan had been caught cheating on a test in fifth grade, and felt he had deserved the punishment he got. Here, the workshop leader takes Stan through his private logic to discover how his belief system was affected by the punishment. She then takes the participants through an alternative scenario that would have led to greater growth:

LEADER: Does everyone agree with Stan that he deserved the F?

GROUP: Yes.

LEADER: Would that have been enough to teach him the consequences of his choices, or did he need the punishment also?

GROUP: Hmmm . . .

LEADER: What do you think, Stan? How did you feel about getting the F for cheating?

STAN: I felt very guilty and very embarrassed.

LEADER: What did you decide from that?

STAN: That I wouldn't do it again.

LEADER: What did you decide after receiving the whipping?

STAN: That I was a disappointment to my parents. I still worry about disappointing them.

LEADER: So how did the punishment help you?

STAN: Well, I had already decided I wouldn't cheat again. The guilt and embarrassment of getting caught in front of others were enough to teach me that lesson. Actually, the worry about disappointing my parents is a real burden.

LEADER: If you had a magic wand and could change the script of that event, how would you change it? How would you change what anyone said or did?

STAN: Well, I wouldn't cheat.

LEADER: And after that?

STAN: I don't know.

LEADER: Who has any ideas you could give Stan? It is usually easier to see possibilities when you aren't emotionally involved. What could Stan's teacher or parents have done or said that would have demonstrated kind and firm discipline?

GROUP MEMBER: I am a teacher. The teacher could have taken Stan aside and asked him why he was cheating.

LEADER: Stan, what would you have answered to that?

STAN: That I wanted to pass the test.

GROUP MEMBER: Then I would tell him that I appreciate his desire to pass and ask him how he felt about cheating as a way to accomplish that.

STAN: I would promise never to do it again.

GROUP MEMBER: I would then tell him he would have to receive an F for this test but that I was glad he had learned to avoid cheating. I would then ask him to prepare a plan for me about what he would do to pass the next test.

STAN: I would still feel guilty and embarrassed about cheating, but I would also appreciate the kindness along with the firmness. Now I see what that means.

LEADER: Now do you have any ideas how you could use your magic wand to change what your parents did?

STAN: It would have been nice if they had acknowledged how guilty and embarrassed I felt. They could have empathized about what a tough lesson that was for me to learn. Then they could express their faith in me to learn from my experience and to do the right thing in the future. They could reassure me that they would love me no matter what, but that they hoped I wouldn't disappoint myself in the future. Wow, what a concept—to worry more about disappointing myself than my parents. I find that very encouraging.

Several points are made by this discussion about non-punitive parenting.

1. Non-punitive parenting does not mean letting children "get away" with their behavior.

2. Non-punitive parenting does mean helping children explore the consequences of their choices in a supportive and encouraging environment so that lasting growth and learning can take place.

3. Most people turn out "fine" even if they were punished, but they might have learned even more had they received both kindness and firmness to learn from mistakes.

Are you satisfied with "fine," or do you want your children to have the kind of nurturing that helps them bloom into the best people they can possibly be?

The Problems with Permissive Parenting

As you saw above, the lack of contribution inherent in permissive parenting robs children of opportunities to develop resilience and grit, and renders them less well adapted to adult life. Permissive parenting often comes in three forms: rewards, praise, and pampering.

Rewards

Early on in her career, before she was trained in Positive Discipline, Joy used rewards charts in her classroom. One little girl had become entranced by the idea of receiving gold stars for helping out with jobs around the classroom. One day the class invited parents to visit and had refreshments to serve. Before even asking, Joy was delighted to see how her little star pupil took initiative and set out the cups and napkins. She then approached Joy with a beaming face and outstretched hand and said, "Miss, can I have my star now?" Joy was shocked to realize that she was teaching children to become dependent on external forms of reward for enjoyment and a sense of self-worth.

Kohn describes several research projects that demonstrated that rewards actually impaired performance, and that children who tried to earn rewards actually made more mistakes than those who were simply told the results of their efforts at performing a task. Current research in motivational theory of adults proves that for anything more than a basic repetitive task, punishment and rewards do not work as motivators. We will be discussing this dynamic in detail in Chapter 16. We have to be clear that the superfluous and flimsy use of rewards is creating a generation of children who are approval junkies, and it will not set them up for the realities of adult life. Working hard for their achievements and being appreciated for their efforts is what will lead to a healthy sense of contribution and self-worth.

Praise

As we saw in Chapter 6, recent parenting trends have been very focused on making children feel a strong sense of belonging, but parents misguidedly often use rewards and praise to accomplish this. Does praise encourage children to appreciate their own self-worth, or does it encourage them to depend on the opinions of others? We think it does the latter, but it's understandable that praise and encouragement are often confused. Praise focuses on the external achievement, while encouragement on the internal motivation and effort.

Is there ever room for praise? It can help to think of praise like dessert. A little can be so satisfying. A lot can be very unhealthy. All children want to know that their parents are proud of them. If their parents have heard about the dangers of praise and therefore never use it, their children may feel discouraged. This became apparent when Jane received the following letter from Jill Fisher in Australia.

QUESTION: *I'm at my wits' end with my thirteen-year-old girl. Our other daughter is nine. We have been following Positive Discipline for about two years now and it's changed so much in our house with how we act and speak to our girls. This last month we are having a problem with the "Praise" word with our thirteen-year-old. She's very clever at school and gets amazing grades; she loves school! So, the last few tests she's had, she's come home and told us the results, and my husband and I have both said to her, '"Wow, amazing results, Zara! You must be so proud. And you clearly did the hard work and it's paid off!" She floored us when she replied, "Why can't you just say you're so proud of me, like all the other normal parents?"*

We used to use Supernanny methods, like send her to time-out or send her to bed early when she had bad behavior. Now she much prefers the Calm Corner, which we all use, and then we talk when we've calmed down, and we use the 4 R's of recovery regularly! We have family meetings weekly, which definitely has changed a lot in our house—jobs, opportunities with mistakes, et cetera. But there's just one thing my husband and I have no idea how to tackle. Should I sit her down and say, "Of course we're so proud of you and you're working so hard at school and getting amazing results but, more importantly, you should be very proud of yourself"?

—*Jill Fisher, Australia*

ANSWER: Hi, Jill. I'm so glad you asked this question. I know you represent so many parents who struggle with this issue.

First I want to clarify an important point: it can be ineffective to use any tool as a "technique" without understanding the principle behind the tool. When you understand the principle and take it into your heart and wisdom, there are many ways to use the tools so they don't sound like scripts. I heard your heart and your wisdom loud and clear when you wrote: "Should I sit her down and say 'Of course we're so proud of you and you're working so hard at school and getting amazing results and you should be very proud of yourself, more importantly!' I'm sure you are very proud of her—so tell her. Admit that you made a mistake and didn't tell her the truth about how proud you are of her because you were afraid that it might make her dependent on the opinion of others. Let her know what a relief it is to tell her how proud you are and that you would also love to hear how proud she is of herself."

Pampering

Pampering (permissiveness, overprotection, rescuing) is at the other end of the spectrum from punishment. Parents who engage in pampering hope their children are thinking, "Thanks for loving me so much that I will never have to suffer. I will be forever grateful and will make it up to you by being the best kid on the block." So the parents give in to their demands for candy in the grocery store or for the latest fashion "because everyone else has it." It is perhaps particularly easy for professionally engaged parents to fall into this trap due to their added guilt, which we explored in detail in Chapter 3. In fact, some parents say their main reason for working is so their children can have more things (although they would prefer the word "advantages"). They may even struggle to understand why their children are so ungrateful and continue to demand more. When parents think about it, however, they realize that their children cannot develop survival and problem-solving skills if they are never given the opportunity to practice. And yes, they can in fact survive disappointment.

Permissiveness is almost always something "other parents do," and most parents recognize its ineffectiveness when they see other parents doing it. Millions of people watched, appalled, a few years ago as a film crew for a popular TV newsmagazine followed parents who took their two children to a large discount store. One child wanted a toy. The parents talked to him very kindly and reasonably about why he couldn't have the toy. The child had a temper tantrum. He grabbed the toy from the shelf and put it in the cart. The mother took it out of the cart and put it back on the shelf while continuing to discuss the matter very firmly. But as the child's decibel level increased, Mom's willpower decreased. Finally she gave in and bought the toy for the child. This provoked a great deal of comment from viewers. Some said, "That kid should have received a spanking the minute he had a temper tantrum." Others said, "I can't believe those parents could be so weak." Or "I would never let my child get away with that."

It is true that the parents were inconsistent and weak. Chances are that these parents would have been horrified themselves had they been watching someone else! It is very easy to judge others when you are not emotionally hooked, totally frustrated, and out of time. It is true that the children were not served well by having their parents give in to them. However, is the only alternative a spanking or some other form of punishment? Of course not! Neither method produces effective long-range results when you consider what children might be deciding in response to either permissiveness or punishment.

What were these parents thinking? We can only guess. Were they thinking, "I can't stand it when my child has a temper tantrum"? Were they concerned about what others were thinking? Or did they finally give in because they just didn't know what else to do? All of these thoughts probably crossed their minds, but the last may have had the greatest weight. Many loving parents simply don't have any tools in their parenting toolbox other than permissiveness or punishment. It is likely that these parents did not accept the punishment option and saw permissiveness as the only other choice.

POSITIVE DISCIPLINE PROVIDES ALTERNATIVES TO PUNISHMENT AND PERMISSIVENESS

It is interesting to note that parents don't need training in the most popular parenting methods: punishment, permissiveness, rewards, praise, rescuing, and overindulgence. Those methods seem to come naturally. Parents occasionally find themselves swinging from one extreme to the other: they are permissive until they can't stand their kids, then controlling until they can't stand themselves. In addition, it is amazing how many parents are fearful that if they are not pampering or punishing, the only alternative is neglect. Neglect is never acceptable. Positive Discipline provides you with many alternatives that are respectful, kind, and firm at the same time, and effective in the long term. However, it does take awareness, training, and practice to use non-punitive methods. It is up to you to practice, make mistakes, learn from your mistakes, and keep practicing. Raising capable, confident, loving children takes time, energy, and patience (and we're well aware that you may be running low on all three!), but it is possible and well worth the effort.

What might some kind and firm solutions be for those parents in the store? When the child asked for the toy, the parents could validate the child's feelings (connection) and then say no only once (firmness). It might sound something like this: "I know you really want that toy, and you can't have it today." Then they could shut their mouths and act by kindly and firmly taking the child to the car, where he could have his feelings (temper tantrum) in private. Or the parents could ask, "Do you have enough money saved from your allowance?" When the child pouts and says no, they could say, "As soon as you have saved enough money, you can have the toy." As another option, the parents could advise their children in advance that they will all leave the store immediately if there is any misbehavior.

You nurture the best in your children when your methods meet the five criteria for effective discipline that we set out in Chapter 2: helps children feel a sense of connection, belonging, and significance; is kind and firm at the same time; is effective in the long term; teaches valuable social and life skills; and empowers children (and parents) to feel capable and to use their power constructively. Yes, effective discipline can help children feel a sense of connection, belonging, and significance. Punishment doesn't. Kind and firm discipline is respectful to the child and to the adult. Punishment, permissiveness, rewards, praise, and rescuing aren't. Effective discipline has positive long-term results. Punitive methods may stop the behavior in the short term, but they have negative long-term results. Last but not least, both of you will feel capable and experience the joy of using your power constructively.

Teaching Parenting Skills

It is a good idea to know what you want for your children. As with all endeavors in life, chances of success increase when we have clarity on what we want. Only then can we better understand how to get there. At the end of this chapter, we have an exercise on defining the characteristics and life skills you want for your children. How do you teach these important characteristics and life skills? To answer that question, you will also be making a list of challenging behaviors you experience with your children. Believe it or not, these challenges are the very opportunities you need. The misbehaviors are clues to how you can change your own behavior and choose the most appropriate Positive Discipline tools.

Like many parents, you may be surprised to discover that changing your own behavior is the most important thing you can do to inspire children to change theirs. Let's illustrate. In our parenting classes, we love to use the example of "not listening" for an activity that demonstrates how parents model the opposite of listening. Instead they *talk*, and they talk by *telling* instead of inviting a dialogue. They tell children what happened, what caused it to happen, how they should feel about it, and what they should do about it. Then they wonder why children not only don't listen (meaning obey) but often "talk back." Then the children are scolded for following their parents' lead.

Instead, we teach the skill of asking curiosity questions with phrases such as "What happened?"; "How do you feel about it?"; and "What ideas do you have to solve this problem?," and we encourage parents to really listen to the answers. When parents role-play the child listening to these respectful curiosity questions, they are amazed at how much they feel listened to and, as a result, how much they feel like cooperating. Think of your own reactions when someone lectures you in the workplace. Do you feel like cooperating, or do you feel like avoiding? You might even wish you could talk back, but you hold your tongue so you don't lose your job. On the other hand, when someone respectfully asks a question and sincerely listens to your responses, how do you feel? Are you now more likely to feel part of a cooperative team?

Let's look at another example. If your child is struggling academically, let's say with mathematics, what do you do? You probably sit down with your child, break the problem down into smaller steps, encourage him or her, show faith that he or she can do it, and have patience. Now, what do you do when your child struggles with one or more of the important life skills? Do you show him a small step? Take time for training? Model patience that he is learning a new skill? Some parents have a hard time modeling patience or many of the other life skills, and revert to punishment and blame. Why is that? They become emotionally involved. Rationally thinking through and helping with something like mathematics is easier—you are not feeling challenged, stressed, or overwhelmed yourself.

The Positive Discipline tools you are learning in this book not only *change negative behavior*, both yours and your children's, but also encourage the development of the *characteristics and life skills* you want for your children (and yourself). Hurrah! Finally, you can start seeing misbehaviors as opportunities and get excited about the idea that every time they happen, you have an opportunity to encourage your child to become a responsible, independent human being!

THE FOLLOWING TABLE summarizes ineffective and effective parenting methods as discussed in this chapter, and can be a useful guide to the attitudes and strategies you want to develop.

PARENTS WHO USE INEFFECTIVE PARENTING METHODS	PARENTS WHO USE EFFECTIVE PARENTING METHODS
See children as possessions	See children as gifts
Try to mold children into what they want	Nurture children to be who they are
Are unreliable friends (or insist that a parent can't be a friend)	Are respectful and supportive friends
Give in or make child give in	Remain kind and firm
Control and dictate	Guide and coach
Strive for perfection (in child and self)	Teach that mistakes are opportunities
Try to win over child	Try to win child over
Lecture or punish ("for your own good")	Involve child in solutions
Treat child as object or recipient	Treat child as an asset
Overprotect	Offer appropriate supervision
Avoid feelings (try to prevent or rescue)	Allow feelings and empathize
Fix for the child	Teach life skills
Bawl out and then bail out	Allow child to experience and then explore consequences of his or her choices
Take behavior personally	Help child learn from behavior
Think only of their own point of view	Get into child's world
Are fearful	Have faith
Are child-centered	Are child-involved

POSITIVE DISCIPLINE IN ACTION

Nicole shares her story of discovering effective parenting strategies: "When our children were little, my husband and I would spank them often, whenever they would misbehave and we were angry. We went on a Positive Discipline course and had a real revelation! We had our first family meeting and told the children (nine and eleven at that time) that we would never punish or spank them again. They did not believe us. We told them that if we ever did that, we were wrong and would apologize. We never spanked them again. For sure there was an adjustment period with lots of conflict and tantrums as the kids were testing our limits and their newfound reality. But we managed, most of the time, to stick to more positive strategies such as positive time-out and enforcing agreements.

"I felt like a weight was lifted from my shoulders. I didn't have to deal with everything anymore and be or make the law. I didn't have all the responsibility; we shared power and responsibility between us parents and the kids. We became a team, working together for the good of the family, helping each other. I am in awe of how wise children are when we give them the opportunity. My twelve-year-old decided at one point to not do screens for a week when he saw how it was not helpful to him. Another amazing result of using Positive Discipline tools (like putting children in the same boat and problem-solving at family meetings) is that sibling fights are almost nonexistent. Positive Discipline has brought such a great team spirit to the family."

POSITIVE DISCIPLINE TOOLS

Teaching characteristics and life skills can be both fun and stimulating when you realize just how many opportunities there are to do so. To know you are on the right track with your own behavior, here are some fundamental Positive Discipline tools well worth learning by heart!

Kind *and* Firm

Firmness and kindness should always go hand in hand to avoid the extremes of either. Begin by validating feelings and/or showing understanding. Offer a choice when possible. Here are some examples: "I know you don't want to brush your teeth, *and* I'll race you to the bathroom"; "You want to keep playing, *and* it is time for bed. Do you want one story or two?"; and "I love you, *and* the answer is no."

Avoid Pampering and Punishment

Parents make a mistake when they pamper in the name of love. One of the greatest gifts you can give your children is to allow them to develop the belief "I am capable." Pampering creates weakness because children develop the belief that others should do everything for them. Punishment may stop the behavior in the short term; however, the long-term consequences can be devastating, as the child develops feelings of resentment and revenge. Sometimes it is the experiences that are the hardest for you and your children that will be of greatest service to them for the rest of their lives.

Curiosity Questions

Instead of lectures that attempt to stuff in, try curiosity questions to draw forth. When children hear a respectful question, they are likely to feel capable and cooperate. The key is using "what" and "how" questions, such as "What do you need to do to be ready for school on time?"; "How can you and your brother solve this problem respectfully?"; "What do you need to take if you don't want to be cold outside?"; and "What is your plan for getting your homework done?"

Natural Consequences

Children can develop resiliency and capability by experiencing the natural consequences of their choices. Avoid lectures or saying "I told you so." Instead, show empathy: "You're soaking wet; it must be uncomfortable." Be comforting without rescuing: "A warm shower might help." And always validate feelings: "Sounds like that was very embarrassing." After allowing your child to experience the natural consequences of a choice, you can ask conversational curiosity questions to help him be more aware of how he has more control over what happens based on his choices.

EXERCISE

Creating a Road Map for Your Parenting

Begin by creating a list of challenges that you are currently facing with your children. The following is a compilation of challenges brainstormed by thousands of parents from all around the world. You may find it comforting to know you are not alone! Although there are some cultural or situational differences, for the most part the challenges we face are age appropriate and part of the natural growth and development of children. Feel free to add any behaviors that are challenging to you that we may have left out.

CHALLENGES

- Demands your attention
- Won't do chores/work
- Doesn't listen
- Back-talks
- No motivation
- Entitled
- Materialistic
- Strong-willed
- Defiant
- Technology addictions
- Constant texting
- Tantrums
- Whining
- Cheating
- Fighting (especially with siblings)
- Biting
- Aggression
- Lying
- Stealing
- Homework problems
- Morning hassles, bedtime hassles
- Foul language
- Interrupting

Now, take a few minutes to create a list of characteristics and life skills you hope your children will develop. Imagine your child as an adult who has come home for a visit. What kind of person would you like to spend time with? Does your list look similar to the following?

CHARACTERISTICS AND LIFE SKILLS

- Problem-solving skills
- Responsibility
- Gratitude
- Cooperation
- Self-discipline
- Self-control
- Communication skills
- Resilience
- Self-confidence
- Courage
- Courtesy
- Patience
- Open-mindedness
- Sense of humor
- Compassion
- Respect for self and others
- Empathy
- Integrity
- Enthusiasm for life
- Interest in learning
- Honesty
- Belief in personal capability
- Social consciousness
- Self-motivation
- Kindness

Add any characteristics to your list that you feel have been left off. Refer back to the chapter and review the ineffective strategies you feel you may have been using. Ask yourself, "Do those strategies promote any of the characteristics I want? And do they strengthen any of the negative behaviors I want to root out?" Then look at effective strategies described in the chapter and think about how they may help you teach and develop the positive characteristics and life skills you are after. Keep your lists handy and refer to them often to verify that the Positive Discipline tools in this book are helping you provide the atmosphere that inspires the development of the characteristics you want, and the strategies for how to deal with the challenges that face you. And remember that it is the challenges that provide us with the opportunities to teach these important characteristics and life skills.

CHAPTER 8

UNDERSTANDING MISTAKEN GOALS

THE BELIEF BEHIND THE BEHAVIOR

In this chapter, we look at the fundamental approach to child be-havior as understood in Adlerian psychology with a tool called the Mistaken Goal Chart. We use the chart to detect mistaken beliefs and learn how to positively correct misbehavior. This chapter is going to get a little technical, so make sure you have a cup of tea at hand and won't be disturbed for a while! Even if it takes a couple of reads, we cannot stress enough the importance of understanding this fundamental Positive Discipline tool. If you master this, you have a key to unlock pretty much any challenging behavioral situa-tion, including with adults. It is that powerful!

POSITIVE DISCIPLINE'S PERSPECTIVE ON THE BEHAVIOR OF CHILDREN

Remember your fantasies about what it would be like to have a child before you actually had one? This child would never have a snotty nose, would always be well groomed and well liked, would behave well, and certainly would never be allowed to talk back. By now you have had your rude awakening, because the truth is that children don't always behave the way we expect them to or wish they would. Has this added to your sense of stress and feelings of being overwhelmed? Feeling even more stressed and overwhelmed doesn't mean that you're a bad parent. It just means that there is a huge difference between fantasy and reality, which can unwittingly lead stressed parents to choose ineffective parenting strategies (after all, they feel discouraged too). Misbehavior is a normal part of both early child development and the adolescent's individuation process. Adlerian psychology provides an excellent framework for understanding child behavior. In this chapter, you will learn it is normal for children to misbehave as they grow and develop and test their boundaries. This should help relieve some of the stress and help you choose encouraging parenting methods.

Why Children Misbehave

It is normal for children to test the waters (misbehave) as they try to figure out how they fit into this world. How do they find belonging, connection, and capability? How do they find out who they are separate from their parents? How do they deal with their perceptions of being less capable than others? How do they deal with the frustration of lacking the skills to accomplish their desires? Often the way they deal with their perceptions and frustrations is to feel discouraged and then to misbehave. Remember what Rudolf Dreikurs said: "A misbehaving child is a discouraged child."

As we discussed in the Introduction, it is often difficult to understand why children believe they don't belong or feel they are not capable. For example, how does a child believe she doesn't belong even though her parents love her? Why does she decide she doesn't belong when her parents have another baby? Why does a young child believe she is not capable just because she can't do something as well as an older child? Her mind has not developed enough to comprehend logic and consequently concepts such as cause and effect and the bigger picture, so instead she feels discouraged. This is why Dreikurs taught, "Children are good perceivers, but poor interpreters." In other words, children observe a situation, interpret what it means (based on their illogical, undeveloped thinking skills), feel something about it, decide something about themselves, others, or the world, and then act based on their interpretation, feelings, and decisions about the situation.[20]

Most parents don't realize that their children are always making decisions. These decisions form the foundation of personality and future behavior. Children are not consciously aware of their decisions, but they make them nonetheless. These life-shaping decisions often fit into the following categories:

I am _____ (good or bad, capable or incapable, fearful or confident, and so on).

Others are _____ (helpful or hurtful, nurturing or rejecting, encouraging or critical, and so on).

The world is _____ (threatening or friendly, safe or scary, and so on).

Therefore, I must _____ to survive or to thrive.

When children make decisions about thriving, they choose behaviors that help them develop into capable people. When they make decisions about how to behave based on their perceptions of how to survive, they usually choose what adults call misbehavior.

Let's take a look at one of the most familiar examples of early childhood decisions. A three-year-old usually feels dethroned by the birth of a new baby. Now, this child has had three years to be queen of the castle. She has received unlimited love and attention, and she rather likes it this way. Suddenly, without consulting her, Mom and Dad bring home a baby. This baby is cute and she does like it (sort of), especially when she gets to hold it or play with it, but she also has become, quite suddenly, less important. Or so it seems. People come to the house, walk right by her, and coo over the baby. They bring the baby presents. Worst of all, Mom and Dad are infatuated. They hover around the baby; Mom nurses it, Dad bounces it, and they talk about it all the time. Our three-year-old pouts and no one even notices. Obviously, something must be done about this situation. Her decision process might look something like this: "I am not important; others are ignoring me; the world is unsafe; therefore, I must behave in a way that will make them care for me again."

It is typical for young children who believe they have been replaced by a new baby to act like babies. She loses interest in the potty, wants her pacifier back, and insists on having milk in a bottle. She also finds that she "can't" fall asleep without being rocked and walked. This behavior makes sense to her and is based on the unconscious belief that "Mom and Dad will give me more time and attention if I act like the baby," but it sure looks like misbehavior to Mom and Dad!

See the Discouragement Beneath the Behavior

Adults usually look at the behavior, the tip of the iceberg, without understanding the discouragement or belief that motivates the behavior (what is under the surface). Instead of seeing a misbehaving child as a discouraged child, these adults give the child all kinds of labels, such as "naughty," "hardheaded," "stubborn," "disobedient," "bad," "strong-willed," "liar," "lazy," "irresponsible," "spoiled," and so on. These words create a very negative mindset. They label the child without seeing what the child is trying to say through the misbehavior: "I'm a child, and I just want to belong."

Dreikurs was able to see past the behavior and identify four mistaken goals that explain the beliefs behind the misbehaviors. They are called *mistaken goals* because the *real goal* is to achieve belonging, connection, and capability. The mistake is that children choose an ineffective way to achieve their real goal. As Alfred Adler taught, all behavior has a purpose. Understanding mistaken goal behavior helps adults understand that the real purpose is hidden, like a code, in behavior that seems illogical. Again, that is because children do not yet have the cognitive ability to express their needs in a more effective and positive way.

FOUR MISTAKEN GOALS OF BEHAVIOR

1. Undue attention ("I'll belong only if you pay constant attention to me")

2. Misguided power ("I'll belong only if I boss you around/if I don't let you boss me")

3. Revenge ("I don't belong, and that hurts, but at least I can hurt back")

4. Assumed inadequacy ("I don't belong and there is no hope that I can, so I give up")

UNDERSTANDING HOW MISTAKEN GOALS WORK

When you understand mistaken goal behavior, you will know that, in a sense, children are actually speaking in code. When you understand the code, you can respond to what the child is saying with her misbehavior in ways that will give your children encouraging experiences that may lead to different beliefs and decisions. When children no longer feel discouraged, when they find belonging, connection, and capability, they respond by behaving in positive, appropriate ways. When we invite adult participants at our workshops to take the roles of children in similar situations, they often find themselves coming to the same conclusions, and gain an insider perspective on their child's attitudes.

The Mistaken Goal Chart

Take a look at the Mistaken Goal Chart at the end of this chapter, or tear out the one in Appendix 2 and keep it next to you (and then stick it on your fridge once you're done with this chapter). Look at the second column: the first clue that helps you understand the child's mistaken goal is your own feelings, as they usually lead to you behaving ineffectively, as seen in column 3. Now, look at column 4:

the second clue is how the child reacts to ineffective interventions (your behavior) as listed in column 3. When you understand mistaken goal behavior, you can take your uncomfortable feelings as warning signs that your child is engaged in one or several mistaken goals. Instead of reacting to how you are feeling and your child's irritating behavior, you can instead focus on what the child is really saying—the coded message. Let's take the mistaken goals one by one and look at the associated typical feelings, misbehaviors, and coded messages together with some of the parenting skills that may help your child to feel encouraged and so eliminate the misbehavior.

Undue Attention

When you feel annoyed, irritated, worried, or guilty, your child is involved in the mistaken goal of undue attention and has the mistaken idea that he or she will belong *only if* you give him or her almost constant attention or undue service (meaning doing things that he or she is capable of doing). The reason this goal is called "undue" attention is that everyone has a healthy, appropriate need for attention. Children are very resourceful. If they believe they don't belong and choose the mistaken goal of undue attention, they may try interrupting, acting silly, whining, crying, pretending to forget, pestering, acting helpless, clinging, clowning around, and manipulating through tantrums.

Although these behaviors are irritating, they often get your attention (especially if you've been spending time at work and already feel guilty about not being there), mistakenly leading the child to believe she will find belonging, connection, and capability. Instead, feeling annoyed, irritated, worried, or guilty may lead you to choose ineffective strategies such as punishment. The coded message for children seeking undue attention is "Notice me, involve me usefully, I want to participate and feel needed." However, their mistaken goal behavior achieves just the opposite. Children do their mistaken goal behavior and parents respond in mistaken ways (see column 3 of the Mistaken Goal Chart), which only convinces children that they don't belong. When parents respond to the coded message instead of to the misbehavior, their response can help children achieve their goal to belong and feel significant. The coded message shows a way for parents to break this discouraging cycle and give children what they really need, which will stop the misbehavior.

Brad is a single father raising three children and working full-time outside the home. As in many homes, his mornings are very hectic. One morning he can't find clean underwear for Emma, his three-year-old. After a frantic search, he uncovers a clean pair and gives them to Emma with the admonition, "Hurry and get dressed." The next thing he knows, Emma comes into the living room stark naked. Brad asks, "Why aren't you dressed?" Emma smiles sweetly and says, "My panties are wet." She has deliberately peed in them. Brad is flabbergasted.

When you understand mistaken goal behavior, it is easy to see how Emma could get the mistaken idea that she wasn't important as her father rushed around trying to get everyone out the door on time. Emma found a creative way to get some undue attention. It doesn't matter that Emma's father loves her very much and knows she belongs. He is doing a remarkable job of caring for his children all by himself while working full-time. Children don't see the bigger picture, and instead they base their behavior on what is right in front of them—in Emma's case, her dad chasing her out the door.

What could Brad have done to help Emma feel a sense of belonging, connection, and capability? It would not take much more time to take Emma by the hand and, instead of searching by himself, say, "I need your help to find some clean underwear. Where do you think they could be?" Also, many of his morning hassles could be prevented by helping Emma lay out all of her clothes for the next morning as part of her evening routine.

Once undue attention is determined as the goal of your child's misbehavior, there are many things you can do to encourage behavior change. A few are listed in the limited space of the last column of the goal chart. Please keep in mind that all the parenting tools in this book are designed to help children feel belonging, connection, and capability, and thus to reduce all misbehavior.

Misguided Power

When you feel challenged, threatened, angry, or defeated, your child is involved in the mistaken goal of misguided power. Your child may have the mistaken idea that he or she will belong *only if* he or she is "the boss," or tries to show you that "you can't make me." Children need a sense of power (or autonomy) and will use it one way or another. It is the job of parents to guide them in the constructive use of power so they avoid the misguided use of power. A few of the creative (though mistaken) ways children seek belonging when they have chosen the mistaken goal of misguided power are defiance, saying "You can't make me," agreeing but then not keeping their side of the agreement, being bossy to others, complying just enough to get you off their back but not up to your satisfaction, making disrespectful demands, and pretending to forget.

Notice that the last behavior, pretending to forget, is a behavior that was also listed under undue attention. Many of the same behaviors can be for different goals. That is why you have to rely on *your* feelings to help you understand which one it is. A child who pretends to forget because she wants undue attention is likely to invite you to feel annoyed. A child who pretends to forget because she wants misguided power is likely to provoke feelings of anger. When you are tired after working all day or running endless errands, it may seem easier to simply bark out orders. However, it would be much more effective to pay attention to the coded message. The coded message for the mistaken goal of misguided power is "Let me help. Give me choices and clear boundaries."

Too many parents boss their children around and then wonder why they rebel. It takes two to engage in a power struggle. Instead of doubling your efforts to make your child comply by using threats or punishment, you can defuse the situation by stepping out of the power struggle and using some of the suggestions in the last column of the Mistaken Goal Chart that respond to the coded message. Sometimes this requires what feels like superhuman effort and self-control.

Nine-year-old Scott was respectful and cooperative at school, but at home he was a little tyrant. He bossed his four-year-old brother and caused trouble just when his father, who worked from home for a tech firm, was under serious deadline pressure. He would stand on top of his bunk bed with his finger pointed at his mother and say, "Get my backpack out of the van now! Move it! I need it!"

In desperation Scott's family marched him to the family therapist's office for help. The parents were shocked to learn that Scott felt like an "alien" at home. During sand-play therapy Scott chose a small silver alien to depict himself. He lined up his mother, father, and little brother across from him in angry, blaming positions. He confided to his therapist that he always felt like he was the one in trouble. He believed that his parents loved little Steven more than him and that they were always too busy for him. He felt blamed for all of the problems between himself and his little brother because his parents would say, "You are older and ought to know better."

Scott was a very unhappy boy. He was feeling discouraged because his core need to belong was not being met at home. That is why this same child could behave so well in one setting (in school, where he felt encouraged) and be a "little monster" in another (at home, where he felt discouraged). Parents who understand that a misbehaving child is a discouraged child know that the best way to deal with misbehavior is to encourage the child, which will help him feel belonging, connection, and capability. When a child feels encouraged, the misbehavior will disappear.

Scott's parents were asked to spend one-on-one time with Scott every day for the next week regardless of his behavior. The father was asked to take Scott on a date of his choosing, without his little brother. The parents were also instructed to avoid taking sides when the boys fought, and instead to simply separate them. One week later the mother said to the therapist, "It is a miracle. Scott is a different child. He is helpful and fun to be around. How did this happen?" When a child believes he belongs, positive behaviors follow. When a child feels discouraged and unloved, the misbehavior returns.

The adult finger is often pointed at children as the "cause" of power struggles. Parents complain, "Why won't he listen to me?

Why won't he do what he knows he should do? Why does she say she'll do it, but doesn't?" In many instances, the finger could be pointed in the other direction—not in a sense of blame, but in a sense of awareness. The child could complain, "Why don't you listen to me? Why don't you talk to me respectfully? Why don't you involve me in decisions that affect me instead of giving orders?" We have never seen a power-driven child without a power-driven adult close by.

If you recognize that you are engaged in power struggles with a child, a good place to start is to take responsibility and apologize for your part. Remember, a power struggle takes two. Be willing to look at your part. Maybe you have been too bossy or too controlling. Apologize and offer to work with your child to find more respectful solutions. Too often when parents insist on winning the power struggle, the child becomes the loser. This hurts, and often is an invitation for the child to seek revenge.

Revenge

When you least expect it, your child may do or say something that invites you to feel hurt, disbelieving, disappointed, or even disgusted. This is a pretty good clue that your child has been hurt and is seeking revenge. Some typical revenge behaviors are name-calling, put-downs, deliberate destruction of property, deliberately failing, lying, stealing, and self-destructive behaviors.

You may have hurt your child without even knowing it. Sometimes children feel unloved or conditionally loved because of their parent's high expectations—"You love me only when I get good grades or live up to your many expectations"—and that hurts. Or they feel they have been neglected. Sometimes they may have been hurt by someone else. In any case, it can be very easy for parents to fall into a revenge cycle: when the child does something hurtful, the parent punishes, the child feels more hurt and hurts back, and the parent punishes more severely. When children feel hurt and are hurting back, it can be extremely difficult to see the coded message, but it is the only way out of the revenge cycle. The coded message for the mistaken goal of revenge is "I'm hurting, validate my feelings." Children who choose revenge have almost submerged their desire for belonging, connection, and capability. They are more focused on their need to hurt back.

Nine-year-old Marina was being difficult. Her mother, Tamara, has a full-time job and an active social life. One Saturday, Tamara took Marina to the bowling alley, where Tamara was looking forward to an afternoon of fun with three of her girlfriends. Her intention was to spend time with Marina while also enjoying herself.

Marina was cooperative at first, and she enjoyed trying to get the ball down the lane. After two hours, though, Marina's patience was gone. She started to scream and threw herself on the floor, pounding her fists and shrieking, "I hate you! You are the worst mother in the world!" Tamara was dumbfounded. She tried to explain to her friends that Marina's behavior was not typical. In embarrassment, she dragged Marina to the car. On the way home, Tamara shamed and blamed Marina. "You're grounded for a week! How could you embarrass me like that in front of my friends?" Several days later, with the family counselor, Marina said she felt her mom cared about her friends, not her. Marina didn't know how to tell her mom what she really wanted. Instead she chose the mistaken goal of revenge.

Two days later Marina felt neglected and started screaming at her mom. This time Tamara said, "Sounds to me as though you are feeling angry and neglected right now. I love you, and we'll talk about this as soon as you have calmed down." Tamara was surprised at how quickly Marina calmed down. She experienced firsthand that children who have chosen revenge usually feel some satisfaction just from having their feelings validated. They may need a little more time before they are ready for a deeper discussion, but feeling understood is a huge first step. A few hours later, Tamara asked Marina if she was ready to talk. Marina agreed. Tamara validated her feelings again and together they brainstormed for some solutions to solve the problem.

Once again you are called upon to use superhuman self-control to avoid reacting to a child who is being hurtful. It is human nature that when hurt, you want to hurt back. But as Tamara discovered, retaliation and punishment will only reinforce your child's belief that she doesn't belong and will only escalate her misbehavior. Validating feelings in the moment and then brainstorming for solutions at a calmer time defuses the revenge cycle and helps the child feel belonging, connection, and capability, thus reducing the misbehavior.

Assumed Inadequacy

When you feel despairing, hopeless, helpless, or inadequate, chances are that your child is feeling the same and has chosen the mistaken goal of assumed inadequacy. Dreikurs called this "assumed" inadequacy because the child isn't inadequate, but assuming inadequacy can have the same results. Children who have lost confidence in their ability to be successful defend themselves by not trying. They are very discouraged and may have deep reservoirs of perceived inadequacy. They often choose to "give up" by withdrawing, seeking isolation from others, making self-deprecating remarks, and not trying.

This child often says "I can't," and you know he or she believes it. This differs from a child who has chosen the mistaken goal of undue attention and who often says "I can't," but you both know she really can. It is common for parents to mirror the feelings of the child who has chosen the mistaken goal of assumed inadequacy instead of understanding the coded message. The coded message for the mistaken goal of assumed inadequacy is "Don't give up on me. Have faith in me. Show me a small step." You may feel very helpless and inadequate when trying to help your child who feels like a failure or wants to give up and be left alone. These children can be very convincing. The worst thing you can do is leave them alone. This tells your child he or she truly is as worthless as they feel. On the other hand, coaxing and nagging compound their profound sense of inadequacy.

Six-year-old Eppie was a very discouraged child who refused to try just about anything. All she wanted to do was cling to her parents and say "I can't." Her parents bought into her helplessness and rescued her and did everything for her. Eppie didn't have a chance to practice being capable, which deepened her belief that she was inadequate. She had a very difficult time leaving her parents to go to school, and she spent much of her time sitting at her desk trying to avoid being noticed. The teacher recommended testing with the school psychologist, who discovered that Eppie was very capable but had simply developed the belief that she wasn't. The school psychologist explained mistaken goal behavior to Eppie's parents and suggested a plan for helping Eppie feel encouraged.

Her parents had a difficult time grasping the possibility that Eppie didn't feel belonging, connection, and capability because they loved her so much. In fact, they had "loved" her so much that they didn't require much of Eppie. They did everything for her, which smothered her. They thought this would make her feel more loved, not inadequate.

When they understood how Eppie came to her conclusions of inadequacy, they started the process of weaning her from her dependency on them. It would have been too much to stop doing everything for Eppie all at once. Instead they took small steps and more time for training. For example, Eppie didn't even want to put on her own shoes and socks. Dad started by saying, "I'll put on one sock, and show you a few secrets such as scrunching up the sock, and you can put on the other sock." Mom would sit down with her during homework time and say, "I'll draw the first half of the circle, then you can draw the second half." As Eppie started doing more things for herself, she had to give up her belief that she was inadequate.

Many experiences could lead some children to decide they are inadequate. It is important to note that different children come to different conclusions from the same experiences. Children who feel that they have not met parental expectations in the past may develop defenses to avoid future expectations. They may be passive, pretend not to care about anything or anyone, and refuse to try.

Others may decide to try harder. Sometimes children are afraid to put forth their best effort. If they don't really try and then fail, they can fall back on knowing that they didn't give it their best shot. If they truly try and still fail, they confirm what they already suspect: "I'm a loser." Other children may feel challenged by failures and simply try again. Some children may develop perceptions of inadequacy because parents have done too much for them and they haven't had the opportunity to develop faith in themselves, like Eppie. Others simply disregard their parents' efforts to do too much for them and insist on doing things for themselves.

Parents' Part in Mistaken Goal Behavior

Considering the part parents may play in their children's discouragement should be done not with a sense of blame but with a sense of awareness. Remember that each child is unique and each may form a different perception from the same experience. Taking a look at these few possibilities (among many more possibilities) may increase your understanding of mistaken goal behavior.

PARENT'S BEHAVIOR	CHILD'S BELIEF	CHILD'S MISTAKEN GOAL
Overprotecting and overindulging	"I belong only if I receive constant attention or special service."	Undue attention
	"I belong only if I'm the boss and others do what I want." ("I haven't learned to problem-solve for win-win solutions.")	Misguided power
	"I don't belong because you don't have any faith in me, and that hurts so I'll get even."	Revenge
	"I don't belong because I'm inadequate, so I'll just give up." ("Everyone else does everything so much better.")	Assumed inadequacy

Controlling	*"I can't get attention in useful ways, so I'll get attention in whatever ways I can."*	Undue attention
	"I don't have skills to use my power in useful ways, so I'll use it to defy or to dominate others."	Misguided power
	"Sometimes it seems as though you care more about my achievements than about me. This hurts, so I will hurt back."	Revenge
	"You don't believe I'm capable, so why should I believe I am?"	Assumed inadequacy
Punishment	*"I don't feel belonging when you hurt me, but maybe getting you to pay even negative attention to me will prove that you love me."*	Undue attention
	"I don't feel belonging when you hurt me, but maybe using power in disrespectful ways like you are doing is the way to achieve a sense of belonging."	Misguided power
	"I don't feel belonging when you hurt me, but at least I can hurt you back."	Revenge
	"I don't feel belonging when you hurt me, so I'll just give up and try to stay out of the way."	Assumed inadequacy

The range of possibilities illustrates again that children will make very different decisions depending on their perceptions. Being willing to see how you may be part of the equation may inspire you to change your behaviors in order to help your children change theirs. To understand in more detail how your beliefs contribute to the decisions you make in your parenting, refer to column 6 in the Mistaken Goal Chart. Of course, there are many other reasons children may develop a belief that creates one of the mistaken goals, and some may be out of your control (for example, peer rejection may cause them to feel they don't belong).

BECAUSE THE DECISIONS children make are not made at a conscious level, we have to depend on a theory called Mistaken Goal Disclosure to parse them out.

Mistaken Goal Disclosure

People used to ask Dreikurs, "How can you keep putting children in these boxes?" Dreikurs would reply, "I don't keep putting them there, I keep finding them there." During his studies with children, Dreikurs would ask, "Could it be that you do this [specific behavior] because this is a good way to get people to pay attention to you?" Dreikurs would look for the recognition reflex. If the child gave a spontaneous grin while saying "No," Dreikurs would reply, "Your voice is telling me no, but your grin is telling me yes." If the child displayed a recognition reflex, Dreikurs would not continue with the goal disclosure questions, but would start brainstorming with the child on how to get attention in useful ways.

If the child said no without the grin, Dreikurs would go on to the next question: "Could it be that you do this to show that you are the boss?" Again, Dreikurs would get either a straight no or a grin with the no. If the child displayed a recognition reflex, Dreikurs would say, "Your voice tells me no, while your grin says yes." Then he would help the child find ways to use his power in constructive ways.

If the answer was no without a recognition reflex, the next question would be, "Could it be that you do this behavior because you feel hurt and want to hurt back?" Again, there might be a sly grin while the child said, "No." However, some children feel understood when they hear this and simply say, "Yes." If yes, Dreikurs would validate the child's feelings and then work with the child to find solutions.

If Dreikurs still didn't get a recognition reflex or a yes, he would ask, "Could it be that you do this behavior because you feel you can't do better and so you just want to give up?" It would be rare to get a recognition grin for assumed inadequacy. It might be more likely for the child to show tears. With this recognition reflex Dreikurs might say, "I have a secret. I know you can. You just need a little training. Let's work on a plan together."

Dreikurs taught that goal disclosure is a way of "spitting in the child's soup"—sometimes the behavior loses its appeal when it becomes conscious. Also, there is something about feeling understood that helps a child feel encouraged so that misbehavior also loses its appeal. Mistaken goal behavior is one way to understand why children misbehave. There are many other ways. Sometimes what seems like misbehavior in children under the age of four is really behavior that is developmentally appropriate; more on that in Chapter 9.

Marie is a mother of three: Mathieu, age ten, Louis, age eight, and Amélie, age four. After spending six years in Hungary with the children attending school in the British system, Marie and her husband moved their family back to their native France. It was not an easy transition for the children, especially Mathieu. When Mathieu started his new French school, he struggled to fit in. He had the stress of keeping up academically in a new school system with different methods. When he was required to memorize and write all the French verbs by heart, he found it very difficult. Marie recalls, "I remember ripping the page out of his book and making him write it over and over again until it was right. I even told him he had to stay in his room until he memorized all the verbs and could recite them to me by heart. One day I went into his room to check on him and noticed that he had completely defaced his desk by making huge holes using his compass. I was confused. Why would he destroy his own desk? I was also hurt because it was an antique desk that we bought while in Hungary, and it had sentimental value for us.

MISTAKEN GOAL CHART

THE CHILD'S GOAL IS:	IF THE PARENT/ TEACHER FEELS:	AND TENDS TO REACT BY:	AND IF THE CHILD'S RESPONSE IS:	THE BELIEF BEHIND THE CHILD'S BEHAVIOR IS:
Undue attention (to keep others busy or get special service)	Annoyed Irritated Worried Guilty	Reminding Coaxing Doing things for the child he could do for himself	Stops temporarily, but later resumes same or another disturbing behavior Stops when given one-on-one attention	I count (belong) only when I'm being noticed or getting special service. I'm only important when I'm keeping you busy with me.
Misguided power (to be boss)	Angry Challenged Threatened Defeated	Fighting Giving in Thinking "You can't get away with it" or "I'll make you" Wanting to be right	Intensifies behavior Defiant compliance Feels he/she's won when parent is upset Passive power	I belong only when I'm boss, in control, or proving no one can boss me. You can't make me.
Revenge (to get even)	Hurt Disappointed Disbelieving Disgusted	Retaliating Getting even Thinking "How could you do this to me?" Taking behavior personally	Retaliates Hurts others Damages property Gets even Intensifies Escalates the same behavior or chooses another weapon	I don't think I belong, so I'll hurt others as I feel hurt. I can't be liked or loved.
Assumed inadequacy (to give up and be left alone)	Despair Hopeless Helpless Inadequate	Giving up Doing for them Overhelping Showing a lack of faith	Retreats further Passive No improvement No response Avoids trying	I don't believe I can belong, so I'll convince others not to expect anything of me. I am helpless and unable. It's no use trying because I won't do it right.

OW ADULTS MAY ONTRIBUTE:	CODED MESSAGES:	PARENT'S PROACTIVE AND EMPOWERING RESPONSES INCLUDE:
don't have faith you to deal with sappointment." feel guilty if you aren't ppy."	Notice me. Involve me usefully.	Redirect by involving child in a useful task to gain useful attention. • Say what you will do: "I love you and ____" (Example: "I care about you and will spend time with you later"). • Avoid special services. • Say it only once and then act. • Have faith in child to deal with feelings (don't fix or rescue). • Plan special time. • Set up routines. • Engage child in problem-solving. • Use family meetings. • Ignore (touch without words). • Set up nonverbal signals.
n in control and you ust do what I say." believe that telling u what to do, and cturing or punishing u when you don't it, is the best way motivate you to do tter."	Let me help. Give me choices.	Acknowledge that you can't make him/her do something and redirect to positive power by asking for help. • Offer a limited choice. • Don't fight and don't give in. • Withdraw from conflict and calm down. • Be firm and kind. • Act, don't talk. • Decide what you will do. • Let routines be the boss. • Develop mutual respect. • Get help from child to set reasonable and few limits. • Practice follow-through. • Use family meetings.
give advice (without ening to you) cause I think I'm lping." worry more about at the neighbors nk than about what u need."	I'm hurting. Validate my feelings.	Validate child's hurt feelings (you might have to guess what they are). • Don't take behavior personally. • Step out of revenge cycle by avoiding punishment and retaliation. • Suggest positive time-out for both of you; then focus on solutions. • Use reflective listening. • Share your feelings using an "I" message. • Apologize and make amends. • Encourage strengths. • Put kids in same boat. • Use family meetings.
xpect you to e up to my high pectations." hought it was my job do things for you."	Don't give up on me. Show me a small step.	Break task down into small steps. • Make task easier until child experiences success. • Set up opportunities for success. • Take time for training. • Teach skills/show how, but don't do for. • Stop all criticism. • Encourage any positive attempt, no matter how small. • Show faith in child's abilities. • Focus on asset. • Don't pity. • Don't give up. • Enjoy the child. • Build on his/her interests. • Use family meetings.

"After being exposed to Positive Discipline and the Mistaken Goal Chart, I understood the reason for my son's behavior—a light went on. Mathieu was hurting and he wanted to hurt me back for making him study so hard without recognizing his feelings. It was so clear to me that his mistaken goal was revenge. Looking back, I can see how discouraged he was. Now I know how to deal with things differently. Instead of focusing on the negative behavior and what I want, I now listen to and validate his feelings in order to connect with him before we focus on solutions. This has built trust and established a stronger connection. He now knows that I care more about him than about the end result."

POSITIVE DISCIPLINE TOOLS

Mistaken Goal Disclosure

Solving the mystery of why your children misbehave can be fun and beneficial. Once you break the code, you will have more information on how to encourage behavior change (see the exercise at the end of this chapter to become a Mistaken Goal Detective). In Positive Discipline, we emphasize the importance of understanding the belief behind the behavior. You can use the Mistaken Goal Chart to accomplish this goal. You will be much more effective in encouraging behavior change when you deal with the belief behind the behavior instead of just the behavior.

Empower Your Kids

All Positive Discipline tools aim to empower your children, and yourself, in the process. Our definition of empowering is "turning control over to young people as soon as possible so they have power over their own lives." When you share control with young people, they can develop the skills needed to have power over their own lives. Some of the quickest and most effective ways to empower your kids: teach life skills, focus on solutions together, have faith in your children, let go (in small steps), and increase self-awareness with curiosity questions such as "How do you feel? What do you think? How does this affect what you want in your life?"

....

EXERCISE

Mistaken Goal Detective Clue Form

1. Think of a recent challenge you had with your child. Write it down. Describe what occurred as though you are writing a script. What did your child do, how did you react, and then what happened?

2. What were you feeling when you were in the middle of this challenge? (Choose a feeling from column 2 of the Mistaken Goal Chart.) Write it down.

3. Now check column 3 of the chart to see if the action you took in response to that feeling comes close to one of these typical responses. If your action is described in a different row instead, double-check to see if there is a feeling in another row in column 2 that better represents how you were feeling at a deeper level. (We often say we feel "annoyed" when, at a deeper level, we are feeling challenged or hurt; we often say we feel "hopeless" or "helpless" when we really feel challenged or defeated in a power struggle.) How you react is a clue to your deeper feelings.

4. Now look at column 4. Do any of these descriptions come close to what the child did in response to your reaction?

5. Once you've identified what the child did in response to your reaction, review column 1. It is likely that this is your child's mistaken goal. Write it down.

6. Now move on to column 5. You have just discovered what your child's discouraging belief may be. Write it down.

7. Next, look at column 6. Does this come close to a belief you have that may contribute to your child's behavior? (Remember, this is not

to blame—only to create awareness.) While you are learning skills to encourage your child, you will also change your belief. Try it now. Write down a belief that would be more encouraging to your child. You'll find clues in the last two columns.

8. Now review column 7, where you will find the coded message about what your child needs in order to feel encouraged.

9. Move once more to the right, to column 8, to find some ideas you can try next time you encounter this challenging behavior. (You can also use your own intuition and experience to think of something you could do or say that would speak to the coded message in column 7.) Write down your plan.

10. How did it go? Record in your journal exactly what happened. You want to revisit your success stories for future encouragement. If your plan wasn't successful, try another tool.

CHAPTER 9

DEBUNKING THE MYTH OF THE PERFECT PARENT— OR CHILD

Fifteen-year-old Stephanie arrives home after a long day of school and sports practice. As soon as she walks in and puts her bag down, her mother starts peppering her with questions: "How was your day? How did practice go? Do you have a lot of homework tonight?"

Stephanie snaps, "It was fine! Just leave me alone," and heads for her room, where she slams the door and throws herself on her bed in exhaustion.

Her mother goes after her: "Don't talk to me that way, young lady! I just asked you a simple question."

Sound familiar?

DREAMS OF THE PERFECT CHILD

Many parents fantasize about having the "perfect child." Some parents who work full-time may feel as though they have to try harder to "make" their children be perfect, to compensate for not being at home with the children all day. We want to assure you that this is a myth. In one of our workshops, when we asked parents about their expectations of perfection, one mom made a profound observation: "I can see that I expect my child to be perfect, even though I'm not."

Most parents know it's not wise to compare children. Still, many will occasionally compare their own children to one another, or to other families' kids. We can perhaps remember our own parents saying things like "Why can't you be more like your sister?" or "At least I have one that doesn't get into any trouble." When parents make these comparisons, they think it will motivate their child to be more like the "good child." The opposite is true. Being negatively compared is extremely discouraging and often invites more misbehavior.

For the "good kid" the long-term result may be to feel significant only if he or she is getting praise. As a result, this child may not be secure enough to test boundaries and to individuate (find out who she is apart from her parents). He or she may be afraid to take risks for fear of making mistakes and receiving disapproval. At the same time the "bad kid" looks for behavior that will either dispute or strengthen that characterization, depending on his or her private logic.

In *Mindset*, Carol Dweck explains that children who grow up with labels such as "good kid" often develop a fixed mindset. Kids with this mindset struggle to handle competition and may fall apart when they make their first big mistake. They often struggle when they are exposed to serious competition in college or at work, as they realize they are not the only "special" person. The child labeled "bad kid" may also develop a fixed mindset, believing he or she is no good and the world is a bad place, so why put in any effort?

The "capable kid," by contrast, is a child who develops the life skills required for resiliency and the ability to apply problem-solving skills through challenges. Dweck calls this a growth mindset. We often wonder how we can help our kids develop this mindset, and busy parents who worry that they don't have a lot of time for parenting need strategies that work consistently. By applying Positive Discipline, we empower children by teaching them that mistakes are opportunities for growth. We take time for training the life skills we know will give consistent results, and encourage our kids to focus on solutions. Does this mean they will never misbehave? No! It is part of their developmental process to individuate by testing how they can use their personal power. However, by using Positive Discipline tools every time your children do test the limits, you are helping them learn socially acceptable behaviors that increase their sense of capability, belonging, and significance.

Not all Positive Discipline tools will be effective with all children at all times. This is why it is helpful for parents to have as many tools as possible and to understand what factors influence the emerging personality of their children. Let's look at some key scientific findings regarding children's development.

UNDERSTANDING YOUR CHILD'S EMERGING PERSONALITY

As any parent with more than one child knows, every child is born with a unique personality. Understanding what their world looks and feels like, and how their brains and skills are developing, is an essential part of effective parenting. This is of course also true in the professional world. In order to be effective in any field, it is helpful to understand the perceptions of other people—to be able to get into their world. The development of the human personality is a very complex topic, but there are a few important aspects that are generally agreed upon, which can give clues for how to parent effectively.

Nature vs. Nurture

Children are a product of their parents' genes (nature) and of the environment around them (nurture). Research indicates that genes and inborn temperament traits play a strong role in the development of the child's personality.[21] However, equally important are the beliefs (private logic) we develop and the environment we grow up in.[22] Since the child's personality is still emerging (responding to nurture), a good starting point is to look at a child's temperament (nature). How does this play out? For example, children in the same home may have completely different ways of dealing with and accepting boundaries. One child may decide, "I like the safety of boundaries," while another may decide, "I feel suffocated by boundaries." When you understand and accept these differences, you can adapt your parenting and choose your tools more effectively to better fit your child's temperament.

In a study of temperaments, Dr. Stella Chase and Dr. Alexander Thomas found that there are two basic temperaments, active and passive. This study revealed that these two temperaments are lifelong characteristics; in other words, passive infants grow up to be passive adults, while active infants grow up to be active adults. Subsequent studies confirm the environment's impact in creating the adult personality.[23] For example, if your temperament is passive, that is a lifelong character trait, but you can still train yourself in more active behaviors. Parents can thus help their children develop behaviors that help create a more balanced personality.

Since both nature and nurture play significant parts in creating the life skills your child will require for a happy and successful life, it's important for parents to take the time to get to know and accept their children for who they are, and adjust their parenting accordingly. Parenting isn't the only factor in our child's environment impacting his or her development. Siblings can have a significant effect as well, so let's take a look at this dynamic in more detail.

Birth Order and Other "Assigned" Roles

How significant are birth order and peers in determining the emerging personality of the child? Researchers have not come to a consensus on this. Still, most of us will feel a strong sense of recognition with the various "roles" seemingly assigned to us depending on where we ended up on the sibling ladder. Are you the "responsible" eldest, the "forgotten" middle child, or the "self-centered" youngest of the family? Or maybe the "love to be different" only child? You may be the second child who took over the "responsible" role because the oldest gave up trying so hard. These roles create misconceptions of ourselves that then become integral parts of the belief system contributing to our personalities. Understanding this dynamic can therefore really help us get into the child's world and better understand his or her private logic.

As you now know, children are always making decisions and forming beliefs about themselves, others, and the world based on their interpretation of their life experiences. Their behavior is then based upon those decisions and what they believe they need to do to thrive or merely survive. It is very common for children to compare themselves to their siblings. This is a natural part of their socialization behaviors—trying to figure out where they fit into the group (the family). If a brother or sister is doing well in a certain area, the other sibling may feel that in order to "survive," he or she may have to develop competence in a completely different area, compete and try to be "better than" other siblings, develop uniqueness by being rebellious or revengeful, or give up because of a belief that it is just too hard to compete.

Being in a family can feel like being in a play. Each birth order position is like a different part in the play, with distinct and separate characteristics for each part. One child's interpretation might go, "Since 'responsible' is already taken by my older sister, I will be the 'dramatic' one" (or the rebellious one, the academic one, the athletic one, the social one, and so on).

As a parent, it is important to avoid assigning roles on top of what the child may already be experiencing due to birth order and siblings' talents. Making sure that everyone is valued and encouraged is key as well as appreciating the differences that come with your children's temperament. The better you know your children, the better you will become at nurturing each one's uniqueness and dealing with any misconceptions based on birth order or on other (mistakenly) assigned roles.

EFFECTIVE PARENTING FOR DIFFERENT AGES

We often ask parents if they would consider trying to get the job of their dreams without an education or training. The answer is "Of course not." Everyone agrees that education and training are necessary whatever the goal, whether it is to be a bricklayer or a brain surgeon. We then ask, "What is the most important job in the world?" All agree that it is parenting. We strongly recommend that every parent take a basic child development class or read a book on child development. However you do it, it is important to learn about child development because so many parenting mistakes are made when parents don't have an understanding of age-appropriate behavior. Let's look at some specific tools that are particularly helpful in the two main life stages that parents usually struggle with the most—toddlerhood and the teen years.

TODDLERS

A father thought he was being a good dad when he took his two-and-a-half-year-old son to a baseball game. He most likely did not stop to consider whether such a young child would be interested in baseball for any length of time. Dad became annoyed when the only thing that interested his son were the treats being hawked up and down the aisles. After listening to his son whine for several minutes and ordering him to "settle down" and "be quiet" to no effect, Dad blew up. He grasped the child's hand firmly and proceeded down the wide cement steps at his own pace. The little boy, his face contorted with fear, seemed nearly to be flying as he was dragged along by his father.

This child couldn't understand what was happening. His "crime" was to be more interested in popcorn and soda than in baseball—a thoroughly appropriate (if irritating) response for a child his age. Although this father loved his son, he failed to understand his little boy's limitations, attempted to control his behavior, lost his own temper, and ultimately frightened his son badly. It will likely be a long time before this little boy wants to attend another sporting event with Dad.

Adults often expect young children to understand things that their brains are not yet capable of processing, which often leads parents to engage in ineffective parenting strategies. When you understand that perceiving, interpreting, and comprehending an event are so markedly different for young children, your expectations as an adult will alter.

Ineffective Parenting Strategies for Toddlers

Lecturing

Research explains much of why children under the age of three don't understand "no" the way you may believe they do. "No" is an abstract concept that is in direct opposition to the developmental need of young children to explore their world and to develop their sense of autonomy and initiative. Your toddler's version of knowing lacks the internal controls necessary to halt roving fingers. Toddlers lack the ability to understand cause and effect. Higher-order thinking, such as understanding consequences and ethics, may not develop until children are as old as ten to twelve. Lecturing children on what they can and can't do is therefore futile. Your child may know you don't want her to do something. She may even know she will get an angry reaction from you if she does it. However, she cannot understand *why* in the way you may think she can. To her it can be a game, or a way to get negative attention from you (remember our discussion of mistaken goals in Chapter 8). Why else would she look at you before doing what she knows she shouldn't do, grin, and do it anyway?

Spanking

Parents often cite the danger of a child running into the street as a justification for spanking a toddler. Reasons include the life-and-death nature of the situation, the need for immediate compliance, and the effectiveness of a spanking for getting a child's attention. But to a toddler who can't grasp the danger of cars, an angry, shouting, spanking parent is far more frightening than any street. So he or she may be watching out for you instead of watching out for cars! Even when parents believe punishment effectively teaches a two-year-old child to avoid running into the street, would they let him or her play near a busy street unsupervised? No. They know, spanking or no spanking, that they can't expect their child to have the maturity or that responsibility.

The same is true when parents try forcing a young child to "say you are sorry." As Bev Bos said in a lecture for the California Association of Young Children, "Insisting that a two- or three-year-old say 'I'm sorry' makes as much sense as insisting that a Japanese child say 'I'm Italian.' They can say it, but it isn't true or meaningful." Toddlers are not yet developmentally ready to understand concepts such as empathy and regret.

Do vs. Don't

Here's a tricky one. When it comes to safety, parents always have the best intentions. However, some parents insist that they can train toddlers not to touch things (e.g., electric plugs). Not only is this a mistake, it is very sad. Touching, exploring, and experimenting are part of the developmental programming for toddlers. It is heartbreaking to know that children are being punished (scolded, hands slapped, spanked) for things they are developmentally programmed to do. Brain research demonstrates that when children are not allowed to explore, touch, and experiment, their brain development is hindered.

Even when toddlers learn to repeat a phrase such as "Don't touch," they have learned it at the intellectual level of a parrot. When Dad put his feet on the coffee table, two-year-old Sage loved saying "No" while she pushed his feet off the table. Everyone laughed and thought that was so cute. Later, she was in her exploring mode and wanted to climb on the table. Everyone thought she was being defiant and scolded her. Actually, she had learned how to get approval (like a trained puppy) by pushing her dad's feet off the table. In her mind, this was totally unrelated to wanting to climb. She didn't really know she should stay off the table any more than she would know she should stay out of the street if she was all by herself.

It's important to understand that our brain doesn't understand the word "don't" in a single step. So when you tell a child, "Don't hit your brother," the child's brain has to process the very thing you told him or her not to do (hitting his or her brother) and then take an extra step of thinking about what to do instead. Not only is it more difficult, it can be confusing because there are many other options (like kicking, biting, etc.). What you're hoping to teach is for the child to keep his or her hands to himself and not hurt his or her brother.

What is most helpful is using "do" language. Instead of "don't hit" you can say "use your words" or "walk away." Giving clear instructions is helpful during this stage of development. And creating a safe space by childproofing your home is essential.

So how can we incorporate this knowledge into our parenting?

Effective Parenting Strategies for Toddlers

Take Time for Training

With young children, it is important to take time for training—over and over—until their understanding catches up with the teaching. Take your little one by the hand when you are walking and want to cross a street. Ask her to look both ways and tell you if a car is coming. Ask her what might happen if the car is coming. (It is amazing how many parents think their children can understand the meaning of a spanking when they don't even understand what would happen if a car hit them.) You repeat this process over and over. You don't let your child cross a street by herself until she is much older, which you probably already know on some level. Continue to take time for training. Just because your young child does not have the capability to understand all you teach is no excuse to stop training. Training must take place over and over until your children are developmentally capable of absorbing what you're trying to teach them.

Supervision, Distraction, and Redirection

Now that you know that young children are not capable of the kind of maturity and understanding you may have believed in the past, it makes sense to accept that it is your job to supervise. One thing that amazes parents, when they think about it, is that supervising, distracting, and redirecting don't take any more time than punishment. Most parents find that they spank or send children to time-out for the same things over and over. Even though what they are doing doesn't work, they keep doing it because they are afraid they aren't being good parents if they don't try to stop the "bad" behavior.

Hopefully you now know that it isn't bad behavior. Even though the behavior isn't bad, neither is it safe or practical to let children climb on tables or run into the street. So you stop the behavior through kind and firm supervision, distraction, and redirection, not by expecting your child to learn to stop because of your punishments. For example, instead of expecting them to understand "Don't touch," supervise closely and intervene when they go to touch something you don't want them to touch. Kindly and firmly show them what they can touch, and know that you will have to do this many times. Understanding child development makes it easier to be patient when you have to repeat yourself over and over. You know that neither you nor your child is defective. Learning is a developmental process that takes practice.

Distraction can take many forms. One mother combined distraction and redirection in dramatic ways when her child would do something inappropriate such as playing in the fireplace. She would say something like "I hear Batman calling. Run to the living room to give Batman the help he needs." Another way to distract is to simply remove a child who is climbing on a coffee table. Adding redirection means to show a child what he can do instead. Instead of saying, "No. No. Don't climb on the table," remove the child and say, "You can climb on your beanbag." Don't expect your child to never climb on the table again until he is much older. Supervision, distraction, and redirection are constant tasks for parents of young children.

Childproofing for Young Children

The amount of supervision required will eventually decrease dramatically, and your child will be safer if you childproof your home.

The toddler years are a good time to decorate "garage sale style," so you don't have to worry about damage to expensive furniture. Put away those sentimental, delicate table decorations and anything else precious to you so that you minimize the number of times you are tempted to utter "no, no." Get plastic plugs for outlets, avoid cords hanging down off blinds, don't leave plastic bags lying in reach of children, keep pot handles on the stove turned inward, and keep anything dangerous (knives, medicines, cleaning supplies) securely locked away from your child. You can find more information on childproofing from your pediatrician, parenting magazines, and other resources.

Some days does it seem as if "no" is the only word you say? Is it any wonder children learn to say "no" long before they understand what it means? Distraction, redirection, and childproofing can help you eliminate "no" from your vocabulary. The parents of one toddler learned about age-appropriate behavior and decided they would childproof their home so their two-year-old would not be hampered in exploring and touching. They also decided they would not say "no" to their child. (This does not mean they were permissive, as they were using kind and firm discipline.) Their theory was that their child would not go through the "no, no" stage if she didn't hear that word.

One day, however, they were shocked to hear her say, "No, no. Bad dog." They forgot that she heard what they said to the dog. This was a powerful reminder that children learn from everything they experience—even when the lessons are not intended for them. They learn from words, actions, attitudes, experiences, and their environment. They are more likely to develop a sense of autonomy in a childproofed environment where it is safer for them to explore and easier for Mom and Dad to supervise and redirect.

Manage Your Expectations Around Cooperation

You may have noticed that sometimes your little one seems very cooperative and loves to help. Other times he absolutely refuses to cooperate. Perhaps it is because "cooperation" is the wrong word to use. What adults think of as cooperation may be part of a fun game for a toddler who acts so proud of himself as he fetches a diaper for the new baby. At other times, he just isn't interested in the diaper-fetching game.

You can increase the chances of cooperation with your young children through many positive discipline methods such as routine charts, but you will drive yourself crazy if you expect more than their brains are capable of delivering. Don't expect a toddler to pick anything up unless you make it a game and do it with him. Even then, it will work only occasionally. They are not being irresponsible or defiant when they refuse to pick things up. They are just not old enough to be responsible. And refusing to pick things up doesn't mean they will refuse forever. Well, they might, but after the age of four it is a little easier to find ways to invite cooperation. Even then it has to be done over and over.

That is what raising children is all about—repetition. Try kind and firm persistence. This means taking the child by the hand (kindly and firmly) and saying, "Let's pick these things up together." If he resists, let him go until he tries to get another toy; then kindly and firmly take him by the hand and say, "You can play with that toy as soon as we pick up what is on the floor." He may resist one hundred times (though ten is more likely) until he realizes you are going to be consistently kind and firm. If a child has been used to manipulating you into giving in or reverting to punishment, he may push for the results he is used to, so it takes longer for that child to understand that you will remain both kind and firm until he is willing to cooperate.

Encourage Contribution

As children grow, they become more and more capable of contributing. However, you may have noticed that "me do it" is a common phrase for your two-year-old. At this age, they want to help. Yet too often they are told, "No, you are too little. Go play with your toys." These same parents then wonder why their children don't want to help as they get older and instead say, "No, I'm busy. I'm playing." Let small children help. Give them a dust pan when you are vacuuming, a small dust rag when you are dusting, a safe chair to stand on while they help you tear lettuce. Take time for training them in these chores, over and over and over. Toddlers are practicing cooperation as they help.

Routines

Even two-year-olds love routine charts with pictures of them doing their routine tasks, but even more important for this age are daily routines they can count on. Young children feel secure when they know what is going to happen on a regular basis such as sleeping in their own bed and having meals and naps at the same time every day. You have probably noticed what happens when you go on vacation and routines get all messed up. Children get cranky and misbehave much more frequently. As soon as they get back to their regular routines, they settle down and are as cooperative as young children of this age can be.

Busy parents may find it tricky to stick to routines, especially for those who may not have the traditional nine-to-five working life. We suggest that, as much as possible, you single out a few important routines that you don't compromise on. For example, if it's hard to have dinner as a family at the same time every night, breakfast may be easier. Same with a set bedtime. Another idea is to have some set routines on weekends that young children can count on, such as spending time outdoors, family fun activities like going to the zoo, or a playdate.

Adapt Other Parenting Tools for Toddlers

You now have a basis to adapt the many other parenting tools to the developmental level of your younger children, or to know when the tools are too advanced. This is a time of life when your child's personality is being formed, and you want him or her to make decisions that say, "I am competent. I can try, make mistakes, and learn. I am loved. I am a good person." Using discipline that is age appropriate while being kind and firm at the same time provides the foundation for the development of good character. Patience, along with a few good parenting skills, will make the journey smoother and much more pleasant for both you and your child.

TEENAGERS

The adolescent brain is not an adult brain with fewer miles on it. By age six the brain is 95 percent of its adult size. In the past, the assumption was made that by adolescence the brain was fully developed. However, recent research now confirms that the brain is not fully developed until approximately age twenty-five. It goes through a significant growth spurt just before puberty. Since the brain matures from the back to the front, the last part to fully mature, the prefrontal cortex, is still under construction during the teenage years. It's completely normal for teens to seek independence from the family unit, test parental values, and keep secrets—this is individuation, and it's important for their development.

Brain development is not an excuse for poor choices and disrespectful behavior, but it can help us understand why teens need connection, patience, and good life skills. It helps parents respond to the negative behavior less personally and, hopefully, feel more compassion for what their teen is going through. It also helps busy parents understand why it is important to respectfully involve teens in family responsibilities so that they balance brain development with capability training.

Ineffective Parenting Strategies for Teens

Control

The teenage years can be a scary time for many parents as their adolescents experiment with different identities, make mistakes that may have more severe consequences, and at the same time may stop communicating with their parents (as Stephanie's mom is experiencing in our opening story).

If you react out of fear and try to control your teenager's every move, chances are the individuation process will turn into all-out rebellion. Trying to control your teen will not work. Instead you need to try to engage her in regular family meetings and in planning special time.

Permissiveness

Some parents get so intimidated and exhausted by their teen's behavior that they "check out" and become overly permissive. Since teens are still children, a lack of structure and routines can affect them and lead to any of the mistaken goals discussed in Chapter 8. The parent of a teen therefore needs to find a balancing act between loosening control to allow the teen to individuate, on the one hand, and providing consistency and security so that the teen continues to feel safe and nurtured, on the other.

Lecturing

Parents who go into lecture mode are usually coming from a place of fear. One of the biggest challenges with lecturing is that your child most likely isn't even listening to you. She may be hearing words coming out of your mouth, but she learned a long time ago to tune you out when you go into lecture mode. Instead of listening, she is watching you very closely and is learning quite a lot from your own behaviors.

Effective Parenting Strategies for Teens

Kind and Firm

Being both kind and firm is extremely important with teens. Here are some kind and firm tools to remember:

1. *Connection before correction.* Connection can be physical touch (although this may be less welcomed by a teen than a younger child), making eye contact, validating feelings, listening and being curious, making sure the message of love gets through, and showing empathy by getting into your teen's world.

2. *Being excited about mistakes.* Remember that mistakes are a natural part of growing and learning. Instead of lecturing and ridiculing, learn to celebrate mistakes.

3. *Joint problem-solving.* When teens are respectfully involved in problem-solving, they are much more likely to keep agreements.

4. *Special time.* Plan for a weekend breakfast together, or time to attend special functions that are of interest to your teen.

Encourage Contribution

Give up all thinking that you need to be a "superparent" to make up for being a busy working parent. Kids thrive on being needed. Skills training doesn't stop because the kids are teens. In fact, it is a time when you can set some higher expectations for your kids in terms of cooperating and contributing to the family unit. If they drive, they may be able to help out with some chauffeuring needs. If they haven't yet started grocery shopping, cooking, and tidying anything beyond the basics, this is the time to really train that. Babysitting, petsitting, and watching the house when you have nights out should all be within the teen's areas of responsibility (with individual variations) and will strengthen your teen's confidence and sense of contribution. We had one parent share that it was a blessing in disguise when she broke her foot. Her three teenage children were forced to step up to the plate and share all her responsibilities around the house for a month. She was pleasantly surprised at how well they were able to cook dinner, wash, dry, and iron their clothes, and even create a schedule so that the older ones could take turns driving the younger one to school and after-school activities. Her children felt so empowered by their independence that even after she had her cast removed, her children continued to take care of their own laundry and even helped with cooking meals. She was reminded that when we give children the opportunity to contribute it provides them with a greater sense of significance and belonging.

Listen

Your teen will listen to you after he or she feels listened to. Notice how often you interrupt, explain, defend your position, or lecture. Try listening with your lips closed: "Hmmm." Many parents have shared that one of the best times to listen to their children is in the car. All it takes is asking a few curiosity questions and they can ramble on for hours. One parent shared how she used to take the longer route home from school because it was the only time her teenage son would open up and talk to her.

Sense of Humor

Who says parenting a teen has to be unpleasant and scary? Humor can be one of the best ways to approach a situation. Learn to laugh and create a fun atmosphere to get unpleasant tasks done quickly.

A Positive Spin on the Teenage Years

The teenage years can be the beginnings of a more adult relationship with your children. Here, professionally active parents can really come into their own. A new opportunity for dialogue can open up around choosing good options, finding and developing your unique skills, and the ups and downs of working life. The teen is trying to find his or her place in the world and can be inspired by a busy parent's life choices. Teens are interested in more adult behaviors and lifestyles, so it can be useful to have a discussion around the life skills that are required to be successful in relationships and professional situations.

Some couples who have dual working lives report fewer problems with teens, as they simply don't have time to hover and micromanage everything their kids get up to. This provides the teens with some well-needed space. Some busy parents also report greater closeness, as they are able to share more of their own adult lives with their teens. In our opening story, fifteen-year-old Stephanie probably could have done with coming home to an empty house, getting a chance to unwind, and having some alone time rather than dealing with an overbearing mother. Her mother also most likely would have enjoyed a more fruitful chat later on if she had been able to give Stephanie that space. Invest early in getting to know your child. By the time she hits her teens, it will be easier to let go a little and give her the space she needs. Then, by using curiosity questions and spending special time, you can strengthen that bond, and your worries about what she is getting up to will hopefully be manageable.

POSITIVE DISCIPLINE IN ACTION

Karen explains how her experience of birth order and changing sibling dynamics led her to look for parenting advice: "Where do I begin with Alexa? My middle girl. She is the reason I felt I needed parenting tools.

"We have four children: our eldest, Jason, is ten, and then we have three daughters, Rebecca, eight, Alexa, six, and Katy, five. Our son is firmly established in the family structure as the oldest child. Rebecca was very comfortable with being number two until Alexa was born. Rebecca lost her defined identity, being now the middle child, and consequently became more insecure. Alexa was a terrific baby—great personality and very beautiful. Our fourth child was a surprise. Her arrival changed the dynamic completely— Alexa had a nervous breakdown. At age one she knew the party was over and she was not the little baby that everyone fawned over. Rebecca, on the other hand, has over the past few years grown more confident and turned into more of a matriarch for her two younger sisters.

"Alexa was never the same after Katy was born. She cried and cried and experienced panic attacks all year. Her threes were terrible for me. She was so unhappy. I wondered if we needed professional help. I think an outsider could have helped, but I felt that deep down the answer was *love* and I just had to give her more somehow. I could do this. I am supermom, I thought.

"The fours were worse because she was no longer a baby. Just a little girl no one wanted to be around. She cut off her friends and only wanted to be home in fear of 'missing' something. I didn't know if her mistaken goal was undue attention, power, revenge, or assumed inadequacy, as it felt like all four at the same time.

"I have used just about every tool with Alexa this year and we are making progress. We have a double fist pump on our chests to signal that we are in each other's hearts if I can't be with her for the moment (if I'm with company or with her siblings). The nonverbal attention puts her at ease. Alexa is constantly looking for her siblings' approval as well and has become the family clown to get attention. When she isn't making them laugh she is often crying. I spend a lot of time validating her feelings. And letting her know that I understand. She is an emotional person and feels a lot. We talk about how those feelings make her who she is and help her sing, dance, and perform with passion. Alexa responds very well to routines, and likes to help with chores. This makes her feel part of a system and our family. We are making progress."

POSITIVE DISCIPLINE TOOLS

In this chapter, we discussed the importance of taking time for training, supervision, distraction and redirection, correction before connection, mistakes as opportunities for learning, and listening as well as the importance of kind and firm parenting without control. Here are a few more tools relating to the topics we have covered:

Put Kids in the Same Boat

When parents interfere in fights between siblings and take one child's side, they reinforce the idea that parents can love only one child at a time—and so the competition increases. This is why we suggest that you "put children in the same boat" and treat them the same. You may not really know who started it anyway. You probably don't see all the subtle things one child might do to provoke another child into reacting. So put them in the same boat to focus on solutions.

Pay Attention

Are your children getting the impression that they are not important? Put down whatever you are doing and focus on your child as though he or she is more important than anything else you could do. Don't forget to schedule special time.

Closet Listening

This is a great tool for observing and getting to know your children. Try to be in the same space as them without engaging and just gently observe and listen to what they say. If they talk, just listen without judging, defending, or explaining. If they don't talk, just enjoy their company.

Don't Back-Talk Back

An essential tool with teens. Try not to be provoked by their behavior and get dragged into a power struggle by talking back. Stay calm and firmly state what you will do, such as "I am happy to discuss this with you but not to let you shout at me. Let's take some time to calm down until we can both be respectful."

···

EXERCISE

Mindful Parenting: Practice Being in the Moment

Imagine this scenario. You've just stepped out of the sports complex into a frigid winter afternoon. You're rushing to get to your car before the parking meter runs out, and to get home in time to get dinner on the table. At the same time, you are carrying your two-year-old with one arm because she's too tired to walk, and you have a huge bag of soccer gear in your other arm. It starts to rain, and your six-year-old is distracted by the icy puddles, which crackle with each step as he slowly moves from one to the next.

What would a "perfect" parent do right now? Would that parent notice how engaged the six-year-old was in the wonderful discovery of liquids turning into solids, and stand back calmly until he was ready to stop? Would that parent wait in the rain and smell the crisp fresh air as the parking enforcement officer slaps a ticket on the car? Well, let's face it; when it comes to the day-to-day grind, most of us feel like we are just trying to survive and don't have time to be mindful, fully present parents. In this situation, how many of you would respond by grabbing your six-year-old by the hand and pulling him toward the car, while trying not to drop anything as you rush to beat the parking enforcement officer who's heading toward your car?

To be a mindful parent is to slow down, to be less busy, to be less directive of your children, and to make the effort to get into their world—allowing your children to go at their own pace, to be free to experiment, to play, to get bored, to be messy, and to use their imaginations. It goes against our current practice of keeping them busy all the time by cramming their schedules with self-improvement activities, and it means letting go of the idea of perfection (remember the myth of the "perfect child" we spoke about at the beginning of the chapter). Of course, all parents at one point feel the pressure to make their children be the best they can be and reach their full potential (again, all in the name of love), but how is this pressure impacting our children's ability to just be kids? Childhood is precious and short, and shouldn't all be about training your child for adulthood.

Your exercise is to spend one week being a mindful parent. Here are some tips that may help you.

DO NOTHING!

Scale back activities in favor of doing nothing for an entire day. Let your children muck around in the park (not just in the playground). Go for a walk with no particular destination. Encourage them to play with mud, sand, and water. Stop and smell the flowers. Look at insects, bugs, and animals. Maybe create an art project with items found in nature.

DON'T AIM FOR PERFECTION, AND HAVE SOME FUN

Let yourself and your children get messy, dirty, and wet. Remember how much fun it was to jump in puddles as a child? Look scruffy on the weekend; let them choose their own clothes and dress themselves (even if a piece doesn't match or is put on inside out). And how about asking them to choose your outfit?

OBSERVE YOUR CHILDREN

Practice the art of observation and passively watch your child playing, eating, or getting dressed without getting involved, micromanaging, or doing it for them. Try to go at their pace, taking their cues, and not correcting or directing them. If your children look to you for instructions, use curiosity questions to help them use their imagination to discover new ways of doing and looking at things.

BE PRESENT

Don't think of work, dinner, shopping, or anything else when you are with your children. And most important, don't use your cellphone. Be focused on what they are doing, feeling, and expressing and what you are doing, feeling, and expressing.

ASK YOUR CHILDREN

What does quality time mean for them? You will often be amazed at their responses.

CHAPTER 10

HELPING CHILDREN THRIVE

Jane shares, "In our family we had what we called the three-week chore-plan syndrome. At the family meeting, we would create a chore routine together that the kids would follow enthusiastically for about a week. They would follow the plan *un*enthusiastically for another week. By the third week, there was wailing and gnashing of teeth over the chore plan. So, back on the agenda chores would go. We would then come up with another plan that would follow a similar three-week pattern." Does that mean the chores chart wasn't working? Far from it! As Jane says, "This three-week syndrome felt a whole lot better than the *daily* battles I used to engage in. I don't know what we would have done without family meetings."

FAMILY MEETINGS

Stress, disorganization, frustration, and anger—are these part of your morning routine? Getting sleepy, uncooperative children out the door on time in the morning can try any parent's patience, but it is especially difficult when both parents have to get out the door and off to work themselves. And why is it that these same sleepy-eyed children are wide awake and full of energy after you've put in a full day's work and it is now time for bed? Have you ever muttered, "There's got to be a better way"? Well, there is. Picture this: Your children wake up on their own, get dressed by themselves, take turns fixing breakfast (including yours), and get their lunches (which they fixed the night before) from the fridge. They then pick up their homework and gym clothes (from the place where they had them all laid out the night before) and give you a kiss as they leave for school with time to spare. Sound good? This could be your home—or very close to it.

We aren't promising that you will never have morning hassles (or bedtime hassles), but we are promising that you can significantly reduce stress, power struggles, and chaos.

Dos and Don'ts of Family Meetings

Regular family meetings are a way to nurture a healthier and more positive home environment. As much as possible, it is ideal to have family meetings on a weekly basis at a specified time. It is easy for the demands of our busy lifestyles to intrude on family time, but it's a great way to connect and catch up on the week. Children need to know that they are as important as any professional or social engagements their parents may schedule. This fosters a sense of belonging and significance.

Format for Family Meetings

Family meetings work best if they follow the same format every time, ensuring consistency and a sense of security for the children. Here is the general format:

1. Start with compliments to create a positive atmosphere from the beginning and to teach family members to look for and verbalize positive things about one another.

DO	DON'T
Remember the long-term purposes: to develop perceptions of connection (belonging, significance, and capability); to exercise power positively and allow everyone to be accountable; and to teach valuable social and life skills for good character such as communication, problem-solving, decision-making, and cooperation.	Don't use family meetings as a platform for lectures and parental control.
Post an agenda in a visible place and encourage family members to write problems on it or anything that needs to be discussed by the family as they occur.	Don't allow children or parents to dominate and control. Mutual respect is the key.
Keep a family meeting notebook where you can record compliments, items that have been discussed, brainstormed ideas, and suggested solutions (circling the one that is chosen). Later you can have as much fun looking at your old family meeting notebooks as when looking at family photo albums.	Don't forget that a family meeting is a process that teaches valuable social and life skills, not an exercise in perfection. Learning the skills takes time (for parents and for children). Even solutions that don't work provide an opportunity to go back to the drawing board and try again, always focusing on respect and solutions.
Rotate the jobs of chairperson and recorder. Of course, children who haven't learned to write can't be the recorder, but even a four-year-old can be a chairperson who calls on people to give their compliments, asks for an evaluation of past solutions, asks someone to read the next item on the agenda to be discussed, etc. She may need help when something needs to be read and reminders of what is next, but she will feel a strong sense of belonging, significance, and capability when taking her turn as the family meeting chairperson.	Don't skip weekly family meetings. Remember what you're modeling to your children—if you don't prioritize family time, they will not feel a sense of belonging and significance. If you need to skip a meeting for reasons outside of your control, make sure you clearly explain to the children why, as well as tell them when the next one will be so they feel secure you are not abandoning them.
Focus on finding solutions, not on who is to blame, and teach that mistakes are wonderful opportunities to learn.	Don't expect children under the age of four to participate in the process. If younger children are too distracting, wait until they are in bed.
Keep family meetings short, twenty to thirty minutes, depending on the ages of your children. End with a family fun activity, game, or dessert.	Don't forget that mistakes are wonderful opportunities to learn.

2. Evaluate past solutions without blame or shame.

3. Discuss agenda items for which the family member who wrote the item can choose to:
     a. Simply share feelings
     b. Invite a discussion for awareness and clarification (without brainstorming for solutions)
     c. Brainstorm for solutions and circle the one everyone is willing to try for a week

4. Calendar time: write on the calendar upcoming events, family fun, need for rides, etc.

5. Weekly meal planning.

6. Fun activity and dessert.

1. Compliments

Sharing compliments is not just about saying and hearing nice things. It is much more profound than that. It helps us focus on and seek out the good stuff, being appreciative of all we have and of one another. Gratitude teaches empathy and compassion and reduces negative feelings such as envy and frustration, which are often some of the biggest stumbling blocks to us achieving our full potential. This is a great life skill to develop and will serve children well in their adult lives when they will inevitably have to deal with setbacks, disappointments, and loss. Compliments also serve to elevate the sense of belonging in the whole family, which guarantees more cooperation and better behavior.

In the beginning, compliments may not be easy to either give or receive. It can take training and practice. A simple gratitude exercise to share with your children is to go to bed and wake up every day reminding yourselves to be grateful, to feel love and appreciation. This can become part of story time and morning rituals. Or it can be private, a journal entry or a list you quietly run in your mind. Sharing compliments during family meetings then becomes the natural extension of this exercise and teaches children the importance of sharing positive emotions.

Part of the education for learning to give and receive compliments is to overcome past notions that it is immodest to receive a compliment, and that it is okay to acknowledge good things about yourself. Gracious receiving is easy to teach with a simple "thank you." Children learn this more quickly than adults, who are used to saying things such as "Oh, it's nothing." It's important to focus the compliment on the person's efforts, helpfulness, and contributions, not on final results or physical traits, as well as to point out that only respectful comments are allowed. During her first family meeting, Jane's four-year-old, Mary, said about her brother, "Mark is nice to me sometimes, but other times—" Dad quickly interrupted and said, "Whoops, no 'buts.'"

Some simple steps can be taken to help children get used to the "compliment habit," such as providing them with daily practice during the week. Place blank compliment sheets on the refrigerator (or another spot) where everyone can write down compliments for others each day. (Young children can dictate their compliments to older members of the family.) This could be a ritual that takes place just before dinner. When you see someone deserving a compliment, write it down. If a child observes something someone else did, ask, "Would you like to write that on our compliment sheet?" Once children develop the habit of noticing compliments, they won't need reminders. At the beginning of each family meeting, family members can read their compliments. Ask for any verbal compliments that were not written down. Make sure every family member receives at least one compliment. After having modeled how to do it, let your kids go first. That way you can make sure to even the score at the end if need be. Place this compliment sheet in a folder, and place another blank sheet on the refrigerator to be filled out during the week.

Another idea: At the end of the family meeting, pass out sheets of paper that are blank except for the phrase "I am grateful for . . ." written at the top. (We call this a gratitude page.) Encourage family members to put the page in a place where they can access it easily and write down the things for which they are grateful. During each family meeting, collect the gratitude pages and place them in a folder. Agree when you will share your gratitude pages. One family we know of read their gratitude pages once a year as part of their Christmas ritual. Others allow time during weekend family meals.

These exercises plus others that you will come up with in the course of planning and conducting family meetings will create traditions that increase family closeness. Even though compliments may feel awkward in the beginning, it isn't long before families become compliment pros. Don't expect perfection! Some sibling squabbling is normal. However, when children (and parents) learn to give and receive compliments, negative tension in the family is reduced considerably.

2. Evaluate Past Solutions

Evaluating past solutions need not take long, yet it is an important piece to help the family evaluate their progress. Read over the solutions that were circled from the last family meeting. The meeting chairperson can ask, "How did it work?" If it worked well, it is nice to hear about it. If it didn't go well, the chairperson can suggest it be put back on the agenda for more brainstorming when it comes up in chronological order. Often it is a good idea to table a problem for another week if the solution didn't work. It could be that the item is too hot and more cooling-off time is needed before family members can find a workable solution. The key here is to not blame or shame whoever was responsible for the solution. It is a team effort.

3. Discuss Agenda Items

The family meeting agenda can help arguing family members to calm down, while ensuring that their concerns will be heard. Suppose your children are fighting. You can ask, "Which one of you would be willing to put this problem on the agenda?" Often that is enough to distract them from the fight while they focus on who is going to put it on the agenda. (If they fight about who gets to put the problem on the agenda, let them flip a coin to take turns writing their version.)

Suppose you are upset because you come home and find dirty dishes left in the sink. Instead of wasting time and energy giving a nasty lecture, you can put the problem on the agenda. When it is time to discuss the problem, the family member can decide whether to simply share his or her feelings, invite a discussion for awareness, or brainstorm for solutions.

Great brainstorming starts by clearly defining the problem (always avoiding blame). You might teach the following slogans: "We're looking for solutions, not blame" and "What's the problem? What's the solution?" After writing down as many ideas as possible, go over the list and let your children practice analyzing which ones are respectful, reasonable, relevant, and helpful. Choose and circle a solution that works for everyone if the problem concerns the whole family. If one family member is asking for help with a personal problem, he or she can choose and circle the one that works best. Sometimes a problem has to be tabled until the next meeting if it concerns the whole family and they can't come to a consensus. If a solution has been chosen, agree to try it for a week. When the chosen solution has been circled, it is easy to look back in the family meeting notebook and find it. Evaluate how it worked (or didn't) at the next family meeting.

4. Calendar Time: Scheduling

Many professionals travel for work. Chaos results when children tell parents at the last minute about rides they need or events they have to attend. Much of this can be eliminated when calendar time is part of your weekly family meeting. Each person can learn to come to the meeting prepared to share the important events for the upcoming week. If schedules clash, alternatives can be found for rides or event coverage, and disappointments can be dealt with if parents will miss significant events. This is an important way for family members to learn to respect their own needs and the needs of others.

5. Weekly Meal Planning

One of the biggest complaints we hear from busy parents is the hassle caused by mealtimes. It isn't just finding time to cook that is the problem, but also what to cook and having the necessary ingredients available. Wouldn't it be nice to think about meal planning only once a week, or have someone else take over for a night?

Mealtime provides a terrific opportunity to teach the character traits of cooperation and contribution. Even small children can take a turn (with supervision and a little help) preparing a simple meal such as soup, grilled cheese sandwiches, a vegetable, and ice cream. It is amazing how much better children eat when they are respectfully included in the meal planning and cooking process. Meal planning during family meetings can eliminate the disorganization and stress from lack of planning, and it can make your dream of occasionally having healthy, homemade meals ready when you arrive home a reality. Here is an example of a meal plan; you may want to leave out weekends if you enjoy spontaneity and going out.

FAMILY MEAL PLAN

COOK		MAIN DISH	VEGETABLE	SALAD	DESSERT
	Mon.				
	Tues.				
	Wed.				
	Thurs.				
	Fri.				
	Sat.				
	Sun.				

At the family meeting, use a copy of the family meal plan to ask every family member to help plan the meals for the week. Each family member can be in charge of the evening meal for one day (if you have only one child old enough to cook, you can of course get creative on solving all the other evenings with take-out, leftovers, etc.). Take a few minutes during the family meeting to have each family member choose the day or days he or she will cook, and note it down on the meal plan. Bring cookbooks, food magazines, or printouts of online recipes to the family meeting. Let everyone choose old favorites or new recipes they might want to try. Find a way to capture your favorite recipes into a family cookbook—take snaps and upload to your family website for a fun family project.

At this point we know some of you are thinking, "You've got to be kidding—when will I have time to get everyone to the store, teach the kids (and my partner!) how to cook, supervise children cooking, and create family cookbooks? Gosh, work is less stressful than this! Surely it is just quicker if I do it all myself." You would be right to think so—in the short term. Positive Discipline is not a quick fix. It is, however, a supremely effective parenting methodology for teaching your children the life skills they need to become well-adjusted and happy human beings. If you really enjoy cooking but you still want to teach your children this essential life skill, you can perhaps have one week a month when everyone contributes. Find a solution that works best for you and your family. Remember, perfection is not necessary!

6. Fun Activity and Dessert

End each family meeting with a fun activity. This could be something as simple as playing hide-and-seek with smaller children, or board games or popcorn and a film with older children. Dessert can be served during or after the fun activity. The important thing is that you are having scheduled fun as a family. You are providing your children with traditions and feelings of family closeness that foster—you got it—belonging and significance! This family fun is not, however, instead of scheduled family fun at a separate time. Those activities are not connected to a "must" such as a family meeting but should just be fun-filled and a time for bonding.

Maybe there will be times in your life when you have the right dynamics to run family meetings with meal plans, schedules, activities, and so on. At other times, perhaps work is so demanding that you can barely make it home in time to see the kids before they go to bed. Don't beat yourself up—be creative. Traveling parents can use video calls to participate, or perhaps just for that week you move the family meeting to another day. Remember ultimately that in everything you do you communicate life lessons to your children. Sometimes the lesson is how to prioritize and not lose your cool in times of chaos!

Create a Family Motto

A fun and insightful activity to do at a family meeting that fosters a sense of belonging is to create a family motto. A motto can be a clear signpost for everyone in clarifying what is important. It guides children to understand that deeper values such as compassion and caring are more important than quick, selfish gains. Developing this together with your children gives them ownership and you a clear reference point when they make mistakes. Let's say the family motto that you have all agreed on is "All for one and one for all." If your youngest refuses to help her sibling with agreed-upon chores, you can refer to the family motto.

ADDITIONAL LIFE SKILLS TRAINING

In Chapter 7 we discussed how helping children explore the consequences of their actions and decisions helps acquaint them with their personal power. How else can you help your child feel a healthy sense of autonomy?

Conscious Irresponsibility

One of the best ways to help your children learn responsibility is for you to be "consciously irresponsible." Parents sometimes spend endless energy and time being responsible for their children. They set their alarm clocks for them, shake them out of bed in the morning, issue incessant reminders to get dressed, eat breakfast, find their shoes, pack their backpacks, and grab their lunch, and still they find themselves driving children to school because they missed the bus. It's a good system for the kids (at least on the surface). But children aren't learning self-discipline and motivation and often become discouraged about their own competence, and parents are becoming cranky, frustrated, and resentful. (You may also want to consider if you have the same dynamics at work and/or with your partner. If you are constantly taking control, what might that invite in others?)

To be consciously irresponsible, let children know what they are capable of doing on their own, then don't do it for them. Don't set the alarm clock, don't remind them to get dressed or eat. As they experience natural consequences, they may choose to be more responsible themselves. After an initial uncomfortable learning stage, they will likely start to enjoy their growing skills and confidence. This is a great way to acquaint them with their personal power in a positive way. What about if their behavior doesn't improve? First, you may need to give it some time. If you've done everything for them up until now, it will take some time for them to unlearn the destructive behaviors, just as it will take some time for you to unlearn them. If things still don't improve, there may be something deeper at play. Review the Mistaken Goal Chart and see if you can get some clues there as to why your children are not responding to your change in behavior.

Money Management

Teaching money management is another essential part of developing responsibility and exploring personal power. Allowances give children an opportunity to learn many valuable lessons about money. Money shouldn't be used for punishment or reward. It then creates an arena for power struggles, revenge, and manipulation. Chores are a separate issue and should not be connected to an allowance. Be sure not to rescue your children when they run out of money by giving them new funds. Learn to say no with dignity and respect. Be kind and firm; be empathetic without trying to fix things. You might say, "I understand you feel disappointed that you don't have enough money left to go to the game." Offer your services as a budgeting consultant, but do not give advice unless asked. You can also offer them a loan and discuss the terms of how they will pay it back (this is not the same as rescuing). Show them how to set up a payment plan and agree together on an amount you can deduct from their allowance. Another possibility is to make a list of special jobs to earn money for extra items or to help pay back their loan. You may want to avoid offering a new loan until the first loan is repaid.

You may also want to set up guidelines, such as "Allowances will be given only once a week during family meeting time. If you run out before then, you have an opportunity to learn what that feels like and what to do about it, such as go without or find a job to earn extra money." Most parents have periodic times (once a year or every six months) when an allowance can be raised. That can provide a good opportunity to discuss with your children what they will use the increased allowance for, or maybe even ask them to explain to you why they need a greater allowance. Some families raise the allowance of all the children on every child's birthday.

Family meetings are a great forum to have periodic discussions about money where you share some of your mistakes and what you learned (without lecturing or moralizing). Encourage others to do the same. Create a sense of fun so everyone can laugh while they learn. Use curiosity questions to help them explore what happened, what caused it to happen, what they learned from it, and how they will use this information in the future. This is effective only if they agree to explore and only if you are truly curious about the perceptions of your children. It is not effective to try disguising a lecture as exploration.

AGE-APPROPRIATE GUIDELINES

AGE	GUIDELINE
2–4	Give children small change and a piggy bank. For each year, add a bit more, and maybe paper money once in a while too. They like putting money in the piggy bank and are starting a saving habit before they know it.
4–6	Take your child and the piggy bank to a bank and open a savings account. Every one to three months, take your child to the bank to make a deposit. It can be fun to watch the balance grow. At these ages, you might want to suggest two piggy banks: one for the savings account and one to save for items on a wish list.
6–14	Schedule a planning session with your child for you to decide together how much money he needs and how it should be allocated for savings, weekly needs such as lunches, and fun. You might also encourage your child to save money to give to community organizations and those in need.
14–18	Add a clothing allowance so teenagers can learn how to plan. Children who learn to handle money from an early age can handle a clothing allowance much sooner. In the beginning, instead of giving them money, tell them the total amount they can spend on clothing; and then deduct their purchases from a running total that you keep. They quickly find out that if they spend too much on a few items of clothing, they don't have enough left for an adequate wardrobe.

Chore Charts

We don't know of a single family, no matter what the parents' work obligations, who don't complain about chore hassles! Parents make all kinds of mistakes that invite lack of cooperation and rebellion among the ranks. They leave lists of chores that they expect their children to do before they get home. Then they lecture and scold them when they don't comply. Sometimes parents punish them by withdrawing privileges or deducting money from allowances. They offer bribes, which may achieve compliance for a short time. However, none of these tactics are effective long-term strategies and they don't help children develop responsibility.

Family meetings provide a great forum for creating chore charts that involve the whole family. Chore charts are similar to the routine charts we described earlier. Discussing and planning for chores at the family meeting may not be a cure-all, but it will be more effective over the long term than punitive measures, and it teaches responsibility, decision-making, and problem-solving. One mother shared, "We created a chore chart during a family meeting and the kids did their chores for about a week. Then they reverted to their old, slothful habits." She was asked, "Have you found anything else that got them to do their chores for a whole week?" She admitted that she hadn't. It was suggested that she keep doing what worked. Even if she had to do it once a week, just like Jane shared in her story at the beginning of this chapter, it was better than the daily nagging that didn't work.

Children can be very creative when they are treated respectfully and allowed the opportunity. Ask your children for their ideas on solving the problem of organizing and getting chores done. Then ask again! You will be pleasantly surprised if you keep at it and allow time for children to learn and practice the skills of problem-solving. They will feel good about themselves and their ability to contribute, and so will you. Even better, it might even take some chores off your plate! Be sure to discuss in advance your family's policy of building each other up rather than tearing each other down as each of you finds your way to do chores. Both children and adults must be asked to refrain from criticism and instead offer solutions or suggestions when asked for how the chore can be done more effectively. It is important to seek improvement, not perfection. Some of the chore routines created by Jane's children were as follows:

1. Draw two chores for the week out of a jar.

2. Make a wheel of chores and put a spinner in the middle. Spin for two chores for the week.

3. Create a chore chart with two slots for each child (a "to do" slot and a "done" slot). Make a set of cards for the chores to be done by each child. The card sets go in the "to do" slot until the child does the chore, at which point it is moved to the "done" slot.

Mark, a single father, dreaded laundry day. His daughter's clothes were rarely in the basket, and he found himself hunting in the closet and under her bed for missing articles. Gwen, age ten, played a lot of sports and left her sweaty socks in damp wads, and Mark detested turning them right side out. Mark believed he had tried everything: he'd lectured, threatened, and made huge heaps of Gwen's dirty clothes on her bedroom floor. Nothing fazed Gwen; she went right on leaving her clothes and wadded socks wherever she pleased. Eventually Mark would gather everything up and wash it.

Mark was groaning about Gwen's habits to a friend one evening. "Why do you keep picking up after her?" his friend asked. Mark discovered that he didn't have a good answer. Gwen's behavior was certainly working well for her! It occurred to Mark that if his daughter was going to live on her own someday, she might need to know how to deal with her laundry.

Mark put the item on the family meeting agenda. "You know, Gwen, I get frustrated looking for your things and peeling your socks apart. Do you have any suggestions for how we can solve this?"

Gwen looked disinterested.

"From now on," Mark went on kindly, "I'm only going to wash what's in the laundry basket, and if you put your socks in there in wads, that's how I'll wash them. Whatever doesn't get washed will be your responsibility. I'll show you how to run the washer and dryer."

Gwen looked at her dad and rolled her eyes. "Whatever," she said with a shrug.

Mark stuck to his guns, and, as he had anticipated, trouble showed up right on schedule when Gwen stalked into his room on a Monday morning. "Where's my Abercrombie sweatshirt, Dad?" she said. "I want to wear it!"

"I don't know," Mark said. "Was it in the laundry basket?"

"I don't know," Gwen howled. "I don't know how to do this stuff. You've always done it all!" She went back to her room, where she discovered the missing sweatshirt behind her desk.

"Looks like you'll either have to wear it the way it is or wash it tonight," Mark said sympathetically, and left the room to finish getting dressed. He heard Gwen muttering to herself in her room but resisted the urge to rescue her or solve the problem for her.

Sure enough, that evening Gwen sat down at the counter while her dad fixed dinner. "Sorry about this morning," Gwen said. "I sorta lost it. Could you show me again how to do the wash? I found my best jeans under the bed."

Mark smiled. "Sure. Come here and I'll show you how to cook pasta. You can tell me about your day. And after dinner we'll have another go at the washer and dryer."

As time passed, Mark discovered that although he and Gwen still battled occasionally over chores, teaching her skills and then having faith in her ability to work things out helped both of them. He was less grumpy, and Gwen began to take pride in her ability to master the everyday tasks of managing her life. The process required energy and patience from both of them, but the long-term results for Gwen promised to be worth the effort.

Positive Discipline Tools

In this chapter, we have discussed one of the most basic and most impactful of Positive Discipline tools, the family meeting. This is a cornerstone. There are other key tools as well that can be used consistently in between meetings to help enforce the learning.

Focus on Solutions

In family meetings but also at other times it is key to focus on solutions instead of blame. You will be amazed by the capability of children to find solutions when they are invited to do so. As always, start with clearly identifying the problem. Then brainstorm as many solutions as possible. Pick one that works for everyone. Try the solution for a week. In a week, evaluate. If it didn't work, start over.

Sense of Humor

Humor can help parents and children lighten up. Remember to laugh and have fun! Use games to help make chores fun: "Here comes the tickle monster to get kids who don't pick up toys." When kids are fighting, gently tackle them and say, "Pig pile!" Use this tool with caution, however, and never use sarcasm. Be sensitive to times when humor is not appropriate, such as when the child is very upset or angry.

··

EXERCISE

Have your first family meeting.

PART 4

PERSONAL WORK

CHAPTER 11

UNDERSTANDING
THE BRAIN

Louise comes home after a long day teaching at the high school where she works, and goes straight into the kitchen to prepare dinner for her family. She enjoys cooking and is looking forward to a family dinner with her children and husband where they can share about their busy day. But as soon as they sit down to eat, the complaining and bickering begins. Nine-year-old Kelly starts complaining about the meal, how she doesn't like this or that, and "why do they always have to have chicken?" Thirteen-year-old Emma starts going at Kelly for being such a picky eater and always whining. Frank has had another stressful day in court and is stonewalling everyone. Louise is feeling underappreciated. As the complaining and bickering continue, she can feel her blood boiling. She loses it and screams, "If you don't like what I've cooked, then you can go to your room hungry. And don't even think about dessert! Frank, can you please say something to the girls?" Frank swallows his last bite and storms off into the study for some peace and quiet. Kelly begins to cry, and Emma continues to call her a baby. Louise sends both girls to their rooms as she clears the table while trying to calm herself down.

MIRROR NEURONS: THE IMPORTANCE OF MODELING FOR YOUR CHILDREN

Now it is all about you! Bringing up children is of course as much about you, the parent, as it is about your children. We want you to feel empowered by that. We all make mistakes and overreact when we are stressed, but a lot of the seemingly overwhelming aspects of parenting and children's behavior are more within your sphere of influence than you might think. But it takes effort on your part. It means occasionally shifting your focus away from your children and onto yourself, and taking an honest look at your own behavior. It means accepting that you cannot ultimately control how your children think and feel and what they decide. However, you can provide the kind of atmosphere that influences them to make better choices. The best way to do that is to model better choices to your observing child. Parenting is a growth process for the parent as much as the child.

Monkey See, Monkey Do

We know that humans learn by looking and copying, starting in infancy. The parts of the brain responsible for this are called mirror neurons. Mirror neurons are a relatively recent discovery. However, parents from earlier generations will attest that they didn't need science to tell them that their kids copied their behavior!

So how do mirror neurons work? Imagine you're having lunch with a friend and she fishes a lemon slice out of her glass of ice water and bites into it. Her face scrunches up in reaction to the sourness of the lemon. Did your mouth water just then? What about if you watch someone stumble, fall, and smash his knee on the pavement? You would probably flinch in empathy with the person's pain. What about when you walk into a meeting room and your colleagues are all laughing heartily—what do you do? You immediately smile. Feelings are infectious. These behaviors are caused by mirror neurons, which are cells in the brain that respond not just when we perform an action but when we witness someone else performing that same action.[24] This is intimately linked to how we learn—by observation. The child's brain is effectively practicing new behaviors by observing others. The child then tries them out.

The impact of this phenomenon on parenting is significant. Whatever you want your children to do, you'd better do it first! Imagine if you come home from work after having a tough day and you're feeling stressed and flustered and say things you will later regret. We call that "flipping your lid"—you're in your primitive, emotional brain and your rational thinking is disengaged. What is going to happen to your kids? They will most likely pick up on your emotions and get cranky and whiny—they flip their lids too. This is a two-way street. If your child comes home from school after a rough day and has flipped his lid, what is likely to happen to you? Go back to our opening story and look at the chain reaction of flipped lids from the girls to Mom to Dad and back to the girls. On the other hand, if you stay calm, what are you likely to invite from your child? The ability to gather yourself and access the rational part of your brain is a critical skill, both for you and for your children.

Mirror Neurons and Private Logic

Parents often say one thing and do another. (Remember the old saying "Do as I say, not as I do"?) Even parents who are aware that their children copy what they do often forget just how keen a child's power of observation can be. Couple that with children's underdeveloped cognitive skills and the fact that they are always making decisions based on their experiences, and you will realize how easily the child can develop faulty private logic. Do you ever come home from work, throw yourself on the sofa, and exclaim, "God, I need a drink"? You may be thinking there's no harm in that, as you have a healthy attitude about alcohol. The observing child, however, may be thinking that alcohol seems to be a way to feel better when we're stressed. That's not necessarily the attitude you want to impart to your child. Or maybe you've told a child,

"Honey, don't smoke, it's terrible for your health!" and then your kid sees you having a cigarette and laughing at a dinner party. Your child's conclusion might well be that smoking makes people feel good in social situations. Maybe these are extreme scenarios, but even something small, like "I'm on a diet, kids—you should eat your meat and potatoes and I'll just have soup," can impart conflicted messages around healthy eating. Asking your child to control her behavior when you don't control your own can be the most conflicting modeling of all.

SELF-REGULATION REQUIRES AWARENESS AND TIME

It will help if we first discover how the brain prioritizes behavior so we can then discover how to effectively work with our brains to self-regulate.

The Reptilian Brain

We are sure that you have certain buttons that when pushed send you into a tailspin. Your children know what those buttons are and exactly how to push them. (This isn't deliberate meanness on the part of your children; they're just exploring the possibilities in their world.) Maybe you have a "fair" button. All your children have to do is say, "That's not fair," and you jump in to do whatever you can to make sure everything is fair. Have you noticed that nothing you do seems to make it fair? You could bring out the finest weight scales to prove that both children have the same amount of cake, and one would whine, "Well, his looks bigger." Your children aren't nearly as interested in what's fair as they are (at a subconscious level) in the attention and reaction they get from pushing your "fair" button.

Let's look again at Louise in our opening story. When her buttons got pushed, she flipped her lid and went into her reptilian brain.

The function of the reptilian brain is survival, and so the only options are fight, flight, or freeze. If you are in a fight-flight-or-freeze state of mind, chances are your children will be right there too. Nothing positive can be accomplished when any of you is operating from that state of mind.

The "Flipped Lid" Explained: Brain in the Palm of Your Hand

In their book *Parenting from the Inside Out*, Daniel Siegel and Mary Hartzell present an easily understandable explanation of what goes on in the brain when our buttons are pushed or we are under stress. In our classes with parents, teachers, and children, this model remains one of the most useful and remembered tools. It's called "Brain in the Palm of Your Hand." What follows is a simplified version of Siegel and Hartzell's model.[25]

Hold up your hand—we will be using the parts of the hand to represent the different parts of the brain.

Your wrist and palm represent the brain stem. They are responsible for survival instincts (fight, flight, or freeze) and for autonomic (automatic) functions such as breathing and swallowing.

Now fold your thumb in. Your thumb represents the midbrain. Included in the midbrain is the amygdala, the primary storage area for memories and emotions.

Fold your fingers over your thumb. Your fingers over your thumb represent the cortex: perception, motor action, speech, higher processing, and what we normally call "thinking."

Your fingernails represent the prefrontal cortex—a primary integration center for the brain, almost like a "switchboard" that makes sure messages get where they need to go. Documented functions of the prefrontal cortex are emotional regulation, regulation of interpersonal relationships, planning and organization, problem-solving, self-awareness, and morality.

What happens when you are stressed, overwhelmed, or tired, when your kids are acting up, or when you are trying to deal with traumatic or painful memories? The prefrontal cortex shuts down;

it no longer functions. (This is temporary, thank goodness!) Let your fingers fly open so that just your thumb and wrist are exposed. Now you have "flipped your lid." You can't use most of the functions above—and you also can't learn without them. This is not the time to try teaching your children about right and wrong. No one is listening. To engage and to learn, you need to calm down until the prefrontal cortex is functioning again.

It's a really good idea to explain to kids what happens in the brain to all of us when we get stressed. With some kids, you can use the example of the "brain in the palm of the hand." They usually enjoy it. You can follow that by saying, "We're not likely to solve the problem when we feel rotten. We first need to calm down so we can think again. When we both feel better, we'll be more able to think of ideas and solutions. Let's agree that if we can't calm down, we will take a break from each other until we feel better." In Positive Discipline, we call that taking a positive time-out. Parents make a mistake when they try to teach children life lessons when they are both feeling upset. The feeling behind your teaching will more likely be one of frustration than kindness. You may think, "But if I don't do something now, I'll be letting my children get away with bad behavior." This is not true. When you exercise self-control by waiting until you can be calmer and more effective, you are teaching your children proper anger management by example.

Time-out deserves special mention, as punitive time-out is a faulty discipline method widely used and even advocated by many parenting experts. There is a *huge* difference between positive time-out and punitive time-out.

Why Punitive Time-Out Doesn't Work

In an effort to correct misbehavior, parents say, "You go to your room and think about what you did!" This is actually a fairly ridiculous thing to say, because they can't control what their child thinks about. Parents like to believe their child is thinking, "Thank you so much for giving me this terrific opportunity to think about the error of my ways and to realize that from now on I must behave better." It is more likely that the child is thinking, "I'll show you. You can make me sit here, but you can't make me do or think what you want me to." Even more tragic is the child who thinks, "I really am a bad person."

Parenting in our hectic world can create a sense of urgency where it seems imperative to deal with each behavior, each crisis, and each problem right away. Children have an impressive knack for frustrating, challenging, and angering their parents, but angry and frustrated parents can't do their best work. Thus, parents frequently find themselves reacting—doing what seems to work for the moment instead of acting thoughtfully for long-term results. Many parents have decided they do not want to use physical punishment, and they think punitive time-out is a good alternative. We often invite parents to think about how they would feel and how they would respond if their spouse, colleague, or friend said, "You go to time-out and think about what you did." They laugh and say something like "Excuse me!" or "I don't think so!" If children made these comments to their parents, they would be accused of "talking back." Why would a child respond favorably to a situation that would certainly not be motivating to you?

The Benefits of Positive Time-Out

Children *do* better when they *feel* better (as do parents). Positive time-out is designed to help children feel better so they can do better. It is a highly effective tool for children and parents alike to learn self-regulation. The old adage "Time heals all things" is true. It is difficult to stay in the primitive brain when you take some time to do something you enjoy. Physiologically, once the stressful element is removed, the stress hormones abate and you start to reconnect with your thinking brain. It is not, as some may think, a reward for misbehavior.

You may find it very helpful if you agreed with your child in advance for both of you to take a time-out by choice. It is even more helpful when you have decided in advance what kind of time-out would be most encouraging to you. Come up with a fun hand signal for time-out. When they see it, they'll know it signals a chance to catch your breath, calm down, and come up with new strategies or plans after you are feeling better. Positive time-out is rarely effective for children under the age of four, and if they can't participate in the time-out guidelines, they are not developmentally old enough for positive time-out. Your children will appreciate the difference between punitive and positive time-out when you use these seven guidelines for positive time-out.

1. Understand that a time of conflict is not a good time to teach and learn.

When you exercise self-control by waiting until you can be calmer and more effective, you are teaching your children proper anger management by example. Sometimes a positive time-out will be enough to stop your child's behavior. If not, you can follow up later, when you are both calm (a no-conflict time), with teaching time (see guideline 7).

2. During a time when there's no conflict, teach the value of taking time to calm down until the rational brain can be accessed.

There are several ways to teach children about the value of time-out and the rational brain. The first way is to model taking a time-out yourself when you go into your irrational brain. Explaining about the "brain in the palm of the hand" and the reptilian brain is very useful. For slightly older kids, you can also teach the following quick steps for calming down. First, realize what is happening—engage your thinking brain and say to yourself, "I'm about to flip my lid." Second, stop whatever you are doing and breathe deeply. If that is not enough to calm down and reengage the rational thinking, it may be best to go to your positive time-out space.

3. Encourage your children to design a positive time-out area that will help them do whatever they need to do until they feel better and can do better.

After teaching the value of taking time to calm down, you can encourage children to design their own area that will help them do whatever it takes until they feel better and can do better. Involving children in the design is key, as is having this discussion during a no-conflict time. Encourage children to brainstorm things that help them feel better. Don't do this for them, though you can ask some questions to get them started, such as "Does soft music help you feel better? What about reading a book, stuffed animals, playing outside, jumping on the trampoline, talking with a friend, taking a shower?" A time-out area could include a little corner where they have some soft cushions, books, and headphones for music. Or it could be something they do, such as exercising. It is good training for them to think about what helps them feel better, and to plan for times when they need it. This is a very powerful self-nurturing practice that goes beyond taking a time-out, so they are learning many essential life skills during this step. Using screens should never be part of a positive time-out area or plan, as they can make the child disconnect emotionally rather than exploring his emotions.

4. Suggest the child choose a name for this area, something other than "time-out."

If punitive time-out has been used in your family, it can be very difficult for both parents and children to adopt the new paradigm of time-out being a positive life skill. Suggest that your children come up with a positive name for their time-out area, a name other than "time-out." Doing this can shift the time-out concept from negative to positive. Children (and parents) can have fun brainstorming for a new name for time-out. Some have decided to call it their "happy place," "cool-off spot," "space" (with cardboard planets and stars hanging in the area), or "Hawaii" (with posters of Hawaii on the wall).[26] When a child creates a unique name for her positive time-out area, it makes the area her special place and gives her a sense of ownership.

5. Design your own time-out area.

Yes, your example is your child's best teacher. Positive time-out is good for you as well as for your children. Let your children know what you will do when you need to calm down. Perhaps a run or walk around the block works for you (if your children are old enough to be left on their own). Maybe you feel refreshed after reading a good novel, meditating, or taking a bath. Whatever your time-out plan, let your children know in advance that you may go to your special place so you can behave better, not as a way to abandon or punish them. Sometimes posting everyone's positive time-out ideas on the refrigerator is a good way to keep the focus away from blaming the offender, and instead showcasing it as a tool for everyone in the family when they are in need of self-soothing.

6. During a conflict, ask your children if it would help them to go to their positive time-out place (using the name they have given it), or for you to go to your own time-out area.

When it has been set up in advance, it can be effective to ask your angry (discouraged) child, "Would it help you to go to your positive time-out place?" The language is very important, which is why you ask the child if he or she will find it helpful. *If children don't choose it, it is punishment, not encouragement!* If your child says no, you might ask, "Would you like for me to go with you?" Most children find it difficult to refuse this offer. Of course, it wouldn't be wise to offer this choice if you are as upset as your child. However, just seeing time-out in this positive way is enough to help some adults make a paradigm shift away from their anger and into a desire to be encouraging to their children. Remember, the purpose is to encourage and shift the mood, not punish. And you probably need the time-out as much as he does. If your child still says no, reply by saying, "Okay, I'll go to my special place." This will be a distracting shock (in a good way) to your children and an excellent model for them. Taking your own time-out is often the best place to start, as your children will learn the most from your example.

7. If appropriate, follow up with teaching time at a later moment, when everyone is feeling better again.

Sometimes positive time-out is enough to stop the behavior and follow-up isn't necessary. Other times repairs or amends may be needed. You can help your children find creative solutions once you are both calm. It will be easier to remember that mistakes are opportunities for learning, not for blame, shame, and pain. There are many ways to follow up. Your child may want to put the problem on the family meeting agenda to get the whole family involved in brainstorming for solutions, or you may want to do joint problem-solving between the two of you. Sometimes curiosity questions are an excellent way to help children explore the consequences of their choices.

POSITIVE TIME-OUT IS a powerful tool to help manage conflict, and over time it will likely lead to fewer struggles. But it won't avoid conflict altogether, or eliminate our instinctual fight-flight-or-freeze response. Even the most loving and thoughtful Positive Discipline–practicing parents have been known to react emotionally or out of habit. (The authors have done considerable parenting "research" in just this way!) It is not easy to think about the long-term results of what we do, especially when we are toe-to-toe with a defiant youngster. Sometimes we get it plain wrong, but there is plenty we can do to recover from our mistakes and turn them into opportunities.

HOW TO TURN MISTAKES INTO OPPORTUNITIES: THE FOUR R'S OF RECOVERY

After being asked how he kept going after so many failed attempts at making a lightbulb, Thomas Edison famously said, "I have not failed. I've just found 10,000 ways that won't work." What a marvelous attitude! In our society, we are taught to be ashamed of mistakes. However, we are all imperfect, and it's important that we begin to shift our beliefs and see mistakes as opportunities for growth. This is one of our most encouraging Positive Discipline concepts, though it is one of the hardest to achieve (especially in our professional lives). There isn't a single perfect parent, professional, or human being in the world, yet many of us are demanding it of ourselves and others.

When parents send the message to children that they must pay for their mistakes, they usually mean well. They are trying to motivate their children to do better. However, they haven't taken the time to think about the long-term results of this method and how it may be contributing to children's belief that they are a disappointment, inadequate, bad, and so forth. There is another way: teaching our children to be excited about mistakes because they may be an opportunity to learn. Imagine hearing a parent say to a child, "You made a mistake. That's wonderful. What can we learn from it?" Often this shift involves working on your own attitude to mistakes, starting with getting comfortable with recovering from them.

First, we want to assure you that if you have ever responded to your children in a way that you regret, you are normal. We don't think there is any parent who has not "lost it" and reacted in anger instead of reacting in ways that would be more beneficial to the child and invite cooperation and learning. However, as adults, we have a responsibility to teach our children what to do when we do flip our lid and may have done or said something that we regret. There are four steps that we teach parents and children in order to recover from our mistakes—we call them the Four R's of Recovery. This tool should be seen as a complement to positive time-out. Sometimes the two will be used together; other times you may want to immediately recover from your mistake without taking a time-out.

Step 1: *Recognize.* "Oops, I made a mistake."

Step 2: *Reconnect.* This can be done verbally by validating the child's feelings: "I can see that my behavior has hurt you." Or it can be done nonverbally, through a hand on the shoulder, getting down to eye level, or holding hands.

Step 3: *Reconcile.* "I apologize."

Step 4: *Resolve.* "What can we do to make things better? Let's work on a solution together."

Parents will find that children are often very forgiving when they use these four steps. Many adults are too. Imagine the power of this type of modeling with your partner or in your professional life as well.

POSITIVE DISCIPLINE IN ACTION

Jonathan, five years old, has bitten his younger brother. Jonathan's mother, Jenna, is understandably very upset with him. As a way to teach him not to hurt other people, she bites him back so he will know how it feels. She immediately realizes that this will only teach him that biting is okay. Jenna knows she has to make amends, and so she follows the four R's of Recovery model: "Jonathan, I made a mistake. I bit you. I was so angry at you for biting your brother, but I did the same thing I was mad at you for. That wasn't very nice of me." Jonathan looks down at his feet and nods in agreement. Jenna reconnects with Jonathan by kneeling down at eye level and holding both of his hands in hers. Jonathan feels a connection through Jenna's action and decides he is safe, so his body relaxes and he is able to now look up at his mother. "Jonathan," Jenna goes on, "I'm sorry I bit you. How do you feel about us looking for solutions how to handle the problem you're having with your little brother that wouldn't be hurtful to anyone? Do you want to talk about it now or should we put it on the family meeting agenda so Daddy can help too?" Jonathan decides to put it on the family meeting agenda.

At their next family meeting, the family discusses what happened. Mom and Dad use curiosity questions to help Jonathan understand how it hurts his brother to bite him. They also help him uncover why he did it in the first place—he felt jealous that his little brother was getting more attention from Mom. Mom and Jonathan decide on some special time later in the week when they will go to the planetarium, just the two of them. They also decide as a family how good it feels to hear someone who has upset us say they are sorry. Mom and Dad are now waiting eagerly for the next time Jonathan makes a mistake to see if he has learned this useful skill.

POSITIVE DISCIPLINE TOOLS

In this chapter, we have discussed the following tools and concepts of Positive Discipline:

Control Your Own Behavior

Example is the best teacher. Don't expect your children to control their behavior when you can't control your own.

Positive Time-Out

People do better when they feel better. Positive time-out is a highly effective tool for managing emotions under stress, as well as for building skills around self-care.

Mistakes Are Wonderful Opportunities to Learn

It is important to respond to mistakes with compassion and kindness instead of blame, shame, or lectures. When appropriate, use curiosity questions to help your child explore the consequences of her mistakes. At dinnertime or during family meetings, invite everyone to share a mistake they made and what they learned from it.

The 4 R's of Recovery

Making mistakes isn't as important as what we do about them. Set out the importance of modeling that mistakes are opportunities for learning. When you make mistakes, correct any harm done by applying the 4 R's of Recovery.

EXERCISE

Create Your Positive Time-Out Space

Positive time-out teaches children self-discipline and self-control through an understanding of the value of cooling off until rational thinking is available to them again. Start by teaching the "brain in the palm of the hand." Move on to designing the ideal positive time-out area. Brainstorm ideas together. Make sure to come up with some fun names too. Analyze the ideas and form a plan for creating and using the space (many spaces include books, stuffed animals, coloring books, music, etc.). The next time your child is misbehaving out of discouragement, don't forget to ask, "Would it help you to take some positive time-out?"

CHAPTER 12

DISCOVERING YOUR STRENGTHS AND CHALLENGES

Fiona runs a thriving catering business. When her best friend, Miranda, asked if Fiona would cater Miranda's parents' golden wedding anniversary celebration for a reduced rate, Fiona was happy to comply. Fiona knew Miranda's family didn't have a lot of money. Philippa, an acquaintance of both Fiona and Miranda, heard about Fiona's generosity and asked if Fiona could cater her wedding for the same reduced rate. Fiona felt obliged to agree although she knew Philippa was not short on funds. Then the problems started. Philippa was extremely demanding and wanted last-minute menu changes, input on staff, the service, et cetera, et cetera. She even expected Fiona to take charge of the flowers. Fiona felt incredibly overstretched trying to juggle Miranda's parents' party and all of Philippa's wedding demands. Both events were during the summer, in the midst of her busy season! Fiona, who loves giving excellent service, struggled to communicate her boundaries and limits to Philippa. She felt more and more taken for granted, all the while worrying that she would not do a good job for her dear friend Miranda.

CONTEXT AND DEVELOPMENT OF TOP CARD

Looking at all our relationships, and particularly at how we behave when insecure and under stress, can help us find areas for personal growth. For children, private logic and the ensuing behaviors generally fall within the categories of the mistaken goals. For adults, these behaviors fall within the categories of "top card." The term "top card" is used to refer to the "first card played"—that is, our "go-to" response—when we are feeling vulnerable. The challenges of your top card are what you do when feeling insecure or threatened about your sense of belonging and significance in the world. When you display the challenging behavior of your top card, you are likely to be less rational (you may have flipped your lid). You adopt "only if" thinking ("I'm okay *only if* I'm right," or "*only if* I'm in control," or "*only if* I'm pleasing others," or "*only if* I withdraw into my comfort zone"). In other words, you misbehave. Your response is reflexive and automatic because you are coming from insecurity and a mistaken belief about how to find belonging and significance—to overcome a sense of not being good enough. In order to understand your response, it is important to look at your private logic, since the beliefs you formed as a child still influence your behavior today. Because many of these beliefs are faulty—formed before you could comprehend logic and higher thinking—it is important to challenge them. Identifying your own top card will give you clues where to start, as that shows the behaviors you engage in.

The Origins of Our Belief Systems

We discussed earlier how children are always making decisions and storing them in their subconscious; so of course, were you. You may not have been aware of your preverbal decisions at the time, or even now feel aware of them, but they were made nonetheless. You made decisions based on your perceptions of how you were treated by your parents, as well as your perceptions of other experiences in your life. As a result, this formed your core beliefs or perceptions of how to best fit in (to belong) in your many social circles, starting with family.

Private logic is the framework within which we interpret experience, try to control experience (develop "tunnel vision"), and predict experience (behave in accordance with our expectations). This is an effective learning mechanism. However, the challenge with this aspect of human development is that we look for evidence to support whatever belief we have formed, and we usually dismiss evidence to the contrary. If the belief is "I am not good enough," this can be detrimental to our development. How we then behave will vary: some may try to cover up this belief by overachieving, others go to the extreme of giving up, and some choose ways of compensating that may be destructive. These behaviors are what we can discern through understanding our top card. Understanding this helps us grasp two very important Adlerian concepts: First, we are the ones who assign meaning to our thoughts, which is important to remember when we struggle with our self-worth. Second, it is imperative that we provide experiences for children that increase the chances that they will decide they are capable, confident, contributing members of society.

Top Card Explained

Every top card has both strengths and challenges. Many observe that the challenges (and ensuing ineffective behaviors) of their top card don't represent who they are. This is true. The assets of our top card come closer to describing who we are. The challenges describe what we do when feeling insecure. Think about what you might do when feeling insecure or challenged—when you get into "only if" thinking. This is not a rational space, so it may not feel like the real you. However, when you see your strengths, you probably smile in recognition. The top card challenges do not tell you who you *are*, but they do tell you what you *do* when you are feeling insecure and fearful.

Now, stay with us for this one: the *strengths* of your top card may also come from a place of insecurity and fear, as they too are based on our mistaken beliefs or "only if" thinking. To use the example of the superiority top card, used by someone who mistakenly feels he belongs "only if" he overachieves: This behavior might look successful on the surface (that is, it appears to be a strength). After all, quite a number of people who have a superiority top card can achieve many things, and the behavior serves them in socially acceptable ways. However, they may still feel insecure inside: "I belong *only if* I excel."

Categorizing behavior is a complex undertaking, and as you read this you may feel there are parts of all four top cards that could apply, as well as parts of your top card description that would definitely not apply. This is true. Human behavior is multifaceted and adaptable. Top card is a tool for understanding yourself and others, not a system of labeling. It is meant to help you feel encouraged to focus on your strengths. It is also meant to increase your awareness of what your behaviors invite from others, and to encourage you to work on your challenging behaviors and to develop strategies to overcome them. Whenever you feel insecure, a good way to work with this is to focus on your strengths to avoid dropping into irrational and negative behavior.

Many of our readers may, in their professional lives, have come across some form of personality profiling, such as Myers-Briggs. It may be helpful to think of top card in the same way, as it describes behavioral preference. The four top card categories (which we will describe in detail) describe typical behaviors of a person with that particular top card when she is stressed and when she is relaxed. You can think of it like your challenges and your strengths, which are likely to come out at different times (depending on the stress you're under from your environment). Top card gives you clear pointers on areas where you can improve your behavior by looking at your challenges. It has clear parallels with trends both in education, where the growth mindset (as set out by Carol Dweck) is at the forefront, and in organizational theory, which currently is heavily focused on strengths-based initiatives (Gallup research). Understanding your top card and your children's mistaken goals will therefore serve you (and them) well in all areas of life.

Identifying Your Top Card

Imagine that you have to choose one out of four gifts—and you won't like any of them.

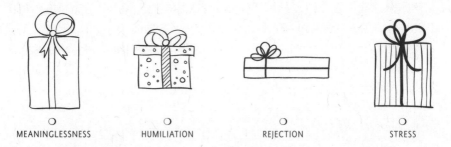

○	○	○	○
MEANINGLESSNESS	HUMILIATION	REJECTION	STRESS

Check the box under the gift that has the experience that you least want to deal with in life, the first one you would give back if you could. Don't overthink it. Follow your gut reaction. This is your top card.

Here is what each gift box represents:

> *Meaninglessness* represents the superiority top card.
> *Humiliation* represents the control top card.
> *Rejection* represents the pleasing top card.
> *Stress* represents the comfort top card.

SUPERIORITY

Most people with a superiority top card do not want to be superior to others. They may have the mistaken belief that they have to be superior in accomplishments to prove (or cover up) their basic feelings of inferiority—which at some level is true for all top cards. People with the superiority top card are often accused of always needing to be right. It may be truer to say they have difficulty being wrong, which they mistakenly interpret as not being good enough.

Superiority "only if" thinking looks something like this: "I belong *only if* I'm doing something meaningful. I feel insecure (and react) when I'm not accomplishing important things, and when others don't agree with my opinions about what is meaningful." Because you want to avoid feeling a sense of meaninglessness, you believe that *only if* you do things right or you are the best can you make life more meaningful and feel important. This can lead to feeling so overwhelmed that you revert to ineffective coping mechanisms—either you try harder and create a vicious cycle of continuing to be overwhelmed or you check out, feel guilty, and beat yourself up about it. Meanwhile, you may be causing everyone around you to feel inadequate.

What the Superiority Top Card Invites from Others

It is useful to think about how your strengths—your assets—enhance your relationships, and how your challenges create problems. On the asset side, adults with a superiority top card may be very good at modeling success and achievement and at encouraging excellence. However, others sometimes see this as "badgering to perfection" and feel lacking and unable to meet the high expectations. Too much superiority may invite children (and others) to feel inadequate. It is very discouraging to think you cannot measure up. Superiority people may see things in terms of right and wrong and lack flexibility, so there is no room for others to engage in brainstorming for other possibilities.

How to Turn Your Challenges into Strengths

Positive Discipline helps parents see how they can operate using their strengths instead of coming from their insecurities in order to help their children (and others) develop effective characteristics and life skills. Although all tools are effective, some may be more effective than others, depending on your personal top card.

Superiority-seeking adults may be more effective if they make an effort to let go of their need to be "right" and "best," practice the skills of getting into the child's (or other's) world to discover what is important to them, support others' needs and goals, practice unconditional love, enjoy the process, develop a sense of humor, be consciously irresponsible, learn to say no to more than they can handle, and hold family meetings where all ideas are valued.

CONTROL

People with a top card of control don't necessarily want to have control over others, but they do want to have control over situations and/or themselves, because they mistakenly believe lack of control means not being good enough. They may jump in and take control of every situation, or procrastinate until they feel more secure.

For this top card, "only if" thinking may look something like this: "I belong *only if* I have control over myself and situations (and sometimes others); I feel insecure (and react) when I think I have been criticized, and when others tell me what to do and/or resent and rebel against my efforts." Because you want to avoid criticism and humiliation, you mistakenly believe you will feel secure *only if* you are in control of the situation, of yourself, and, sometimes, children and others. Since it is impossible to control everything, you may avoid trying (procrastination), or become bossier, and create the thing you are trying to avoid (criticism) when others rebel.

What the Control Top Card Invites from Others

On the asset side, adults with a control top card may be very good at helping their children and others learn organization skills, leadership skills, assertiveness, persistence, and respect for order. However, control-seeking adults often choose a stricter style of parenting and leadership, and can have a tendency to be too rigid and controlling of their children (and others). This may invite rebellion or resistance or even unhealthy pleasing.

How to Turn Your Challenges into Strengths

Control-seeking adults may be more effective if they recognize their need for excessive control and practice the skills of letting go, offering choices, asking curiosity questions, involving children (and others) in decisions, and using family meetings.

PLEASING

People with a pleasing top card may have difficulty saying no to any opportunity to please others—until they feel resentful when others don't appreciate all they do. They may feel hurt when others don't "read their minds" to know how to please them (because it isn't special if they have to tell them). They mistakenly believe that not being appreciated means they aren't good enough.

"Only if" thinking for the pleasing top card usually goes like this: "I belong *only if* others like me and validate me. I feel hurt and insecure when others don't appreciate what I do for them, and when they don't make an effort to know and do what pleases me." Because you want to avoid rejection and hassles, you believe that *only if* you value everyone's needs will you be included and have a sense of worthiness.

What the Pleasing Top Card Invites from Others

On the asset side, adults with a pleasing top card may be very good at helping their children learn friendly, considerate, and non-aggressive behavior. However, pleasing adults may also choose a permissive style of parenting or leadership and as a result may become doormats and feel taken advantage of. They may do too much for their children (in the name of love). This may invite manipulation, demands for undue attention, resentment, depression, or even revenge from others. It does not provide a model for children to articulate what they need and want in ways that are respectful to self and others. The energy of pleasing that comes from insecurity can be very annoying to others, especially when they sense there are strings attached to your pleasing (you expect something back), and they may avoid you—inviting you to feel rejected.

How to Turn Your Challenges into Strengths

Pleasing adults may be more effective when they stop focusing exclusively on others' needs, and take care of their own needs first. They need to have faith in their children's (and others') ability to please themselves; they also need to practice and teach emotional honesty, engage in joint problem-solving, learn how to give and take, set boundaries, and use family meetings.

COMFORT

Most people don't like the name of their top card, objecting to what the name represents. People with a comfort top card may be the exception. They don't understand why anyone would choose anything but comfort—and that is the problem. They may not push themselves to learn and grow, and others may find them under-stimulating and predictable.

"Only if" thinking for the comfort top card usually looks something like this: "I belong *only if* I stay within limits that are safe and familiar, and I don't want to do anything that is stressful. I feel insecure (and react) when others don't want to join me in comfort, or pressure me to join their agenda." You may believe that *only if* you avoid emotional and physical stress, the problems will go away and you will feel balanced.

What the Comfort Top Card Invites from Others

On the asset side, adults with a comfort top card may model the benefits of being easygoing, loyal, diplomatic, and predictable. However, comfort-seeking adults often choose a more permissive style of parenting and leadership, and therefore may create a tendency in children and others toward being spoiled, demanding, or developing a sense of entitlement. Avoiding some challenges can stunt your personal growth and seem boring to others. Or you may try so hard to make others comfortable that you create stress for yourself.

How to Turn Your Challenges into Strengths

Comfort-seeking adults can be more effective when they come out of their shell and get their children (and others) involved in creating routines, setting goals, and solving problems together. They need to allow their children to experience the natural consequences of their choices (even though it is hard not to rescue them) and involve them in family meetings.

WHICH TOP CARD do you think Fiona has in our opening story? What advice would you have for her to manage the situation with her business and her two friends? Growth happens when we learn to maximize our strengths and turn our liabilities into assets. For Fiona, who probably has the pleasing top card, her ability to give great service is a key reason why her business is a success. However, there is a risk that when she gets stressed she will bend over backwards to please, as her "only if" thinking is telling her that pleasing is the only way to avoid rejection. As a result, she has invited manipulation from Philippa. Learning to set some healthy boundaries (joint problem-solving) and saying no (emotional honesty) would be useful skills for Fiona to practice.

As you gain insight and awareness, growth can be exciting and rewarding. Understanding your own top card and how it influences your relationships with your children, other family members, and colleagues can help you learn, with time and patience, to be the most effective version of yourself.

POSITIVE DISCIPLINE IN ACTION

"Learning about top card was a real revelation for me," says one of the authors, Kristina, after participating in the Positive Discipline for Couples workshop. "My top card is clearly superiority, and my partner's is undoubtedly comfort.

"My biggest issue with both myself and others is my unrealistically high demands—I'd even say perfection. Then when either I or my partner (or others) wouldn't reach them (in other words all the time!), I would feel disappointed and despondent. I would react with judgment and criticism. In the past I even know I lost some friendships over my unrealistic demands for people's commitment to me and my ideas.

"With my partner, I would go all cold and harsh whenever he did something 'flawed.' My biggest issue was my perception of his lack of taking personal responsibility for his situation and of his lack of desire to want to work on himself and grow. This was so alien to me, and I thought many times that it would be the end of our relationship.

"Understanding top card made me realize my part of the equation. The more I criticized and demanded, the more he retreated. Since I'm trying to accept that I can't change someone else (a tough one for superiority), I've decided to focus on changing myself. So, I stopped judging (most of the time at least) and instead whenever he, in my eyes, is looking for excuses and shortcuts, I try to either leave him to it, or encourage him with small steps.

"The magic is that my partner is now more open to self-work and change. My lack of judgment has made him feel more secure and appreciated, so he doesn't have to retreat into his 'cave' quite so much. I am also learning from him how to be more accepting and forgiving, which is really helping me deal with my own insecurities."

POSITIVE DISCIPLINE TOOLS

Everyone has a top card, which is our go-to behavioral response when we feel insecure. Understanding your own and others' top cards will help greatly in finding behavioral challenges to address. As we've seen in this chapter, some tools will be more useful to you depending on your top card. Here are a few more general tools, which will help you work with your top card and support you in your personal work.

Perception

Everything is in the eye of the beholder, and we perceive the world through the filter of beliefs formed in childhood. No two people's filters are exactly the same. This is why we all interpret the same experience slightly differently. Being aware of this can be hugely helpful in dealing with our changing circumstances and the effect it has on both ourselves and others. In times of stress, conflict, or disagreement, try to pause and figure out what belief is behind your interpretation of what is happening. Then ask yourself about the interpretation that might be behind the other person's behavior. Try to notice how being aware changes your experience of the situation and see if you can let go of conflicting emotions. Then you can focus on how to be encouraging to yourself and others.

Responsibility

Take responsibility for what you create in your life. Dig deep and figure out how you created the situation you complain about. Responsibility does not mean blame or shame. Awareness of personal responsibility gives you power and options to create what you want. Make a plan to achieve what you want without blame or expectations from anyone else.

Differences

Opposites attract! Think of a characteristic or trait in your partner that sometimes bugs you. Since your partner had this quality from the beginning, how did you once see it differently? Did you once think it was adorable or that it didn't matter? Has your partner changed, or have you? Work on appreciating (or at least respecting) differences. How about keeping a list of your partner's strengths and regularly reading it? Take time to verbalize your appreciation daily.

....

EXERCISE

Understanding Your Top Card

Understanding your top card can be confusing when you first learn about it. Top card is a process that "keeps cooking," and over time you will become more aware of your "only if" thinking and begin to realize when you are engaging in this kind of thinking. This self-reflection activity, designed to help you discover your own private logic, will help you go through that process.

1. Review your top card. Think of a time you experienced what is inside your top card box, or a time when you behaved according to your challenges. What happened? Write it down.

2. When that happened, what were you thinking?

3. What were you feeling? Be sure to use feeling words that are different from the word inside your top card box (a feeling word is one word: "angry," "guilty," "anxious," etc.).

4. What did you do when the experience happened?

5. How did it work for you?

6. Do you have some advice for yourself about what you might do differently?

CHAPTER 13

WELL-BEING

Josh, father of two toddlers, says, "I used to be in great shape before we had kids. I ran marathons and lifted weights three times a week. But that all changed when I had to juggle kids and work. I hate my body now, and I miss how great it felt physically and emotionally to be in good shape."

Far too many busy parents feel like the proverbial hamster on a wheel—running as hard as they can just to keep up with the sheer volume of commitments, both professionally and at home. They feel trapped in an endless cycle of duty and responsibility. The pursuit of individual happiness, however, is a worthy and honorable goal. Heard all this before? Maybe. We are hoping, however, that realizing the impact your personal well-being has on your children will help with that extra bit of motivation to take action.

DISCOVER WHERE YOU ARE OUT OF SYNC

Is the pressure to be 100 percent in all areas wearing you down? Modern life invites us to run at a more frantic pace than ever before. But here is the bottom line: if you aren't happy, nobody is happy. Your unhappiness affects everyone you care about—your children, your partner, your coworkers, and your friends. Unhappy people are less effective parents and professionals, and they don't make good company. Children know intuitively if you are happy and enjoying life as a parent. One mother was shocked to realize that her stressful, overloaded schedule was teaching her son that being a working parent was miserable. She overheard him tell a friend, "I'm never having kids. It's way too much work, and it looks like a total pain in the rear." If you are a busy working parent, it is imperative that you find your own way to seek peace and refuge from the strain and pressure in your daily life. It is an integral part of self-care to clock out of your worldly life on a regular basis in order to find a broader, more enlightened viewpoint. This is what we refer to as seeking spiritual or personal growth. Often we are so busy climbing the ladder of life that we fail to notice that our ladder is leaning against the wrong wall!

The first step in achieving joy in life is to correctly diagnose where the problem really lies. Using the Wheel of Life, a well-known coaching tool, will help you identify the trouble zones in eight very important aspects of your life.

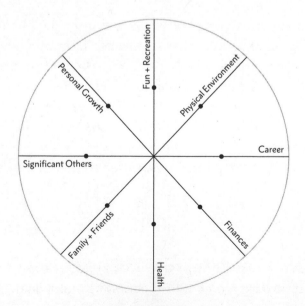

Take a moment to rate your current level of satisfaction in each area from 0 to 10, with 10 meaning you are completely content and satisfied. View the center of the wheel as 0 and the outside edge as 10. Draw a line in each section that correlates with your current level of satisfaction to create a new outer edge (see the example below). When you are finished, you will have a visual depiction of where you are most out of balance. If you've ever driven a car with a tire that is uneven and low on air, you'll know it creates a bumpy, difficult, and uncomfortable ride. The lowest-scoring sections in your wheel are most likely the source of your greatest unhappiness. At this point we need to stress that achieving a 10 in all areas at all times is *not* the purpose of this exercise. That is entirely unrealistic. More realistic is to accept that life is a flowing process of ups and downs. It is still useful to identify where the biggest problem is *at the moment* so that you know where to put your focus right now. Then at some point it will shift to another area—it's a constant process.

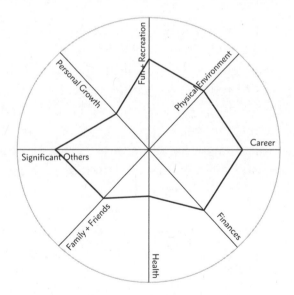

PERSONAL WELL-BEING COMES FIRST

The first step in creating a happy, well-functioning family is to make sure you are a happy and well-functioning individual. This will require you to rigorously guard your physical health, focus on your mental health (including managing stress), and cultivate meaningful relationships. These are the cornerstones of your personal well-being. Let's zero in on the areas that most affect self-care. Using your Wheel of Life answers, remove Career and Finances and look at the remaining six categories. If you scored yourself lower than 5 in any of them, attend to that area of your life first. Implement the suggestions in this chapter that will help you reach a higher level of contentment in those areas. Once you have achieved a higher score in your self-care, only then are you ready to tackle Career and Money.

Let's take a deeper look into the three cornerstones of personal well-being, starting with your physical health.

PHYSICAL HEALTH

Physical health includes focusing on a consistent exercise plan, maintaining a healthy diet, and protecting sleep. (Managing stress also has a great impact on physical health, and we will cover that in the section on mental health.) Taking care of our physical selves is usually where we start to slip up once we become tired and overwhelmed by career and family pressures. How many times have you thought something along these lines: "Once I'm through this particularly stressful time at work, I'll join that running club" or "I can't function on so little sleep without sugar and caffeine—once the kids are a bit older I'll get back on a healthier diet." True, in the short run that strategy might work, but it easily becomes habit, with ensuing poor health, depression, exhaustion, and apathy.

Staying Fit and Healthy with Regular Exercise

Physical exercise is unequivocally the best vaccination of all time. It inoculates us against a host of life's evils. It staves off obesity, heart disease, diabetes, stroke, and stress. It is a natural antidepressant and reduces anxiety by offering a powerful "endorphin cocktail" that can cure the foulest moods in as little as twenty minutes. It elevates our body image, enhances our sexual vitality and fertility, and produces an overall sense of well-being. One mother confessed, "When I am particularly grouchy, my kids beg me to go for a run. They know I'll come home a more patient and tolerant mom."

With the media constantly promoting the benefits of exercise (and we've all seen this by now), why aren't more of us committed to a regular exercise program? The cry of most overwhelmed parents is "It's impossible—there is so much to do and so little time!" Many busy parents have to get creative to find time to exercise without feeling guilty about focusing on themselves. Often that means combining exercising with time for family, friends, or colleagues. It also means managing expectations—you don't have to train for an Ironman or exercise for hours. Leave that for another time in life. Thirty minutes of walking three times a week can be enough, and small amounts of time may be easier to find. The key is to identify a time and place where you can do it regularly.

Whatever you do, find an exercise you enjoy—you will never stick with it if you hate it. Think about how it fits in with your other obligations and ambitions. If your kids are small, put them in a double running stroller and walk or run with them after work or on weekends. Let older children ride bicycles or scooters while you walk or jog. That way you spend time with them, you get your exercise in, and they learn the importance of exercise and wellness too. Another idea is to buy a treadmill or other piece of exercise equipment and use it at home when the kids are asleep or while they are watching a show on television. This can also work well if you and your partner work together tag team style. For example, he helps with the children's homework while you exercise, and then you start dinner while he exercises. Exercising with your partner and choosing an activity you both enjoy (maybe an activity you used to do together before the children came along) is another great way to get fit and maintain a strong connection with each other. Don't forget to check online. These days there are plenty of great exercise classes and even personal trainer sessions available that you can do from your own home.

If you opt for using a facility (gym, swimming pool), make sure it is easily accessible from either home or work. If it's too far out of your way, it becomes much more difficult to fit it into your busy schedule. If you tend to carry work stress home, take half an hour before coming home to exercise and "sweat to forget." On particularly stressful days, one mother called her in-home babysitter to ask her to put her exercise clothes outside the front door so she could get them, go to the gym, and come home in a better frame of mind before interacting with the kids. Or take a yoga class and kill two birds with one stone by exercising and managing your stress levels. If you want to combine exercising with social connections, exercise during lunch. Combine walking or going to the gym with friends from work and you meet two core needs. You will find you have far more energy for the rest of the afternoon. And for the early birds, get up a half hour early and sneak to the gym before the kids are up.

Focusing on Your Diet

Eating well is important to your overall sense of health and well-being. However, you may share Sondra's concern. "My mother stayed home full-time when I was a kid. She cooked a homemade meal every night of the week. Half the time we are too exhausted to cook, or it is impossible to find the time between soccer practice and piano lessons. We order pizza or go through the drive-through more nights than not. I feel guilty about how I'm feeding the kids, and I'm embarrassed by my ever-widening girth."

The reality is that if you have a career, you probably don't have time to cook elaborate meals every night. Let go of the guilt on those unavoidable fast-food nights and try to plan some quick, easy, and healthy home meals for those nights when you are tired and busy. Make technology work for you—pressure cookers are hands-off and can reduce cooking time drastically. One mother's strategy was to cook a double recipe when she could, and stock the freezer for those nights when everyone was on the go. Often it isn't finding the time to cook that is the problem, but figuring out *what* to cook and having the necessary ingredients available. There are many companies and cookbooks now that offer simple, healthy recipes that can be done in under thirty minutes, and all the fresh ingredients and portions can be delivered straight to your door each week. There are also companies that prepare the meals for you and you just need to heat them up. It's time to get creative here.

In Chapter 10 we discussed how mealtime provides a terrific opportunity to teach the character traits of cooperation and contribution. Even small children can take a turn (with supervision and a little help) cooking a simple meal such as soup, salad, sandwiches, and dessert. Cooking with your children allows you to have meaningful special time with your children and creates a sense of belonging and contribution. Having jobs that are shared within the family helps children feel capable by helping out at home, and it invites parents to feel less resentful than when they have to take on all the household duties. A great idea to make sure both you and your kids eat healthily is to have a "healthy snack shelf" in the fridge stocked with cut-up vegetables, hummus, fruits, nuts, and other good-for-you snacks (you might want to have a similar drawer at work). And don't forget to drink plenty of fresh water, as thirst is often mistaken for hunger and dehydration leads to increased fatigue.

Getting Enough Sleep

In a survey done by the authors, less than 50 percent of the adults surveyed answered yes to getting a good night's sleep (most nights), and 80 percent said that their children get enough sleep most nights.

The Mayo Clinic, a prestigious medical institution in the United States, recommends that adults get seven to eight hours of sleep each night. In fact, Americans are now more sleep-deprived than at any other time in history. In 1850 the average American got nine and a half hours of sleep per night. By 1950 that number was down to eight hours. Currently it is seven hours and still declining. A 2009 study by the Centers for Disease Control and Prevention found that 35.3 percent of Americans reported that they typically got less than seven hours of sleep daily.[27] Sleep deprivation leads to inability to concentrate and fatigue, and prolonged fatigue causes lethargy, irritability, and decreased immune function. Exhaustion and burnout are well-known contributors to depression and anxiety. In short, tiredness impairs our coping skills in all areas of life. And when we are less able to cope, we become less effective parents, mates, and professionals.

One mother relayed an incident when she was exhausted and lectured her children with her periodic "martyr tape," which sounded like this: "I work so hard around here. I work forty hours a week, come home exhausted, and all I want is a clean kitchen—and you can't even do that for me. After all I do for the three of you, cleaning up your own messes shouldn't be too much to ask. I am sick and tired of being the family maid." Her fifteen-year-old interrupted her litany of self-pity by saying, "Mom, I think things would look a whole lot better if you'd go and take a nap." She admitted: "His comment infuriated me, but the truth hurts. I was exhausted, and I was becoming a royal pain to be around."

The first thing you need to do is renounce the cultural bias that says you are "hard-core" if you sleep less. Why take pride in sleeping only six hours a night if you function best on eight? Listen to your body and allow it to tell you when it is time for bed. Decide how much sleep you need to function at your best, and make it a priority. Your coworkers and loved ones will thank you. It is important to model good sleep habits for your children. Tell your children when you have "hit a wall" with exhaustion and are no longer fit to be around other humans. If it is a weekend nap or an eight-thirty bedtime that is needed, ask your kids and your partner to support you. It is your responsibility not to burden your family with your bad mood. Often the culprit is exhaustion.

There are a number of steps you can take to make sleep easier and more beneficial. Avoid caffeine and alcohol if you have difficulty sleeping. Alcohol may create the relaxation conducive to two to three hours of good sleep, but it may then interrupt the sleep cycle and cause middle-of-the-night wakefulness. Caffeine interrupts sleep for many. Go for a jog instead. Regular exercise reduces insomnia and deepens sleep. Just make sure not to exercise too late at night, as this may impact your ability to get to sleep. Make sure you create a relaxing bedtime routine and stop all activities that require alertness (work, reading intellectually challenging material, or stimulating phone conversations) at least one hour before bedtime. Listen to soft music, read something easy, drink a cup of herbal tea or warm milk, make simple preparations for the next day, or have sex. In other words, signal your mind and body that it is time to let go by turning the lights down low and quieting yourself. Try to turn off all technology at least one hour before you go to sleep. Screens can stop or slow down the release of melatonin (the sleep hormone), which can make it difficult to fall asleep.

If you are suffering from chronic insomnia, it may be worth speaking to your doctor or going to the nearest sleep disorder clinic and receiving diagnostic testing. It is estimated that 50 to 70 million Americans suffer from chronic sleep disorders that are treatable.[28] One dear friend of the authors with chronic fatigue and depression discovered he had sleep apnea. Surgery restored his sleep and consequently his energy and enthusiasm for life.

If, despite taking all necessary steps, you still can't get seven to eight hours of sleep in because of a busy schedule, discover the power of the micro-nap. These are short moments of deep relaxation that can have amazing restorative benefits. Find fifteen to twenty minutes during the day where you can be still, comfortable, and undisturbed, and exercise deep breathing with your eyes closed (using an eye mask is great too). Lying down is preferable but may not be possible if you are at work; finding an empty meeting room or even sitting in your car can work. Set a timer on your phone or watch so you don't have to worry about falling asleep or forgetting the time. The idea is not to fall into a deep sleep but rather to refresh and reset the mind.

MENTAL HEALTH

Fortunately, it is becoming more and more acceptable to talk about the importance of good mental health. Unfortunately, poor mental health is reportedly on the rise, particularly among young people, and our society is currently suffering from an epidemic of mood-controlling drugs being given to children to help manage behavior that could be corrected by changes in parenting and education. We must be willing to take our own mental health seriously and start modeling healthy habits to our children. In this section, we will discuss two fundamental aspects of mental health—handling stress and developing a sound internal monologue. Apart from that, we are great believers in coaching and therapy, as well as cultivating spiritual health.

Managing Stress

In our survey of working parents, nearly half (41 percent) felt stressed half of the time in a typical week, and nearly a third (27 percent) most of the time. What is stress? Stress is the physical and mental response we have to a perceived threat. The body's survival mode kicks in and we go into our primitive brain, which triggers our fight-flight-or-freeze response (as we discussed in Chapter 11). During this time, our body produces the hormones adrenaline and cortisol to help us survive. In the early days of humanity, life was very dangerous, full of real, physically threating situations (like being chased by a tiger), so these hormones kicked in and helped us survive by enabling us to run faster or get super-strong so we could fight the threat. This was a very useful response to an immediate threat. But it is not a rational thinking state (our lid is flipped). In modern life, many of our stressors are not life-threatening, although at the time they may feel that way. Often they are not even physically threatening, and so sometimes they are referred to as "paper tigers." Survival is still the overriding need of every human, and because it is an irrational, instinctive response, we have the same biological hormonal response to the paper tigers as our ancestors did to the real ones. But do we behave the same way now as early humans did back then?

If we were being chased by a real tiger, we would run and our stress hormones would be used up in the body. Because many of our paper tigers are mental—relationships, work pressures—we usually don't physically react by running or fighting; instead we stay put and deal with it verbally, or suppress it and don't deal with it at all. What happens to the stress hormones that have not been burned off? They can sit in the body and wreak havoc with the immune system, the digestive system, the reproductive system, and our overall mental health. This can lead to chronic stress, which is when we never get a chance to recoup and come down from the stress high, so we have constant high levels of cortisol and adrenaline in our system.

It is important to note that a certain amount of stress is good for us and enables us to perform better, thereby achieving desired outcomes both mentally and physically. This is called positive stress: the brain is functioning fully and releases another hormone called DHEA, which is associated with brain growth—that is, with learning. *This works only when we feel challenged but not threatened.* If we feel threatened, survival mode and the fight-flight-or-freeze response will kick in and we get flooded with stress hormones. Can you think of examples where stress may be good? For instance, in sports, competition can help us perform and improve our skills. However, in sports we also use the tool of taking a time-out to regroup, strategize, and recover from stress.

How can we learn to handle and recoup from stress better at home and at work? A first step is to start using positive coping strategies. Instead of using negative coping strategies (procrastinating, eating, drinking, smoking, etc.), which may give only short-term relief, focus on positive coping strategies, such as exercising (which will burn off those stress hormones), talking to someone, journaling, art, or deep breathing. When you slip up—and who doesn't?—don't beat yourself up about it. Just vow to start again tomorrow. In our survey of working parents, the top three stress-relieving activities were sleep, exercise/yoga, and watching TV. Here are a few more ideas to help manage stress.

Let Go

Some of us spend a lot of energy worrying about, or trying to change, things that we have no control over. Work on letting go of the things you cannot control and focus on the things you can control. "How, how, *how*?" we hear you ask. Indeed, not an easy task. Several tools and exercises throughout this book are aimed at helping you find balance in life and refrain from overreacting, thereby allowing you to be a better parent, partner, and colleague. The first step is always awareness, so spend some time figuring out what you are trying to control, and why. Mindfulness, the ability to be calm and present in the moment, is an incredibly powerful tool to help with this (more in Chapter 17).

Ask for Help

Many of us are not good at asking for or accepting help, often seeing it as a sign of weakness. We disagree! Knowing when you need help and asking for it is actually a sign of strength and self-awareness. It is also a great way to encourage those around you—kids in particular can feel very empowered when asked to help (although we do not advocate off-loading your problems on your kids—this is more about asking them to alleviate some of the burden of running the home). Working with a therapist or coach is a fantastic way to ask for help.

Deep Breathing/Quick Meditations

Do you often find yourself looking to the future for comfort or reason ("When this or that happens, I'll be happy") or to the past ("Because this or that happened to me, I can't be happy")? This kind of thinking takes your attention off the present moment and creates uncertainty. When you learn to breathe in and out deeply and with focus, you bring your mind back to the body and thereby the present moment. This releases tension. If you practice deep, mindful breathing for just five to ten minutes each day, you will naturally remember to come back to your breathing the next time a strong emotion or stressful situation arises. It is one of the most effective instant solutions when you feel yourself getting stressed, losing it, and slipping into a fight-flight-or-freeze response. Deep breathing slows the blood pressure and stops stress hormones from being produced and circulated.

Find Your Internal Locus of Control

Do you look to others for direction? Is it someone else's job to make decisions for you—your partner, your boss, your children? Since we have little control over others, this kind of thinking causes a lot of stress. Much better, then, to rely on our own intuition and experience to make decisions at any given moment, without needing someone else's input. Make a conscious decision to accept that you are responsible for your own decisions, and be forgiving toward yourself when you get it wrong.

Walk in Nature

Nature is incredibly healing. It has been scientifically proven that when you're in nature your brain behaves differently. It can calm you and soothe your nerves. Being in nature has been found to reduce stress, fight depression, improve sleep, and boost immunity. Even if you live in the city, find a park or a water feature to sit near and breathe.

Get a Pet

Caring for and cuddling a loved pet has been proven to release oxytocin, the "cuddle hormone." This is the same hormone that mothers release when they breastfeed their babies, and it is believed to contribute to the bonding process. Experiencing the joy of having a pet in your life can help greatly to boost well-being and reduce stress. It also teaches kids the importance of caring for others and the joy of the natural world. However, for some, having a pet adds more stress due to the responsibility to train, feed, and walk on a daily basis, so make sure it fits into your lifestyle.

Treat Yourself to a Massage or Spa Day

If funds allow it, a regular massage is a brilliant stress buster and has fantastic therapeutic benefits both physically and mentally. It releases tense muscles and gets rid of toxins stored up that can otherwise lead to illness and depression.

Self-Talk: Developing Your Inner Truth

An integral part of sound mental health is the verbal interactions that you have with yourself. Many people are unaware of what they are saying to themselves and so they continue a cycle of negative self-talk—for instance, telling yourself you can't take time for yourself to go to yoga, or that a massage is a luxury you don't deserve.

Negative self-talk can often be set off by changes in our circumstance that put us out of our comfort zones. What if you had an extremely important job that it feels like no one is acknowledging? You're responsible for people's lives and well-being, and you consistently work overtime, but you don't get paid. In fact, you're often made to feel that your job isn't even a job at all, you're not very skilled, and you're not contributing much to society (or at least it feels that way). If you are, or ever have been, a full-time stay-at-home parent, you might recognize this job description. Then when it's time to transition back to work, you feel entirely out of practice, and just when you had started to get the hang of this parenting thing, you're back to square one. It's no wonder that this can be a very stressful time and may trigger feelings of self-doubt and criticism such as "I'm not doing it right," "I can't do it all," and "Am I doing enough?" Some of the universal questions that arise during this transition that can set off negative self-talk are: "Who am I? What is my purpose? What is my worth? What am I able to contribute to my family and to society?"

What stories are you telling yourself? When you've done something good, do you tend to put yourself down, or do you verbally pat yourself on the back? Consider what kind of monologue is going through your mind when you think about doing something that is just for you. Self-care starts with the words you speak to and about yourself or about the action of self-care. Would you say to a good friend what you say to yourself? Would you say the same thing to your child? If so, then you are on the right track. If not, then you need to change your story. What kinds of stories are you telling yourself about other people who make self-care a priority? Are you supportive of their decision to take care of themselves? Or do you sit in judgment and quietly question their commitment to their family or to their job?

Where does this self-talk come from? Remember, your beliefs, or habitual thought patterns, were shaped when you were a child. Maybe you recognize this: "My mother worked really hard. She was the first one in her family to go into the workforce and work full-time outside the home. There were so many great things that she role-modeled for me, and yet self-care was not one of them. It was always everybody else first," said one mother. Not only is that not sustainable, but it can lead to feelings of resentment, self-pity, and burnout. The power of modeling self-care for your kids cannot be ignored. How else are they to learn such an important life skill?

Understanding self-care and practicing self-care are two very different things (remember, nurturing yourself is a necessity, not a luxury). In Chapter 17 we discuss the importance of drawing energy from your strengths and working on turning your challenges into positives. This is the work required to reprogram the brain; you have to change your private logic in order to root out faulty belief systems. Here are a few more ideas on how you can help yourself develop a healthy inner monologue.

Give Yourself a Break

Perfectionism is the enemy of self-care. It's enormously freeing (not to mention a huge stress reducer) to stop holding yourself to impossibly high standards. Give yourself the same empathy you'd show a friend. Reach out to support groups and share your struggles in order to find support from others. It helps to know you're not the only one going through something, and at the very least it will validate your feelings.

Communicate Your Self-Care Plan to Your Family

There should be space for both partners to implement self-care, and no one should ever have to justify or explain why they are doing so. Standing up for your needs strengthens your inner core. It's important that both partners set their own standards and choose what activities work best for them. Celebrating differences is essential.

Put a Positive Spin on Things

Challenge your version of the story. Catch yourself being negative and change your language. For example, instead of telling yourself, "I'm so disorganized, I never get anything done," train yourself to say, "How can I get this done?" or "I may not get this done today, but that is okay, I can give it another shot tomorrow." This isn't about ignoring your problems but rather about retraining your brain and asking yourself, "How can I look at this differently?"

Affirmations and Visualizations

Create your own positive affirmations or mantras to help you cultivate joy and enrich your life. This allows you to eliminate the negative script in your head that judges and criticizes. You have the power to choose your thoughts, and it's much healthier to fill your head with love rather than with fear and negativity. For example, tell yourself out loud or during meditation, "I am more than enough" or "I am just right as I am." Running a gratitude list in your head at waking and before sleeping is another great way to keep negativity at bay (and help with sleeplessness). Visualizing relationships and future events in a positive light is another very powerful tool to help train the brain.

Find Your Purpose

This is so important that we have designated pretty much a whole chapter to it—and it's coming up next! It's about finding the right ladder to climb and making sure it is leaning up against the right wall. It's about creating space in your life for reflection, questioning, and searching. Before we pause and do all that work, let's talk about the importance of nurturing all important relationships.

CULTIVATING MEANINGFUL RELATIONSHIPS

Studies consistently find a link between nurturing friendship and personal well-being. We also know that we both enjoy and are more successful at work when we nurture strong relationships with our colleagues. Gary shares a common problem for working parents: "Before we were married with kids we had a lot of friends. We went to sporting events, I'd play poker with the guys, and we'd go on vacation once in a while with other couples. Now there is only time for work and the kids." This is a common and heartbreaking sentiment.

There is a huge correlation between depression and social isolation, and in our modern world loneliness and isolation are becoming much more common, possibly made more acute by the apparent "connectedness" of our digital screen–based age. Human beings are hard-wired for connection. Good relationships are the foundation of personal happiness and well-being, and it is not true that your spouse, children, and work are enough.

Fitting Friendship into Your Schedule

In our survey, when asked "How often do you spend time with friends face-to-face without the kids?" 40 percent of parents said only every few months. You need good friends and sometimes extended family to help you through the ups and downs of life. Catching up with your girl/guy friends and perhaps siblings is like "inner jogging"—it renews your soul and arms you with a fresh perspective on life. Attentive listening and empathy are therapeutic in and of themselves.

We are more likely to do something when it's a habit, so it is a good idea to create with your dearest friends rituals and traditions that happen regularly. Gary had monthly poker nights and vacations with other couples on his list. If you're friends with the parents of your kids' friends, perhaps you could do a family vacation together. That can be made into a yearly tradition. Try to find people who will share your interests, whether it's galleries, museums, shopping, or sporting events. It's helpful to make plans for another meetup at the end of your time together. Use the digital world to your advantage by having social media groups with your closest friends to make it easy to book lunches or events. Local friends can be perfect for a weekly coffee catch-up. And of course, with your best friend, make sure you have some non-negotiable traditions, such as New Year's Eve parties or yearly birthday spa days.

Negative People

As tricky as this can be, you might want to limit your time with negative people. They can be toxic to your emotional health and make it harder to develop a positive internal monologue. If you are spending time with people who bring you down with their pessimism and criticism, and you feel you have done all you can to support them, it may be wise to keep your distance until they improve.

Building Your Parenting Network

In Chapter 14 there will be plenty of tips on how to develop and nurture your professional network. For now, think back to those early days of parenthood. Did you feel lonely and isolated? This is quite common for new parents and why a strong sense of belonging is more important than ever in parenthood.

Friends and extended family aren't the only people you want to nurture a relationship with, even after you settle down to a partnership and children. To sustain our energy, we need to connect with other people who can encourage and support us. Building a community of like-minded people is essential to our social health. Be proactive, take the initiative, and invite someone you appreciate to do something fun. Get to know your community. Investigate local daycare centers, children's stores, kids' play centers, bookstores, religious centers, and so on, and see what activities they offer. Also, make sure to offer to help out and volunteer. That is often the best way to get some help when you need a helping hand. Same goes for neighbors. There might be local parent-child groups you can join—maybe mother-and-baby exercise groups or online parenting communities. Reach out to your acquaintances and colleagues. Especially in the early stages of parenthood, you might find yourself making closer friends with people you previously knew only casually, because you are now in a similar life stage.

SELF-CARE NEEDS TO be taken very seriously. Many new parents struggle to get the balance right, with serious implications for their mental and physical health, as Alicia shares in her story.

POSITIVE DISCIPLINE IN ACTION

"I thought being selfless would make me a good mom. I was a failed natural-birth warrior, and then I was selflessly devoted to my daughter for the first eight weeks of motherhood, until I crashed and burned. I found myself in therapy because at my post-cesarean checkup I told my doctor, 'I feel like I am falling apart.' I was recommended to a therapist, who asked me, 'What are you doing to take care of yourself?' I replied, 'Well, nothing. I am too busy taking care of the baby.' My prescription was self-care, and to begin at least going for a walk or having a cup of coffee by myself. Indeed, the little moments of self-care I gave to myself added up and I began to heal.

"As I've gone from one to four kids, I've learned to set realistic goals and keep my self-care routine a priority. Otherwise, I am completely overwhelmed: I yell more, and I snap . . . I am just downright unhappy. Sometimes self-care is as simple as taking a 'mommy time-out.' If I am feeling frazzled, I will put one [kid] down for a nap, another in front of the TV, make myself a cup of coffee, and just sit and drink it in silence without doing anything else. Generally, my days are filled with small moments of self-care involving meditation (five minutes makes a difference), nourishment (I eat whole foods and I'm never 'too busy' to skip breakfast), exercise (even if it's taking my kids for a bike ride or doing a few yoga poses while the littlest toddles around), inspiration and flow (I read constantly, and get up early to write), practical beauty care (I wash my face twice a day, moisturize, and quickly put myself together before I walk outside the door so I feel stronger out in the world), and breaks (just about every week I get a babysitter for date night and escape with my husband, even if it's only for two hours).

"Since choosing self-compassion over guilt and setting realistic goals I've found a way to do the things I need to be strong enough to maintain my stamina as both a mother and writer. Self-care has made me a resilient mom and that's how I am able to show up with the love and patience my kids need to thrive."

—*Alicia Assad, www.aliciaassad.com*

POSITIVE DISCIPLINE TOOLS

We have covered plenty of strategies in this chapter for increasing and nurturing our physical and mental health as well as our relationships. Here are a few more general tools.

Happiness

Happiness is an inside job. If you expect someone else to make you happy, you are doomed to failure. Sometimes the possibility for happiness is right in front of you and you don't see it. What steps do you need to take to be happy (or to recognize your inner happiness)? One of our favorite roads to happiness is to practice gratitude.

Sense of Humor

Not only is laughter the best medicine, but a sense of humor can create magic in a relationship when things get tense. We cannot stress enough the importance of laughing and having fun! When you find yourself getting too serious, look for the humor in the situation. Together with your children and partner, you can create silent signals that will remind you to lighten up. Just be mindful about using sarcasm, which can be misunderstood and hurtful.

Share Expectations

Do not expect your partner and your children to read your mind. Share what you want and why it's important to you. Plan your weekly agenda and make sure to include these three categories: individual fun, couple fun, and family fun. Express appreciation when you get what you want and forgive when you don't.

Pay Attention

Love grows when it is nurtured. That goes for self-love and in relationships. Make it a priority to pay attention to your own needs and to the needs of others. Stop whatever you are doing and really listen. Experience the wonder all around you. Is there anything you have been taking for granted (your partner, your work, your children, yourself)? Make a commitment to pay attention and try to meet your own needs in order to meet the needs of others.

EXERCISE

Make a list of things you can do to help increase your level of satisfaction in the sections of your Wheel of Life that get the lowest satisfaction rating. Make a commitment to do at least one of those things each week. Don't forget to reflect on the process.

CHAPTER 14

YOUR DREAMS COUNT

Geetha works full-time from home running her own online card and gift business. When she brought her new baby home, she was operating under the false idea that she would be able to work while her baby slept. After all, newborns usually sleep up to eighteen hours a day, right? Within the first few weeks of being home she found herself very behind on her work. She had no idea where the time went during the day! By the time she had fed and changed the baby and completed a few household chores, she had to start all over again. Before she knew it, her husband, Ravi, was home from work. All the while her in-box grew with unfulfilled orders. Exhausted and exasperated, she felt this was not going at all the way she had expected.

LIVING YOUR LIFE VISION

Here are a couple of truths that are worth accepting: First, pregnancy isn't something you can just power through. It takes an enormous amount of energy and resources to grow and carry a baby, and that energy needs to come from somewhere. It is therefore important to take a realistic look at your commitments, obligations, and relationships and review what changes need to be made. Second, once the baby has arrived, your life has changed forever. You are from now on a parent with a lot of responsibilities, challenges, worries, joys, and new experiences. And you're new at the job (at least with the first baby)! Some people feel eminently prepared and suited to the job, others not so much. When asked "What was your biggest surprise after your baby was born?," 46.5 percent of parents said, "My baby's round-the-clock needs." Up until now you may have been very focused on your own life. All of a sudden you have a new baby relying on you, demanding tremendous amounts of your time and energy. To not lose sight of your life vision, one action that can help working parents is to do some career and life planning. Having a semblance of order in the parts of life you have more control over can help immensely when you feel overwhelmed by your new circumstances.

Career and Life Planning

At the end of Chapter 4 we asked you to write down a vision statement. It is time to review that now and start breaking it down into manageable goals. The purpose of the exercise is to ensure that you are putting effort in the right places. Ask yourself: "What will my life look like two years from now? Five years from now? Ten years from now?" The picture is likely clearest in the short term and more nebulous when you think of the long term. That is totally normal. It is hard to know where your life will be ten years from now in such a rapidly changing world. It is still worth investigating. It is true that you often have to make short-term sacrifices for long-term goals. That is not a problem unless you don't know what your long-term goals are. If you don't, there is a risk that your choices will be a short-term reaction to what is right in front of you, and unaligned with what is deeply valuable to you. You may be more vulnerable to external influences and struggle to see your unique path.

When looking at goals, a good idea is to use the mind-body-spirit concept. Mind denotes intellectual and professional achievements, further learning, and qualifications. Body denotes fitness goals, physical experiences such as adventure holidays, and personal feats such as marathons. Spirit involves bigger life goals, spiritual and religious goals, volunteering and contributing, and the like. Think about where you want to be in terms of all three areas. If you want to break it down further, you can revisit the Wheel of Life categories (now including Career and Money), or divide it by personal and family goals. However you do it, make sure your goals are not conflicting too much, while accepting that some short-term sacrifices are often needed to achieve long-term goals.

For the purposes of this example, we'll use the mind-body-spirit categories. Let's say your vision reads something like this: *I live a full life; develop and use my gifts and talent; and am appreciated and remembered as a loving, contributing, and honest person by my family, friends, and colleagues.* It is a good idea to write your vision and goals in the present tense. Subconsciously that increases your sense of ownership, and can even help them to become mantras as you get into the habit of reviewing your vision and goals regularly. Here is a start on how this might break down:

	2-YEAR PLAN	5-YEAR PLAN	10-YEAR PLAN
Mind	I am promoted to the next level in my field	I have my master's degree	I have received at least one more promotion within my field
Body	I am back to pre-baby shape	I experience at least one adventure on my bucket list	I maintain health and fitness; experience at least one more adventure on my bucket list
Spirit	I meditate daily; I volunteer at my charity of choice once a month	I am doing at least one week-long retreat; I am teaching my kids how to meditate	I go on retreats once a year; I contribute regularity to my charity of choice

Of course, your list would be much more detailed than the example.

Jane shares that when she was a young adult, she received some advice that drastically changed her life. A wise person told her to consider taking just one college class a semester, and pointed out that by the time her children were grown she probably would have a degree. Jane took this advice. It took her eleven years and five children to get her B.A. in child development and family relations. Her sixth child was born in the middle of the three years it took to gain her M.A., and she started her Ed.D. program when her seventh child was ten months old. Of course, she had plenty of help, with a very supportive husband and a live-in nanny.

How to Not Freak Out

For some people, there is a lot of fear and anxiety around life planning. It can feel insurmountable to try to achieve it all, or indeed that others seem to achieve it all while you don't. Comparing yourself with others is futile, as you never know fully what goes on in other people's lives. In truth, there is no guarantee about how anything will pan out for any of us. However, if you set aside some time and effort to plan for success, you increase your chances of getting there. You hopefully also enjoy the journey more, because you are awake; life won't pass you by. Instead you are present to grieve the sorrows and celebrate the victories. Being present in each moment as it happens is part of mindfulness practice. This is hugely beneficial for mental and physical health. Close attention to your goals also makes it easier to make adjustments as you go along to ensure you stay on course.

If you're feeling gripped by fear, it can help to remember that fear is an emotion—that's all! Emotions come and go. Just let yourself feel it, breathe, and know that it will pass. Then, when you're ready, do something that makes you feel good. Taking action is a great way to abate fear. Exercise, call a friend, or read a good book. (One of the authors likes to tidy up—somehow seeing order around her makes her feel calmer!) A little bit of fear and anxiety is absolutely normal throughout life, and in particular during times of big changes such as pregnancy. In fact, fear can be beneficial, propelling you forward and helping you avoid stagnation. But if you have recurring, irrational anxiety that does not go away during pregnancy or after the baby arrives, it is essential you see your doctor.

Change is always difficult and somewhat painful. It is, however, inevitable, and an essential ingredient in your growth and subsequent well-being as a human being. It is a good idea to accept this reality. Let your planning guide you and provide some signposts as the fog thickens.

Another important aspect of becoming a parent is the inevitable change in your relationships. You and your partner will go through some intense moments together, and the dynamics of your relationship might shift. The beauty of Positive Discipline is that the tools work universally well on people of all ages. What about friendships? If you are a parent and your close friend is not, that can be a challenge for you both. It can help to remember that over time, your friends will also become more used to changes in priorities and schedules and these issues will be less of a problem.

There will undoubtedly be changes to your professional life as well, at least in the short term. Many women worry about this, and rightly so, as many workplaces still lack a parent-friendly policy. In the following sections, we will look at a lot of strategies for managing this change as smoothly as possible, starting with how to strengthen your professional reputation.

BUILDING A SOLID PROFESSIONAL REPUTATION

Regardless of what profession you are in, career success is greatly dependent on your professional reputation. A lot of people don't put any conscious thought into this. They get on with work, try their best to meet expectations, perhaps exceed them, and then hope for a promotion. However, it's an unfortunate reality that many women experience an unwanted slowdown in their careers once they have children. It can therefore be worth investing some time and effort into cementing your professional reputation.

There are three areas for you to focus on: yourself, immediate others, and your wider network. We'll take a look at these areas in turn to discover how this might help you. As you go through these sections, see them as tips and ideas, not things you must do. Pick out the suggestions that chime with you, and don't try to do them all. Remember that you are probably already doing many of these things and that perfection is *never* required (and doesn't exist). The most important aspect that will help you with a good professional reputation is to enjoy what you do and let that shine through. As with all personal work, it is also about timing. For instance, if you've just had your first baby and you're feeling overwhelmed, don't add extra stress by worrying about your professional reputation. Focus on enjoying the phase you're in and come back to this section when you have more time and head space to think again about your professional goals.

Invest in Yourself

Think about being a friendly person. This may sound deceptively simple, but the truth is that people want to work with people they like and trust. You are more likely to be chosen to participate in exciting projects and be promoted if superiors and clients like having you around. You will be more missed and more welcomed back after parental leave too. Be generous with your time and energy, show integrity, honesty, and dependability, and be a role model at work as well as at home.

Be yourself. Focus on your strengths and see how you can use them more to your advantage. Check your weaknesses so they don't create blind spots and sabotage your efforts. We all have good and challenging qualities. We also know that we can work on ourselves, and that with discipline and effort we can put our best foot forward. That is all well and good, but you should never try to completely change who you are. Authenticity is essential in order to feel mentally healthy and aligned with who we are, as well as to come across as reliable in the workplace. Most people find it refreshing and reassuring to spend time with someone who just seems to be him- or herself.

Remember to smile often. Remember the mirror neurons in the brain that make children learn? Well, we have them as adults too. When we smile the world smiles, right? Smiles and laughter release endorphins. You don't need to be best friends with everyone, but it's a great way to spread positivity. It also works in reverse. When you make a conscious effort to smile and be friendly, you will release endorphins in your own body, which will help ease fatigue and stress.

Invest in Others

Work on building trust. Invest in quality time with all stakeholders—colleagues, senior staff, and clients. One of the best ways to establish trust is to share personal experiences and offer to help when needed. Ask curiosity questions and really get to know the people you work with. Engage in active listening by asking open questions and listening attentively to the response without being distracted or thinking about what you will say next.

Don't be afraid to show your passion. Be clear on what it is about your work that engages you, and communicate that to colleagues. You may at the same time be helping someone who is struggling to find the meaning and passion in their own work. Check your ego. How do we find the balance between sharing our successes and sounding arrogant? No one likes a brash and boastful person. One great way to find that balance is to shine a light on the efforts of the team. Always highlight other people's successes. Then you can also mention your own contribution without sounding ego-centered. Even if you work for yourself, you undoubtedly have collaborators who contribute to the success of your venture. Be sure to show your thanks and appreciation.

Invest in Your Wider Network

A great way to show commitment to your place of work is to find ways to give back. Taking time and effort to develop others comes high on the list, so get involved in training and development. This is also an area where your parenting skills can really come to the fore, as you are constantly guiding your child at home.

Depending on your industry, there are many different ways to network. If you are part of a large organization, networking internally can be very useful. Look for internal mentor programs and clubs you can join. Read internal newsletters and reach out to featured colleagues. A lot of people will be happy to share their successes, and you're making good connections in the process. Don't be afraid to ask for advice and guidance. Then there are conferences, professional bodies, and trade shows, all great places to make connections. Once you have made contacts, follow through. Invite them out for coffee or lunch and come prepared with some interesting topics to discuss, including how you can potentially help them. They may feel more inclined to meet with you if they feel the benefit is mutual.

An excellent way to establish yourself in your field is to speak at events. Many people have found it very helpful to join Toastmasters to improve their speaking ability. Toastmasters International (www.toastmasters.org) is a world leader in communication and leadership development with more than 352,000 members.

If public speaking isn't your thing, perhaps you can publish in a trade magazine. It can also be helpful to take a class on writing at a community college. Maybe your industry has awards you can put yourself or your team up for. Most organizations these days are involved in some kind of corporate responsibility or pro bono work. This can be another great and very rewarding area in which to establish yourself. You may also be doing your boss a favor, as she knows it needs to be done but may not have the time or inclination to be involved personally.

ALL OF THESE activities will fill up the goodwill account that you may need to draw from when you are starting or extending your family. It will also bring you peace of mind that you are managing your professional life well and allow you to take the foot off the gas for a while without too much anxiety. With a strong professional reputation established, there is also plenty you can do to smoothly manage the transition away from and back to work after parental leave.

MANAGING PARENTAL LEAVE

When it comes to safeguarding your professional dreams, there is a lot you can do around parental leave to ensure that the transition happens smoothly, with minimum impact on your professional standing. If you are self-employed, it is just as important to plan for this. Perhaps even more so, as Geetha in our opening story has discovered. She relies on being at the forefront of her clients' minds for their business and wouldn't want them to think that she is now leaving work behind. Putting your professional house in order will help you enjoy time off with your baby and older children. It will ease guilt and fear around needing to give up on professional goals and dreams. It will help you to stay focused in the moment and enjoy family at home, and work at work.

Before You Go on Leave

First of all, you may want to do some financial planning with your partner to determine how much each of you will work once the baby has arrived. This may also impact how long your parental leave should be. For many, this is less of a choice and more directed by workplace policy. Others may have some flexibility and it can come down to negotiation skills (see pages 252–253 for tips on how to develop your negotiation skills).

If you are employed, you want to investigate workplace policy in relation to parental leave, flextime, and part-time. You may feel confident now that you will return full-time, but circumstances can change and it's good to be informed of all your options. If you work from home, start researching and planning for how you can continue once the baby has arrived. If you have enough space, you may be able to continue to work with the baby and caregiver in the house. However, most new mothers returning from leave struggle to concentrate while being in the same place as their baby, so it is a good idea to start looking around for work-friendly spaces in your area such as freelance hubs (some even have childcare such as entreprenursery.co.uk), libraries, and cafes. And don't be afraid to give yourself time to be a new mother and bond with your child, which will be easier if you have planned ahead.

When the time is right (for most women in the second trimester) and you are comfortable talking about your pregnancy, do so. It is important to ease any fears your line manager, colleagues, or clients might have around how to manage your workload when you're gone, as well as your commitment to returning to the job. Clarify with both colleagues and your boss what their expectations are for keeping in touch while you're away. Some employers pay for parental leave and may not look favorably on you being totally unavailable. Establish an ally at work who can be your go-to source for information while you're away. Connect with other new parents at your place of work and join any parent networks or clubs your organization may have. If you have direct contact with your customers, you want to clarify the level of engagement you will have with them while on leave, as well as who will cover for you when you are away. This is crucial if you are running your own business, where customers may be used to dealing only with you. Whatever your circumstance, a good tip is to not expect special favors or services because you are pregnant. Chances are that would not endear you to colleagues and superiors, many of whom may not be parents.

There is a lot you can do to stay connected to your industry. Identify what sources will help you stay on top of key issues, and plan for how you can stay connected (e.g., take out a personal subscription to a trade magazine, or sign up for newsletters with your personal email address). Identify key players and events in your industry, connect with them, attend a few extra events, and look ahead at what will be in the pipeline while you're away. This means that once back, you can quickly get back up to speed and not feel out of the loop. Look for role models in or out of your industry. Can they mentor you? Or even just offer some advice? People are usually happy to share when earnestly asked for the secret to their success.

Finally, ask yourself if time off is an opportunity to revisit your career choices. If a change in role or job is something you've always desired, this might be a good opportunity to start researching so

249

that you are ahead of the game when you come back from parental leave. Some may also decide to be a stay-at-home parent for a while, if finances allow.

While Away

In our survey of working parents, 41 percent said they kept in touch with their work a couple of times while on maternity or paternity leave. Another 18 percent said they kept in touch weekly or a couple of times a week. Many new parents, both mothers and fathers, find parental leave heavenly—a time to get a break from the grind and focus on something unique and magical in their lives. For them it is an opportunity to completely disconnect from work. Others want to keep a toe in to ensure they are not quickly forgotten and do not feel left behind. Again, there are no right or wrong paths; you have to decide what is best for you given your unique family and professional situation. If you run your own business, staying connected is often a necessity.

The key is to honor any agreement you made with your manager or clients prior to taking leave. Check in regularly with your workplace ally to get updated on changes and politics. Keep in touch with the parent network and wider professional community. Perhaps some colleagues who are also on parental leave live nearby. Even if you are not at work daily, you may still be able to grab a coffee with someone in your industry or a mentor. Continue to read up on current events in your industry; if you are feeling particularly industrious and have a baby who sleeps well (lucky you!), you can identify a particular area of interest and do some extra research. That way you will come back to work full of ideas and initiative.

Back on the Job

Okay, so now you are back on the job and the reality of being a working parent has hit! Childcare has been organized, and what you need now is some on-the-job survival skills.

First of all, if you have negotiated a part-time schedule, make sure it is clearly communicated to all concerned, and manage your time effectively. Set boundaries so that colleagues and managers are clear about if and how they can contact you on days you are not at work. Make sure you stick to the agreement as well. Don't keep checking in with work on days you are not working. It is confusing to colleagues, and adds stress for you. This may be harder if you are self-employed and need to make yourself available when your client is so as not to lose their business. If so, have a contingency plan in place such as a collaborator who can step in when needed. Then make sure you take some extra time to rest up if you've had to un-expectedly work late. Look into having some emergency childcare provisions on hand for last-minute deadlines.

Time and energy are precious when you're a new parent, so think hard about what projects you can get involved in and adjust your expectations accordingly. Making your business grow may not be feasible while your baby is young; if that's the case, focus instead on providing top-quality service to your existing clients. Make sure that you emphasize what you do achieve. Be proud and vocal about your accomplishments.

For your own sanity, and for the sanity of those around you, communicate how you are feeling if you are suffering from fatigue or separation anxiety. It is important that colleagues (and your own family) understand that your crankiness is not their fault. It will make them more compassionate when you don't agree to late meet-ings (if you can avoid them) or too many social lunches (you may need to take it easy during lunch).

For now, accept good enough. It won't be forever. Remind your-self from time to time that work is just work, not life and death (unless, of course, you work in emergency medicine or another life-saving or life-threatening profession). Chill out and take the long view! Change your routine. Realize that what you've been through is life-altering and you may need to recharge more than you're used to. Don't overdo it and expect to be back at top productivity right away. Snack regularly on healthy snacks and stay hydrated to avoid fatigue. Maybe you're too tired for your usual turn on the tread-mill in the gym at lunchtime, but perhaps they offer yoga classes instead. Finally, stay focused while you're working, but don't bring your work home with you.

TOP TIPS ON NEGOTIATING

Forty-seven percent of parents surveyed asked for flexible part-time work after their parental leave.

Any working parent will do well to master the art of negotiation, as you are likely going to need the skills from now on—with your employer, clients, childcare provider, schools, partner, and of course, your children! The fundamental principles are the same regardless of whom you are negotiating with. In the following example, let's look at your professional negotiations.

Before you speak to your employer, prepare. Investigate the organizational policy around your area of concern (let's say flextime) and speak to other colleagues in your situation. Then have a written proposal ready. This will make you look professional and can alleviate fears on your manager's part about how your suggestions will work in practice. You can detail how and when you will stay in touch and meet your commitments. Know your numbers. Anticipate what your counterparty will want, and build some margin into your calculations so you have room to negotiate. Be realistic, but don't sell yourself short!

Once in the room, let the other person speak first—a well-known winning strategy in all negotiations. Show confidence: look the person in the eye, smile, and take your time. Remember, you rarely need to make an on-the-spot decision. If you are unsure, ask to reconvene at another time to give yourself a chance to think things through. Be kind and firm: stand your ground while showing regard for your employer's concerns. This shows respect and integrity for both yourself and your employer. Asking open-ended questions and actively listening to the other person's answers will help you to find a mutually favorable solution.

Focus on what is in it for your employer. Perhaps flextime and working from home one day a week fits in well with the organization's new flexible working policy. It's about finding win-win solutions. Then propose a trial run. Set a time limit, after which you and your employer will reevaluate the arrangement; if they feel there is an opportunity to revisit the decision, they may be more inclined to grant your request. Finally, have a plan B prepared. Can't get flextime? What can bring you the same benefit? Half days on Tuesdays and Thursdays? Friday off? Think creatively about what might work.

POSITIVE DISCIPLINE IN ACTION

One of the authors, Joy, spent many years trying to get pregnant—which in itself felt like a full-time job to her and her husband, Max! She was ecstatic when, after several failed attempts, the IVF treatment finally worked. Two years prior, Joy had already begun to reassess her commitments, goals, and relationships. She had requested to be part-time at the school where she worked, to enable her to focus on two important life goals: starting her own consultancy business and preparing for a family. This included getting a dog and spending more time in nature for a more balanced lifestyle. Fortunately, her employer valued her and agreed to a one-year trial run. It helped that Joy came to the meeting prepared with a win-win solution, including a part-time colleague who wanted to become full-time to take over some of Joy's responsibilities. This new arrangement was instrumental in giving Joy the flexibility and balance she needed to fulfill her dream of becoming a parent and an entrepreneur.

Joy's long-awaited pregnancy was not easy, so she had to revisit her commitments and obligations toward work and relationships. She and her husband were clear that certain financial sacrifices would have to be made, but agreed it was worth it to have time to bond with their baby. They decided that she would take a full year off from her part-time employment and four months off from her consultancy business. Since much of her consultancy work included travel, she would then slowly ease back in. They decided which business trips they could turn into mini family holidays so that Max and the baby could come along. In addition, they started looking into other childcare options for the occasions when Joy had to travel alone. This kind of creative thinking and willingness to consider alternative solutions led to Joy and Max finding balance in their new roles as working parents.

This may sound too good to be true. However, it's important to note that Joy was prepared to take the risk and leave her employment altogether if her employer did not agree to allow her to go part-time and/or take a full year of maternity leave. She had decided what she was willing to do and was prepared to follow through with her agreement to herself and her family.

"Envisioning and planning what I wanted my life to look like two to five years down the road and having the confidence to take the risk were the keys to making it all a reality. It was important for me to focus on the things I had control over (my career) and let go of the things I didn't have control over (getting pregnant and then managing a difficult pregnancy). Some of the skills I had to implement on many occasions were effective communication with my husband and employer, creativity, problem-solving, focusing on solutions, flexibility, and learning to ask for help, which was a tough one for me."

POSITIVE DISCIPLINE TOOLS

Many Positive Discipline tools can help us achieve greater balance and help in our life planning. However, here are a few that can be particularly helpful in times of change.

Decide What You Will Do

This tool looks deceptively simple: "Of course I'm the master of me, so I will decide what I will do!" However, especially when we are emotionally involved, it can be very hard not to falter in our convictions when circumstances change drastically. Unfortunately, inconsistent behavior does not inspire confidence and communicates to others that we can be influenced or even manipulated. Consistency is key in all areas, be it with family or colleagues. Try to identify potential trigger situations in advance—in the workplace, for example, it might be timeliness, accuracy of work, or expectations—then clearly communicate what your expectations are and what you are prepared to do. For example, "We will start the meeting at ten o'clock sharp, and if you can't be there on time, please catch up with one of us afterward." Make sure you communicate with kindness and firmness, never sarcastically or scolding. Always follow through with what you have said and/or agreed.

Listen

People will listen to you *after* they feel listened to. How often do you interrupt with defensiveness, explanations, or advice? Listen as though what the other person is saying is about him or her, not you. Ask questions that invite more information: "Can you give me an example?" You or the other person may figure things out just because you were listened to. This is an essential ingredient in ensuring that both you and others stick to agreements. It can also help you find your own answers if you are unclear on what you want. You buy yourself some time by listening quietly to the other party, which can help you get clarity about your own situation.

Focus on Solutions

Accept that parenting brings change and be open to working with those around you to find creative solutions. With your employer, be clear on what you want, be prepared for what they might want, and employ a kind and firm style to negotiate for win-win solutions.

Partnership

Successful partnerships are based on the foundation of equality, dignity, and respect. That is true for all partnerships, including parents and their children. Are you stuck in some outdated gender roles that are creating conflict and/or resentment? Whether at home or at work, it is important to brainstorm solutions for sharing responsibilities in a way that feels respectful to everyone. Review your important partnerships and work on ensuring they adhere to these basic principles.

EXERCISE

Turn Your Vision Statement into a Life Plan

CLARIFY YOUR GOALS USING THE GROW MODEL, AND SET SMART GOALS FOR LIFE AND WORK

For this exercise, we are going to borrow two established concepts from the coaching world: the GROW model and SMART goal setting.

GROW Model

The GROW model is an easy and elegant way to get clarity around what our goals really are. G = Goal; R = Reality; O = Options; W= Way Forward.

1. Take out your goal chart (page 242). Take each goal in turn and ask yourself questions following the model. Let's use the example of the two-year professional goal: "I am promoted to the next level in my field."

GOAL	REALITY	OPTIONS	WAY FORWARD
I am promoted to the next level in my field	Ask yourself honestly if this is realistic—are you next in line for promotion? Do you have the relevant qualifications? Do you have enough time and energy to devote to this goal?	Ask yourself if there are any other options that can satisfy your original desire (to gain professional recognition). Maybe a lateral move? Changing role or profession?	If you are satisfied, after having reviewed your reality and options, that your goal really is achievable, you now need to map out how you are going to get there. This is where we introduce SMART goals.

2. If, during the process, you realize you need to modify your original goal, just redefine it and then go through the steps again.

Repeat as many times as you like until you feel you have a truly achievable goal.

SMART Goals

Making sure your goals are SMART improves your chances of actually achieving them. In the acronym SMART, S = simple; M = measurable; A = achievable; R = realistic; T = time specific.

1. It is now time to apply SMART goal setting to flesh out your way forward from the preceding exercise. This effectively answers the question "How will I do it?"

GOAL: I AM PROMOTED TO THE NEXT LEVEL IN MY FIELD

SIMPLE	MEASURABLE	ACHIEVABLE	REALISTIC	TIME SPECIFIC
Specify all the actions you need to take to achieve this, such as taking an internal accreditation course. Repeat the following steps for all actions you identify.	Here you ask yourself which parameters equal success. In our example: "When I have the accreditation diploma from the internal course in my hand."	It is important to identify any obstacles or contingencies that may come up. In our example: "The internal course is very competitive. Do I have the right profile? Need to research application process."	Time to review: How realistic is this in relation to the time, energy, and resources available to you? Are any of the obstacles insurmountable? Do you need to rethink?	Be specific and write out a timeline for when your benchmarks need to be hit. In our example: "Internal accreditation application due September; get recommendations by October; promotion process starts January."

2. Go back to your other goals and repeat both the GROW model and the SMART goal-setting exercise.

This may feel like a laborious process, and it will take some time to do the initial plan. The key is not to get each box perfectly checked off, but rather to go through the process of investigation to see what actions you need to take and by when to ensure you reach your life goals. Undoubtedly life will happen in the meantime, and you will need to revisit and tailor your timeline and goals many times, especially for your long-term goals. That is fine—perfection is neither required nor the purpose of the exercise.

PART 5

THE BIGGER PICTURE

CHAPTER 15

LIFE AS A COUPLE ISN'T OVER BECAUSE BABY HAS ARRIVED

Simon and Sarah share how the pressures of work and children got on top of them and led to a breakdown in their relationship. Simon remembers a particular conversation: "I don't want to *work* on our relationship! I have enough of *work* at work!" Simon remembers feeling fed up. Sarah had yet again suggested they should do a couples course to "get closer." Surely relationships were either good or bad—they either worked or they didn't. Wasn't it enough that he worked sixty-hour weeks and still found time to take the kids to both tennis and dramatics on Saturdays? Sarah, on the other hand, felt despondent: "Why can't you see that part of the problem is exactly that—you don't seem to realize that with so little time just for us, we need some help in reigniting the spark?"

CREATING A HEALTHY, LASTING RELATIONSHIP

In order to create lasting well-being in life, the key is to see and apply similar tools and attitudes across all relationships and situations. The magic of Positive Discipline is that it is applicable to all human relationships. The principles we will be discussing in this chapter apply not only to our partners but indeed all our close relationships. Our perspective for this chapter is for co-parenting partners who are living together. If your life looks different, see if anything here resonates with you and can help you make sense of past relationships, and perhaps set you up for your next one. Throughout this chapter, we would encourage you to also reflect on how these behaviors are mirrored in your professional life.

Build Solid Foundations

Most relationships start off with the belief "He/she really loves and admires me." These beliefs meet the greatest need of human beings to belong (to feel connected and capable), and lead to loving and respectful behaviors such as affection, romantic gestures, special dates, regular fun and recreation, a lot of compliments, and frequent sex. In other words, a very close, connected, and loving relationship. This is often called the honeymoon period. Once we've been in the relationship for a while, most of us will recognize that the dynamic changes. The key is to build solid foundations, so that the relationship solidifies into something loving and lasting, not something unsatisfying. This requires being aware of those fundamental needs that guide all human behavior—the need for belonging and the need for significance—as well as learning fruitful ways to handle change.

Family therapists frequently ask the unhappy couples they work with, "Did you used to have fun together and enjoy each other's company?" The following response is typical: "Well, we used to, but that was before we had kids and other responsibilities. Those days are over. We're not kids anymore." This is a tragic belief, both for the adults, who have renounced enjoying life as a worthy pursuit, and for their children, who learn by their parents' example that commitment to parenthood also requires a vow of poverty in the fun and self-care departments.

It is not easy to be a good parent and model positive behavior if you're unhappy in your relationship. Fighting between members of a couple increases misbehaviors in children. Angry and defiant children are often mirroring the behaviors they observe in their parents' relationship. Even when you try to hide your anger or dissatisfaction, children can feel it in your energy. Children in homes with unhappy and tension-filled partnerships will intensify their misbehaviors in a subconscious attempt to bring the parents together, or in more desperate cases to break them apart.

Distressingly, children may later carry a lot of guilt if they believe they created a separation by their misbehavior. For the sake of your children, as well as your personal well-being, creating a happy relationship is clearly a worthwhile endeavor. Ask yourself if you want your children to repeat a relationship like yours.

Develop a Growth Mindset

As relationships mature, there is a greater onus on both parties to prioritize and work on the relationship. Imbalances in approach to this can lead to disagreements and disappointments. Depending on your and your partner's upbringing and personality, you both may have very different ideas about what constitutes a happy relationship. We have already discussed in detail in this book how our underlying belief systems affect how we see reality and our subsequent choices and behaviors. This is further evidenced in the work of Carol Dweck, the author of *Mindset*. She has researched personality types for several decades, and her conclusions are significant when looking at our approach to relationships.

Dweck's research indicates that we are often based in one of two mindsets, or underlying belief systems: the fixed mindset or the growth mindset (as we touched upon in Chapter 9). People with these different mindsets have very different ideas of what a happy relationship is. Dweck believes the fixed mindset often has a fixed idea of the "perfect" person, usually set at the time of meeting and falling in love. The fixed mindset often struggles to see challenges and changes in life as something inevitable and as opportunities for learning and growth, perhaps like Simon in our opening story. They may instead feel utterly disappointed when their partner does something hurtful or even just makes a mistake: Finally they get to know the "real" person. The honeymoon period is over! Someone with a fixed mindset has an external locus of control, meaning whatever is "out there" is the reason why that person feels the way he does. This often robs the individual of an opportunity for personal responsibility and growth—hence the "fixed" description.

People with a growth mindset, on the other hand, see challenges as opportunities for learning and often wonder what they can do to change and improve, like Simon's wife, Sarah. They have an internal locus of control. They realize that relationships are not fixed and perfect and need work like all other aspects of life. This comes very close to the encouragement model we propagate in Positive Discipline.

It may be worth thinking about your own and your partner's mindset and have a discussion around this. It could certainly help Sarah and Simon. Mindset profoundly impacts our ability to agree on a way forward and the level of actions both parties are prepared to take in order to work on the relationship. It impacts our ability to communicate with each other, express love, practice forgiveness, and satisfy our partner's primary goal of belonging.

Nurture a Sense of Belonging

The primary culprit in most unhappy relationships is that the most basic human need to feel a sense of belonging is not being met for one or both people. We have underscored the importance of giving your children a sense of belonging through experiences that help them feel accepted, capable, valued, and connected. When children don't believe they belong, they feel discouraged and may misbehave. Likewise, when you don't feel loved, valued, and accepted by your partner, you are unlikely to put forth your most kind and loving behavior. Misbehavior based on a sense of not belonging creates a repetitive cycle of destructive feelings and behaviors, which, if left unchecked, will sabotage the relationship. Let's look at these destructive behaviors in more detail.

DESTRUCTIVE BEHAVIORS THAT UNDERMINE BELONGING AND SIGNIFICANCE

Relationships are always moving; they are never stagnant. At this moment, your relationship is in either a positive or a negative feedback loop, depending on whether you both perceive you are cherished and admired by your partner. The cycle is either going in a positive direction, which reinforces beliefs that support a sense of belonging and the attending positive behaviors, or in a negative direction, which reinforces beliefs of being unloved and the ugly behaviors that keep those beliefs in place. The cycle progresses like this:

1. If your beliefs are:
   - "He/she does not love me" ("I don't feel I belong")
   - "I can never do it well enough for him/her" ("I don't feel capable")

2. Then those beliefs invite the following misbehaviors in you:
   - Withdraw (silent treatment)
   - Criticize and attack verbally
   - Withhold affection (and sex)
   - Avoid spending time together
   - Romantic gestures and kindness abruptly stop
   - Revenge, "tit for tat"
   - Uncooperative in helping with the kids, housework, etc.

3. Which invites similar misbehaviors in your partner in response to your misbehaviors.

4. The result is the relationship starts to deteriorate.

This unhappy cycle repeats itself over and over in a chain reaction in which both parties feel unloved, unappreciated, and hopeless, and don't know how to reclaim the love and passion they once shared.

Why do we engage in these behaviors? It can of course be a reaction to our partner's misbehavior. It could be our own mistaken goals—our own belief system, which may be a result of unsatisfied needs in our childhood that trigger these behaviors in us. It is also common for new parents to feel neglected when a baby becomes 100 percent the center of attention. Actually, this is partially true throughout the child-rearing phase. What matters is what we can proactively do about it. As with all difficult insights, the key is to become aware of the behaviors first. Only then can you start working on rooting them out.

When you feel challenged in your relationship, you often stop being in the here and now and time-travel into the past. Your partner may do or say something to hurt your feelings. If you were more present, you might respond logically and say something like "That hurt my feelings. I know you love me, so I'll assume you are feeling hurt or upset about something. Let's wait until we both feel better and we'll work on some loving solutions."

The following five closely related common behaviors are extremely damaging to a partner's sense of feeling capable and admired: being controlling, demanding perfection, criticizing, refusing to allow participation, and (the flip side of that) refusing to participate and/or take responsibility. Each of these behaviors sends a message: "I don't trust you to do it well enough," "I don't respect or admire you," and/or "You/we are not a priority for me." These messages are usually unintentional and may stem from mistaken goals set in childhood. Nevertheless, they are hurtful and invite misbehavior from the other person. In other words, your partner's behavior may trigger certain expectations and insecurities in you, which affects your behavior negatively. As you read through this, you'll be able to see parallels with your individual top cards.

Controlling

Ever have the nearly irresistible urge to rearrange the table after your partner has set it? Or the dishwasher, laundry cabinet, storage shelves, their priorities—in fact, their whole life? The question to ask is why it has to be your way. Ask yourself: "What is more important; my efficiency or the other person's freedom to express differences?" Are you communicating disrespect by insisting that your partner (or children) do it your way? If you give them autonomy to do things their own way, even if it is very different from how you operate, that communicates that you believe they are capable and lovable the way they are. Ask yourself: "What will happen if I stop controlling everything and let them do things their way? Will I die?" (Sometimes it is worth getting some perspective on our foibles!) Of course not. Will it be uncomfortable? Yes, probably, but if it makes the other person feel valued and loved, is that not worth it? And over time, as you become used to your new behavior (and your brain creates new preferred neural pathways to that behavior), the discomfort will wear off.

Perfectionism

Often people with a need to control and a need to be superior have unrealistically high standards for themselves and everyone around them. They feel very tense when things are not done "perfectly" or "right." It is important to understand that many perfectionists come from a place of wanting to get things right and to maximize potential. They don't know how discouraging this is to their children and others. Perfectionists do not view mistakes as opportunities to learn. They may even view them as opportunities to correct or even punish. This is a very discouraging mindset that invites rebellion and a sense of incapability in our loved ones. Perfectionism is rooted in insecurity and a deep need to prove one's worth by doing things flawlessly.

The cure for perfectionism is to accept that there is no absolute measure that determines what is "perfect." How can your version of "perfect" be any better than someone else's? Actually, perfection is a discouraging goal. Adler and Dreikurs taught us to work on improvement, not perfection. We can start by learning to accept our own imperfections. How?

Accept that perfectionism is a destructive mindset. Do some soul-searching to find out where it came from. And work on letting it go with the help of meditation, affirmations, or in some cases therapy. When you can love yourself and give yourself grace when you make mistakes, you will be able to accept the imperfections in your loved ones. If you are a perfectionist, we highly recommend you practice what Rudolf Dreikurs called "the courage to be imperfect," as well as the courage to allow your partner and children to be imperfect.

Criticism and Negativity

Do you have the bad habit of chronically criticizing your partner and children? Criticism destroys feelings of being cherished and admired. If you grew up in a critical household and learned to be critical, it can be tough to avoid perpetuating this destructive behavior. Criticism can be closely related to perfectionism and equally rooted in hidden feelings of insecurity. People who are negative may have a fixed mindset and find it difficult to accept change. They may see life from the "glass half empty" perspective and look for the worst. In truth, we all have a choice whether to focus on the positive or negative. If you struggle with criticizing and negativity, then it is worth reminding yourself of the good things in life. Running a daily gratitude list in your head and working on encouragement are key. Work on developing a growth mindset, an internal locus of control. Know that you have control over your beliefs and choices.

Refusing to Allow Participation

It is discouraging to children and adults when they are not invited to help with household chores and other responsibilities. Many children and partners stop trying to contribute because they are told they aren't doing it well enough or "right." Their sentiments are,

"I'm just going to do it wrong anyway, so why should I try? I'm just setting myself up for failure." When partners feel unappreciated in their efforts to help, they may avoid being hurt by spending more time away from the home or doing solo activities. Usually not allowing participation is just another form of control.

Refusing to Participate and/or Take Responsibility

Usually this is a more passive behavior. This person refuses to participate in shared household activities and/or family fun and may come across as aloof and/or disinterested. The partner may also try to avoid taking responsibility for his or her part in the relationship. It can stem from a desire to avoid criticism and/or stress. There can also be deep-rooted feelings of worthlessness coming from the mistaken goal of assumed inadequacy set in childhood. It could be based on old ideas of male/female roles. In any case, the receiver may feel ignored or unimportant. The antidote here is to agree on routines and chores and to have frank discussions about what everyone's expectations are about contributions to the partnership or family unit. Starting with small steps is key, as is a lot of encouragement and appreciation.

THE ENCOURAGEMENT ANTIDOTE

Since discouragement is the root cause of the pain and anger that lie beneath the destructive cycle of misbehavior in relationships, the obvious antidote is encouragement. (Fortunately, you are already learning to practice this with your children.) There are some specific actions you can take and attitudes you can develop so that both you and your partner can learn how to strengthen the other's sense of belonging, connection, and capability. Start by practicing these five essential behaviors: spending special time as a couple, conveying a sense of belonging and significance through affection and sex, getting into your partner's world, giving compliments and appreciations, and appreciating and accepting separate realities.

269

Spend Special Time as a Couple

As we saw in our opening story, many relationships are taking a backseat to the urgent demands of work and children. Little to no time is carved out to enjoy each other. This is a huge mistake. Children benefit when they witness a happy and loving partnership. Your children learn about relationships by observing you.

Some people believe that the children should always come first. We do not agree. It is healthier for both the parents and children when the relationship comes first. Ideally the children should be such a close second that they hardly know the difference, but the difference is important. Why is that? Deep down, your children want to know that their parents have a good relationship. They enjoy seeing the two of you hugging and cuddling on the couch and going on dates together. This helps them feel safe and teaches them that a passionate, wholehearted commitment to another is a wonderful thing and doesn't end when children come along. It is important for you and your partner to have clarity around this and agree as much as possible. You have made a commitment to love and respect each other. If you compromise that pledge, you are compromising your integrity. That leads to frustration and stress, which will be reflected in your behavior and the behavior of your children, your partner, and everyone else around you.

Special time should be a priority over other time commitments so that the relationship isn't always downgraded to last on the list, which can easily happen if both partners work. The feeling of "belonging" will run dry sooner rather than later if the relationship isn't nurtured. And just as it is hard to be a good parent when you're in an unhappy relationship, it is also hard to be effective in your career. You owe it to your professional self as well to get your priorities right.

Convey Belonging Through Affection and Sex

Affection is one of the most powerful ways to make your partner feel cherished. Regular affection sends a powerful message of belonging, which summons our most loving behaviors. Affection meets the core need to feel special and deeply cared for. Holding your partner on the couch, spooning him or her in bed, giving backrubs, holding hands, and frequent hugs all communicate closeness and acceptance. Affection and sex strengthen the belief "I am loved," which always moves the relationship toward a positive cycle of behaviors.

An area to explore is your preferred way of expressing and receiving love and affection. Some people feel that thoughtful gifts and doing things for their partner express love, while others care more about hearing loving words, physical touch, or spending special time together. Much has been written on the idea that we all have a preferred "language of love." Understanding and speaking the love language of your partner can put new sparks in your relationship.

Get into Your Partner's World

During courtship, most couples recall how they would talk for hours about everything in their lives. Their sweetheart would listen to every last word. There is a special sense of connection when you share your innermost thoughts and feelings, hear the innermost thoughts and feelings of your partner, and find similarities to marvel at. The need for meaningful conversation continues throughout the relationship, and it is painful to both parties if intimate sharing stops. The cost to the relationship is loss of closeness and connection and—you guessed it—belonging!

When you think of the person in your life who has offered you the most encouragement and unconditional love, chances are you will recall a person who listened to you with real enthusiasm. Good listeners make you feel special. They send you a loud and clear message: "You matter to me. I care about everything that is going on in your life!" If you or your mate is feeling a lack of love and acceptance, listening and asking questions are surefire ways to elevate the sense of belonging in your relationship. Learn to become proficient in using the same "what" and "how" questions we have encouraged you to use with your children. Questions such as "What is still missing from your career?" or "What specifically could I do to help you with your stress?" or "How can I be a better partner for you?" will help you know the internal thoughts, feelings, and needs of your partner. There are four barriers to listening: defending, explaining, blaming, and fixing. Practice listening without engaging in any of these barriers. Instead, listen to understand not only what your partner is saying but what he or she feels and what he or she means at a deeper level. In other words, listen with your heart to hear his or her heart. Don't try to solve the problem unless you're invited to brainstorm for solutions. You can provide comfort, caring, and a therapeutic benefit to your loved ones just from listening compassionately and allowing them to be heard.

Give Compliments and Show Appreciation

In an earlier chapter, we discussed in detail the importance of compliments and appreciation to foster an energy of positivity in the family. The same is of course true between the two of you as a couple. Compliments and appreciation significantly bolster the sense of belonging and significance. It is much better to receive compliments without having to fish for them. Make it a daily habit to appreciate the little things. Compliments such as "Thank you for working so hard every day" or "I really appreciate how you always tidy up the kitchen before we go to bed" go a long way toward making the other one feel loved and appreciated.

Appreciate Separate Realities and Give Your Partner Unconditional Acceptance

Many couples have conflict because one partner is unable to appreciate the separate reality of the other individual's thoughts, feelings, desires, and beliefs. Or sometimes both partners deny the other his or her separate reality. The relationship stays healthier if each partner retains individuality and unique personhood. It is very risky if one or both parties have the attitude "I know what is best, so you must do it my way!"

The idea of "separate realities" can sound scary to some, who may think, "Does it mean my partner has a secret life I am not allowed into?" That thinking can undermine a sense of security and belonging. We are not advocating secrecy, only that both parties are free to see things differently based on their personal beliefs, and that those differences are accepted and valued by the other. It is okay to disagree on things, and we want to avoid either party feeling as if they have to give up their way of seeing the world. They can't. It is about appreciating that we may like and need different things. Is your ideal evening cozying up on the sofa together with a classic movie, and your partner's a night on the town with a group of friends? Discussing this is important, as one party may have a greater need for independence than the other, or be more of a social butterfly than the other. Finding out each other's likes and loathes and balancing your time together is well worth it. It is true that opposites attract. Your differences attracted you in the first place but will often annoy you later. Rekindle your appreciation for the assets of your partner's differences. When you feel gratitude for your partner, the annoyances will disappear.

Are you and your partner primarily introverts or extroverts? These concepts often get confused with how open or chatty a person may be, as opposed to closed and quiet. But those concepts refer not to external behavior but rather to where we get our energy. And our particular orientation does impact how we choose to, and need to, spend our time in order to recoup and recharge. The introvert recharges from the inside, by going within, so introverts often need an element of introspection, quiet, and solitude to recharge. The extrovert recharges from the outside, so extroverts get energy from activities, events, and people. Most people are not all one or the other, and the balance within any one individual can also change somewhat over time, with most of us tending to want a calmer environment as we age. Think about where you get your energy and take a look at your partner (and your children). A very introverted person who is constantly thrust out into the world by extroverted family members may get very exhausted and act up, and vice versa.

It is of course a great thing when you have shared interests as a couple. We encourage you to find activities you like to do together and continue to share them as time goes on. You do not need to be either into or knowledgeable about your partner's interests in order to be a supportive mate. Often it is sufficient to show interest and wonderment at your partner's enthusiasm and to encourage him or her to explore those interests as much as possible. Your partner will feel truly valued and accepted, and will hopefully encourage you in your interests in return.

Acceptance is a choice. Some people have an easier time accepting their children's imperfections than their partner's, because they understand that young people are supposed to make mistakes. The truth is that older people are also still learning and need to be allowed to make mistakes and/or to be who they are. By making a conscious decision to give acceptance to your partner and children, you are communicating love and belonging. You are communicating that they are safe to make mistakes. You are also mirroring the behavior you would like in return. It is your decision: Would you rather be happy, or would you rather be "right"?

Acceptance is a hugely complex and deep process, and it may sound flippant to dish out advice such as "accept your partner." In Chapter 13 we discussed the importance of learning to let go, which is a big part of this work. In Chapter 17 we will widen our perspective to consider effective ideas and tools from the world of science and spirituality to help us further with this deep personal work.

POSITIVE DISCIPLINE IN ACTION

Paul angrily complained in therapy, "As soon as I walk in the door, I am barraged by Linda's demands and my children's needs. I fantasize about flying a plane again or playing golf, but I don't even ask. It would start World War III."

Paul and Linda had been fighting for months. Both of them worked full-time outside the home and shared responsibility for three young children. There was no time allotted for personal fun. They both felt overwhelmed by the magnitude of their obligations, and they resented each other for their unhappiness. Their communication had descended into childish tit-for-tat retorts such as "I changed the diaper last time. It's your turn!" or "I guess you expect me to help Bradley study for his spelling test!"

At the suggestion of their marriage counselor, they sat down to do an exercise called "Reveal Your Desired Agenda." The purpose was to find a way to meet their individual, couple, and family needs.

First, they individually brainstormed as many ideas as possible of things they would like to do in the following three categories: individual fun, couple fun, and family fun.

Next, Paul and Linda were asked to select one item from each of the three categories to put on the agenda for that particular weekend. Linda's desired weekend agenda looked like this: *Individual fun: go to lunch and shop with Carla. Couple fun: go out to dinner with Paul. Family fun: take the kids to the park.* Paul's desired weekend agenda looked like this: *Individual fun: bike riding with the guys. Couple fun: romantic dinner with Linda. Family fun: movies with the kids.*

Then they were to create a weekend agenda that would work for both of them and the children. The couple fun was easy—both of them wanted a nice dinner together. They scheduled dinner for Saturday night, and Paul agreed to call a babysitter. Linda felt that going to the park with the kids would offer more quality time than the movies. In order to be respectful to children, it is usually best to invite them to brainstorm their ideas. As it turned out, the kids preferred going to the zoo, so that activity was scheduled for Sunday afternoon. Linda happily agreed to be with the kids while Paul went bike riding with his friends Saturday morning, and Paul was content to take over so Linda could enjoy lunch and shopping Saturday afternoon. For the first time, they both were free to have fun without guilt because they had respectfully involved and honored each family member in planning the weekend.

Linda was happy with the arrangement but worried that the fun would result in too many undone household chores, which would spoil her peace of mind in the coming workweek. She and Paul then listed the top four chores that needed to be done on the weekend, and they divided the list. In this way, they reduced the stress that could be caused by too much play (leaving work undone) or too much work (leaving no time for play).

This new arrangement made both Paul and Linda feel much more in tune with each other's needs. This made it easier for them to rekindle the spark and turn their relationship cycle in a positive direction.

POSITIVE DISCIPLINE TOOLS

If Linda's and Paul's planning is incorporated into regular couple and family meetings, chances are that a lot of misbehaviors will abate. Let's review a number of important Positive Discipline tools that will create positive habits.

Schedule Regular Couple Meetings

Regularly scheduled couple meetings will prevent problems and resentments from building up and keep the lines of communication open. Keep the format the same as family meetings. Start with appreciations, brainstorm solutions, commit to a solution that both are happy with, review upcoming events, and plan special time as a couple.

Couple meetings should never replace regular open communication. Meetings should be seen as an additional activity that helps you formalize some of the trickier conversations. (1) Putting a challenge on the couple meeting agenda serves as a cooling-off period before the issue is discussed. (2) Just as in family meetings, starting with compliments sets a positive tone—and a reminder of the things you appreciate about each other. (3) The focus is on finding solutions that are agreeable to both. (4) You are modeling the kind of attitude and focus on solutions that you want to teach your children.

Couple meetings should be separate from family meetings. Don't fall into the trap of skipping them, thinking, "We cover these things anyway during family meetings." Parents need some grown-up time too, to bond and strategize.

Make Agreements in Advance; Negotiate Labor

An excellent tool for avoiding conflict over who should be doing what with the children and the household tasks is to negotiate a plan that works for both of you. You may want to write down a desired division of labor, especially if both of you work outside the home. Agreeing in advance on the division of labor for taking care of the children and household maintenance and repair will avoid a lot of unnecessary arguments and hurt feelings. Both of your likes and dislikes should be taken into account; if one of you hates taking out the garbage but enjoys weeding, make a deal! This exercise will empower both of you to clearly understand your roles and responsibilities at home. Finding a *fair* division of labor depends on what both of you think is fair. Make a list of all that needs to be done on a weekly basis and decide who in the family will do what. It is important that children are given age-appropriate tasks so that they can contribute in a meaningful way to the family as well; see the section on family meetings for more detail.

Balance Kindness with Firmness

Too much kindness toward your partner can be harmful to self (and also teach your partner to take advantage), while too much firmness can be harmful to your partner (and your relationship). A simple rule to remember in balancing kindness and firmness is "Always honor self and other at the same time." When we are kind, we are respectful to others, and when we are firm, we set boundaries that are respectful to ourselves. How can we do both? First, we'll advise you what *not* to do.

Many people are overly kind and generous to others (a trap for those whose top card is pleasing). We define "overly kind" as doing for others even when it does not fit for you and may be detrimental to you. When you give too much, you will ultimately feel resentful and taken advantage of. When you are kind to yourself by using boundaries to take care of your needs, you will be in a much better position to respect your partner as well.

At the opposite extreme is the overly firm person, the blamer. Blamers are very firm in asserting their rights and needs. Their motto is "It's your fault. Why can't you get it right?" Overly firm individuals are very good at honoring their own needs, but in doing so they trample on the needs, rights, and feelings of others. It is always someone else's fault. In reality, however, blaming often masks a deep sense of inadequacy and insecurity. The person is overly firm to defend and protect him- or herself from being hurt. This can be a very lonely place, with a lack of a sense of belonging and significance.

Overly kind behavior results in unhealthy enmeshment: one person gives up his or her individuality to be in the relationship. Too much firmness leads to alienation and resentment. If you can make a sincere effort to meet your partner's needs, your differences will be bridged and your partner will feel loved and appreciated.

Positive Time-Out for Couples

Okay, so have you decided that everything we have discussed in this chapter makes sense and you are going to do it? Hurrah! However, unless you are a saint, you will make mistakes along the way (we speak from experience). There is nothing like a love partner to bring up all the old, unresolved issues from your childhood, and you can rest assured you're doing it back to him or her as well. You are likely to become upset many times and revert to your reptilian brain.

The impossibility of resolving a conflict while upset is just as true for couples as it is for children and parents. You will have a much more respectful and encouraging relationship if you decide in advance that you will take a positive time-out when you are upset. This will not feel like the "silent treatment" so long as it is planned and disclosed in advance. This also models to the children that it is okay to get angry but it is not okay to take it out on each other. Instead we deal with it ourselves by removing ourselves from the situation. Sometimes it is difficult to remember to take a time-out when you are angry, but it will get easier with practice. In one family we know, parents Michelle and Harry and their kids decided to make it a contest to see who could catch himself or herself (not each other!) in a reptilian state first. Often the fun of being first was enough to make the others laugh and the need for time-out would be gone. Other times, one or the other would say, "Okay, I can see what is happening, but I still need a time-out. I'll get back to you when I feel better."

EXERCISE

Have your first couple meeting and put your special time plans on your calendars.

Couple Activity

1. Separately create a list of things you would like to do with your partner.

2. Get together and share your lists. How many of your items are the same?

3. Brainstorm together some other things (that may not be on either list) that you would like to do together.

4. Now divide this list into two categories: "routinely" and "bucket list." Under "routinely," list all the things you like to do together on a regular basis. Under "bucket list," write down all the big things you would like to do at least once.

5. Get out your calendars and schedule time together. Make this a final part of your regular couples meeting every week.

6. Spend some time talking about your next "bucket list" adventure.

7. Journal about the difference this activity creates in your relationship—and then share with each other.

CHAPTER 16

POSITIVE DISCIPLINE IN OUR PROFESSIONAL LIVES

Amy wants to tear her hair out in frustration! She has made a point of coming in early because she knows her boss, Steven, wants to get all the patients' Seasons Greetings cards out first thing. She has prepared all the envelopes and cards for signature the night before and is good to go. She has even put stamps on all the envelopes! As she approaches her desk she sees that her things have been rearranged, which means that Steven, as he always does, has sat at her desk after she'd gone. How did he not realize how intrusive that was? Not only that, but he has taken one of the envelopes, where admittedly the stamp is a *tiny* bit crooked, circled the stamp with a red marker, and written across the envelope, "This is unacceptable, Amy!" Amy feels angry and deflated. With a little one at home taking a lot of energy, Amy feels her place of work needs to be supportive and positive. She loves her other colleagues, but . . . well, this is unlikely to be her last job anyway, so why accept this kind of bullying?

MOTIVATION UNCOVERED

When you're in the middle of starting and running a family, it can be hard sometimes to feel motivated at work. Understanding the factors affecting your motivation (and the motivation of those around you) will help you to focus your limited time and energy in the right places. In *Drive*, his book on human motivation, Dan Pink makes the case that for any task requiring even a rudimentary level of complexity (which means the majority of working activity today regardless of profession), the traditional stick-and-carrot model of motivation does not lead to greater performance. In fact, it makes it worse. The same is true for motivating our children.

Pink further concludes that the three most important motivators that drive professional engagement are autonomy, mastery, and purpose. Let's break all this down into Positive Discipline terms:

- *Stick and carrot* are the same as punishment and reward. We have already talked extensively about how you can achieve short-term compliance but long-term damage with this model. Since punishment and reward demotivates children, it is hardly a surprise that it also demotivates adults, as in our opening story.

- *Autonomy* can be understood as a sense of personal power and influence. We have discussed how children have an innate sense of personal power, and training and guidance on how to exercise it usefully is an essential part of parenting. If children don't get a chance to usefully use their personal autonomy, they misbehave and feel discouraged. So do adults who are given little autonomy in their professional lives.

- *Mastery* means gaining a sense of capability through taking time for training, learning problem-solving and new skills, enjoying growing, and getting better at something through encouragement. It is interesting to note that the desire to learn does not stop because we have grown up. Instead it continues to play an essential part in personal satisfaction.

- *Purpose* means looking for and developing a sense of belonging, understanding, and contribution. Simon Sinek calls this the "why" of what we do, and his is another voice that confirms the importance for personal and professional success of understanding our purpose. Children need to be usefully included in decisions that affect them, in order to strengthen their sense of belonging and contribution. Adults need to understand the purpose of what they are asked to do in their professional lives. If we don't understand the purpose, it is harder to engage and even harder to enthusiastically share or "sell" what we are doing. A lack of clear purpose can lead to an existential crisis for both the individual and the organization.

The parallels are clear: if you train yourself and your children in Positive Discipline, you equip yourself and them with the very life skills that will make you both happier and more effective professionals and colleagues. The culture of the working parent is one of increasing fragmentation as well as time and effectiveness pressures. Ours is a solution that works as well privately as professionally. Become an encouragement expert with yourself, your family, and your colleagues, and you will see remarkable improvements in your own life experience.

WHY ENCOURAGEMENT WORKS

The reason encouragement works is that it goes to the very heart of who we are as human beings. The modern world broadcasts some rather superficial values at times, which can understandably confuse our inner compass. Materialism, physical beauty, social superiority, and so on seem to have eclipsed compassion, sharing, and humanity. In contrast, we often wonder at the seeming unaffectedness of children and how they can be so spontaneously loving and sharing (well, sometimes, anyway). Yet modern parenting continues to be very focused on academic and vocational success, selling the idea to our kids that what you *do*, not who you *are*, is what will lead to success. If we look at the research cited above, those seem like outdated values.

The same is true in the professional space. Current working practices point clearly in the direction of less hierarchy, flexible work, and positive reinforcement. A recent article in *Forbes* made the case that business could learn from child psychology—particularly Positive Discipline, which advocates mutual respect—in its relationship to business partners and employees.[29] One of the clearest examples of the horizontal leadership trend is the development of the coaching style of management. This effectively means a manager sees him- or herself more as a coach who is there to support and encourage, not a general who directs and leads from the front. This coaching style can be utilized by anyone, not only managers. For this more enlightened form of collaboration and leadership, it is important to recognize the brilliance of each individual and encourage everyone to grow. It is about finding a way to nurture their unique strengths so they feel happy and motivated to produce their best work. That way, you as a professional (and as a parent) produce your best work through inspiring and encouraging others.

A HAPPIER WORKING LIFE LEADS TO GREATER PEACE OF MIND

Personal Self and Professional Self

Are you one of the many people who adjust your behavior in your professional engagements? At home you may feel relaxed and let your guard down, but professionally you feel the need to downplay your personality in order to progress, impress, and avoid offending anyone. One woman in a recent workshop shared that she was known at work for being steely and disciplined, while she felt privately that she was emotional and easygoing. That can be situational—her work may have required her to display those behaviors. It would be a concern only if she felt her professional persona made it hard for her to establish close and meaningful professional relationships. It would also be a concern if work pressures to perform and "be perfect" were so great that she then came home and took out her frustration on her family.

If you find yourself struggling with inconsistencies, it is worth reviewing your expectations. If you feel it is easier to be encouraging with your colleagues but harder with your family, ask yourself why you expect more of your family. The same goes, of course, for the other way around. You may also be expecting more of yourself professionally than personally or vice versa. Ask yourself if you are playing one role at work and another at home and why you are not giving the same weight to both. If this hits the mark, we encourage you to address your work-life balance and look at your priorities. Perhaps revisit the Wheel of Life exercise in Chapter 13. Ask yourself what your visions and goals are for each area. Then start practicing encouragement with everyone using the ideas in this chapter, starting with yourself, and you'll begin to feel a greater sense of harmony. (In Chapter 17, we deepen our discussion around role-playing and its effect in all areas of life.)

Leadership and Professional Fulfillment

Earlier, we saw that parenting has at least twice the effect on the child's behavior as any (quality) childcare does, hence the importance of looking at parenting behavior and attitudes. In the same vein, a significantly dominant factor affecting professional satisfaction is the relationship with a manager, hence the importance of looking at managers' behaviors and attitudes. Even if you are not a team leader, your impact as a colleague or collaborator has a substantial effect on other people's sense of professional enjoyment.

Dissatisfaction with leadership is a huge issue for many organizations that struggle to retain talent. Younger people in the workforce (millennials, iGen) have grown up under much more uncertain circumstances and are pretty clear that there is no "job for life." Subsequently, they may prioritize personal fulfillment and adventure over loyalty to any particular organization. This is a big mental shift compared to the majority of their managers and bosses, whose mindset hails from an earlier generation, one where you were instilled with, and rewarded for, loyalty to professional or societal elements. Certainly it is a problem for Steven in our opening story, who is likely to lose a valuable team member. No matter how much Amy may enjoy both her other colleagues and the actual work, a draconian boss is likely going to lead to her leaving the practice.

Regardless of what your professional situation looks like today, at some point you were probably managed by someone else. Reflecting on that experience can help uncover your beliefs around leadership and remind you of the feelings that good or bad professional relationships evoke. Take a moment to compile a list of the traits of the worst and best managers you have had in your life.

You may feel some anger about how you were treated by your worst manager(s), even if it happened many years ago. It is equally likely that you remember your best manager(s) with fondness. Perhaps your list looks something like this:

WORST MANAGER	BEST MANAGER
Controlling	Empowering
Unavailable	Open-door policy; available
Tears down through criticism	Builds up through encouragement
Micromanages	Gives autonomy
Rigid	Flexible
One-up/one-down relationship: "I'm right, you're wrong"	Equal relationship: "We both have a valid viewpoint"
Disrespectful	Respectful
Problem-solves alone and then tells you	Problem-solves with you
Creates rules alone and then tells you	Creates rules with you
Self-absorbed	Caring and empathetic
Takes all the credit	Promotes team effort
Doesn't care about anything other than your output at work	Takes an active interest in who you are as a person
Blaming communication	Respectful communication
Instills the beliefs "Only your output matters" and "You are not capable"	Instills the beliefs "You are valuable as a human being" and "You are capable"

Looking at these lists, we can clearly see that good leadership is aligned with the encouragement model of Positive Discipline: empowering, kind and firm, takes time for training, and so on. The benefits of making your workplace a place where you feel supported and heard will trickle down to your family life and help you feel a little less overwhelmed. If you are a manager, take the above list to heart. If you are not, perhaps it's time to evaluate whether your workplace is a toxic environment.

Positive Discipline Supports Today's Working Practices

Earlier, we looked at the five criteria for Positive Discipline. They effectively show the attitudes and actions of encouragement, or what you can do to positively impact your environment. In the table below we will translate these ideas into the professional space. The language might be different, but as you can see, the attitudes you can develop and the actions you can take as both an effective parent and an effective professional are essentially the same. This should come as a relief and quite an insight for some who may have struggled to reconcile their personal and professional selves. Read the following table from the point of view of how you, as a team member, can influence the team dynamics and management policy of your particular place of employment. Regardless of where you sit in the hierarchy, adopting these behaviors will make your life easier in the long run. Self-employed? The same ideas apply to clients, suppliers, and networks you may belong to.

CRITERIA	PARENT ATTITUDE AND BEHAVIOR	PROFESSIONAL ATTITUDE AND BEHAVIOR
Helps children/ adults feel a sense of connection, belonging, and contribution	Make sure the message of love gets through by consistent appreciation and encouragement of effort, and by focusing on solutions together.	Make sure the message of respect and caring gets through by celebrating successes, sharing compliments, and spending time getting to know your team personally. Promote group problem-solving in which everyone's ideas are heard. Redefine success as a cooperative activity with your team so everyone is on board.

Balance kindness and firmness	Show kindness for your child along with firmness to respect yourself and the needs of the situation. Get into your child's world rather than lecturing your child about your feelings.	Clear communication is key. Expectations, time frames, and benchmarks give structure; flexibility and understanding promote buy-in and ensure best results over time. Walk in their shoes and avoid judgment.
Effective in the long term	Think through your long-term goals for your kids; be careful of short-range methods that may hurt their character development. Take plenty of time for training.	Think through your long-term professional/organizational/team goals; avoid quick wins that sabotage long-term cooperation. Ensure/ask for training that is not just about technical skills but also aimed at enhancing communication and emotional intelligence in the team.
Teaches valuable social and life skills	Model good character. Make a connection before correction: physical contact, hugs, looks, smiles, and reassuring words make your child feel loved and validate his feelings. Then you can address the troubling behavior.	Model independence, compassion, and resilience. Honor your own and your collaborators' need to develop mastery of the work. Practice active listening as part of a coaching leadership/collegial style; spend one-on-one time; plan team-building activities; ensure you have all sides of the story before correcting mistakes.
Empowering for children and adults alike	Don't do for your children what they can do for themselves. Children feel respected when asked for input; teach that mistakes are opportunities to learn and to discover the unexpected. Decide what you will do and follow through. Practice positive time-out. Don't take sides in family squabbles.	Don't micromanage; give everyone autonomy to perform in their own way. This frees up time and energy for you to focus on strategic tasks (if that is part of your role). Ask for input. Have a clear problem-solving protocol. Enforce agreements. Celebrate mistakes as opportunities for learning and creativity. Encourage a time-out when things get heated. Don't take sides in conflicts, and communicate your belief that others can solve their problems. Look for win-win situations.

If you take these criteria to heart, develop the attitudes, and take the necessary actions, you are likely going to transform your professional experience into something positive, supportive, and more human. You will probably also gain some real friends in the process.

We have heard plenty of examples of encouragement in action. Some creative managers throw a ball to each person in the room and give a compliment to whoever has the ball. Fellow team members can also throw the ball to their colleagues followed by an appreciation. Appreciations are extremely encouraging. They elevate each person's sense of belonging and create an energetic, positive, cooperative, and creative atmosphere for work to take place. If you work predominantly for yourself and rarely see your collaborators or clients face-to-face, you can still share a lot of encouragement and appreciation virtually. Send links to thought pieces and ideas that you think would inspire; send thank-you notes and holiday cards; send "congratulations on the promotion" notes via professional networking sites. And don't forget to encourage yourself! If your job can get a little lonely, make sure to reward yourself for achieving important goals or reaching a milestone.

POSITIVE DISCIPLINE IN ACTION

PART 1: MANAGEMENT USING POSITIVE DISCIPLINE

Melanie manages the customer service department for a large manufacturing company. A group of internal and external auditors told her that she was required to produce a "how-to" manual documenting every policy and procedure in the customer service department, step by step. This was a daunting task for Melanie and her team, who were responsible for answering nonstop customer service requests and handling complaints. Melanie immediately called a meeting with all of her direct reports, explained the difficult assignment, shared her concerns, and expressed her need for help and support. She asked everyone to share their ideas for how they could meet the requirements and still keep up with their daily responsibilities.

After brainstorming, Melanie's group decided that each person would volunteer to write one of the step-by-step procedures. Every person then committed to meet a non-negotiable deadline. Melanie expressed gratitude for their willingness to take on this extra challenge and acknowledged the difficulty they would face in juggling this new task along with nonstop customer service orders. She assured them that she would be with them each step of the way to help them through any obstacles that could prevent them from meeting the agreed-upon deadline. She also suggested that when it was all over, they would celebrate with hot fudge sundaes and a party.

Realizing that her team was going the extra mile, Melanie met with them frequently to offer support and encouragement, giving them the freedom to use their knowledge and creativity for each procedure. She gave public appreciation to those who completed the assignment. She asked those who were struggling what support they needed from her to be successful. Some of them expressed frustration because they were not good at getting their ideas down on paper. Melanie would then ask for a volunteer to help them put their ideas in written form. She would compliment each of them on their progress and give practical pointers and tips for getting the job completed. Sometimes it required moving the workload around so those who were behind would have uninterrupted time to write their procedures. Those who were struggling were offered help and support rather than criticism or blame.

Melanie was already skilled at investing time in getting to know her team personally and professionally. She knew what was going on at home and gave support and showed caring when children or family members were sick or when there were personal challenges. In her regular team and one-on-one meetings, she asked many curiosity ("what" and "how") questions in order to fully understand different points of view.

In the end, every single person in Melanie's department met the deadline. As a group, they created an outstanding product in which everyone in the department could take pride and ownership. True to her word, Melanie organized a party for the team complete with hot fudge sundaes! The team all felt cared about, appreciated, valued, and capable. Melanie felt thankful and proud that together they had succeeded. Everyone in the department used the manual and followed the protocols. Because every team member was involved and had clearly understood the purpose of the assignment, and everyone's name was included as co-authors, they were all "sold" on the final product.

PART 2: MANAGEMENT WITHOUT POSITIVE DISCIPLINE

Barbara is the accounts receivable department manager at the same company where Melanie works. She was also asked by the auditors to create a step-by-step "how-to" manual for all of the policies and procedures in her department. In her rush to please the auditors with outstanding work, Barbara holed up in her office and worked long, grueling hours detailing the procedures in her department. She didn't explain the project to her team or seek any formal input. She came out of her office once in a while to seek clarification on certain aspects of their work, but she never told them what was happening. The team members suspected something was going on because Barbara seemed so stressed and overwhelmed. When they finally caught wind of her attempt to write a procedures manual without them, they rolled their eyes and said, "How would she know? We're the ones who do the work every day. She ought to be asking us!"

After weeks of hard work, Barbara contacted the auditors to tell them she had completed the manual. She then called a meeting with her team to deliver the finished product. She was exhausted but proud of her success in meeting the audit deadline. She handed each of them a procedures manual and told them they would need to be diligent in following all of the steps and guidelines it contained. Now that the auditors had received it, they were all committed— their future reviews would be based on how well they performed in accordance with the stated policies and procedures.

As her team members thumbed through the document, hands were raised in frustration as they objected to policies they felt were unrealistic, unfair, or just plain incorrect. All of them resented being told how they had to do things when they had never been asked to give input. They felt angry that they were committed to doing things that were unrealistic given the sheer volume of their daily responsibilities. In the end, the team felt so overwhelmed by the requirements and so disrespected by Barbara that they ignored the manual and carried on doing business as usual. Barbara was furious that her team had so little regard for her hard work and frustrated that they refused to comply with the guidelines.

When the credit department complained that credit memos were not being done in the stated twenty-four-hour period, Barbara would attack the offending team member for not meeting the regulations. The team in turn commiserated behind Barbara's back. They felt misunderstood, discouraged, unappreciated, unvalued, and unimportant. They were not motivated to help Barbara succeed, so they quietly sabotaged her behind her back.

POSITIVE DISCIPLINE TOOLS

We hope that by now you see how much of the Positive Discipline philosophy and tools are applicable in the workplace as well as at home. Let's single out a few crucial ones that will ensure greater professional well-being and success.

Model Positive Behavior

Remember our earlier discussion on mirror neurons? They don't stop working just because we're now grown up. This is why, for example, yawns and laughter are infectious. Starting with yourself, look at how you can model some of the behaviors you would like to foster in others. Make an effort to really understand the bigger picture to find out what the purpose really is and then talk about it with your colleagues. Not everyone has the ability to see the bigger picture; perhaps your investigation will help someone connect the dots. Take more time to really listen to your colleagues; ask open-ended questions about "what," "when," and how." Remember people's birthdays; ask about their family life and hobbies. Share compliments and appreciations as often as you can. In short, treat others the way you would like to be treated.

Become a Top Card Detective

Try to guess a discouraged colleague's top card. Review the list of challenges associated with a particular top card and what it invites from others to get clues on how you can support the person to feel more secure and flip back into his or her strengths. Apply a coaching style by asking open-ended questions and showing real interest in the person's situation. Share experiences from your own life that may be relevant and help the person focus on solutions. However, always remember that the top card should never be used to label someone. It is just to give you clues on what strengths and challenges a person may have.

If you're feeling overly frustrated yourself, it may be a good idea to check in and make sure you're not falling back on the challenging behavior of your own top card.

How to Run Regular, Effective Team Meetings

Team meetings (like family and couple meetings) are important and serve multiple purposes: communicate new ideas and information, set goals, allow team members to inspire and motivate one another, solve problems, build consensus on policies, engage in team-building, and boost morale. When team meetings are well run and kept short, they are an enjoyable and effective way to meet these purposes. In effectively run meetings, people freely share ideas. They tend to leapfrog, not in a competitive way but in a synergistic way, which allows each idea to improve with input from the entire group. One group of junior doctors on a busy ward dubbed their weekly team meeting the "huddle." During extremely challenging or busy periods they would call daily huddles to help everyone succeed by moving the workload around so the whole group could meet their goals. Review the guidelines for family meetings and adjust them accordingly. The key is not to lose sight of encouragement and the regularity of the meeting without it running on too long and being wasteful of everyone's time and effort. Get creative in involving off-site members by using video or conference calls. Don't forget to plan/suggest regular team fun.

Never Take Sides During Conflict

Stay neutral and let those who have a conflict work it out. If you take sides, you will leave someone with the sense that he or she does not belong or is not valued. This will invite the conflict to escalate and exacerbate both parties' efforts to prove they are "right." If you are their manager, they will use you as their proving ground. If they get you to side with them, they will feel justified and "right." Taking sides is damaging to both parties and will invite more rivalry in the future. Your best bet is to have them brainstorm solutions together after a cooling-off period. Admonish them to "focus on solutions rather than assign blame," and ask them to come up with a creative way to honor both sides.

EXERCISE

Turning Your Place of Work into a Positive Place

In your journal, go through the five criteria for Positive Discipline and assess on a scale of 1 to 5 how well you feel you score in your professional life. Then make a plan for what active steps you can take to transform your experience. Review your goal-setting from earlier, and make sure your goals are measurable and time specific—in other words, write down clearly what you will do when, and how you will measure if you have been successful or not. Work this into your routine and check in regularly with your progress. As you go along, take note of any changes you experience in your professional relationships. Has anything improved? Do you feel more confident and secure in your role? Do you feel more content at home and at work?

CHAPTER 17

KNOW THYSELF

If you've consistently worked your way through this book, you are fully prepared by now to put all your newfound Positive Discipline skills into practice. Now we wish to leave you with some food for thought and inspiration for your journey ahead. We have consistently asked you to consider the long-term consequences of your parenting—and, indeed, of your behavior in general—and the impact it has on your children and others. This may be a scary thought, and yes, the sense of responsibility is huge. We don't say that to frighten you. We say that to empower you to make effective life choices. Hopefully you will find comfort in grasping more deeply how you can change your reality by changing your belief system and behavior.

CHANGING YOUR BELIEFS

Since the discovery of DNA, the notion has been propagated in science and healthcare that your genes determine who you are. This has created a rather deterministic view, meaning you inherited either good genes or bad genes, and your health and life prospects will play out accordingly. Reality, as it turns out, is more complex than that. Why else do people with similar DNA (for example, siblings, and identical twins in particular) sometimes have wildly different physical and mental health and abilities?

In the last few decades, science has turned to the environment for clues. There is now a school of thought within biology called epigenetics (look at the work of Bruce Lipton for further exploration). Epigenetics essentially shows that the environment has a deciding impact on your gene expression (the activation of your genes). In other words, the environment creates either favorable or unfavorable circumstances, and the genes, to ensure the survival of the cell that hosts them, will switch on or off in response. At all times, then, the cell is therefore either in growth mode or in survival (protection) mode, depending on its environment. Survival is more important than growth, so at the smallest hint of threat, survival will always take over. Since you are a collection of all your cells, this means that you do not grow and develop to your full potential if you are always fighting fires. Stress can actually stunt your growth. This is huge! It means you have a much greater responsibility for your physical and mental health and the health of those in your care than was previously thought. It is also hugely empowering, as it disputes the deterministic view of life that says there isn't much you can do to impact your experience. Indeed, you can, and in spades!

"Hang on," you're thinking. "This all sounds very theoretical and far removed from my everyday life." Not really. Have you ever experienced road rage? Or felt deeply offended when someone at work took credit for your project? Or felt outright murderous when a loved one lied to you? Remember that rush of emotion? That is the fight-flight-or-freeze response in action (as discussed in Chapter 11). It is the body responding to a perceived threat. This response is a very clever survival mechanism, as it overrides your ability for rational thought and instead makes you act in a way that will ensure survival. This response is six times more powerful than the rational response, and is therefore much more likely to kick in when you experience stress. It is an illustration of what each little cell is going through. Anyone who has either taken an exam or been in a job interview and completely lost their ability to string together a thought or a sentence will understand. It is not a growth and learning mode—in fact, when you're in that state you can't even access all your existing knowledge, never mind learn new things. Imagine the effect over time if a person is in nearly constant fight-flight-or-freeze mode. How can anyone maximize his or her potential? A lot of latent talent and ability may never be developed.

Why does this matter for parenting? Well, remember our earlier discussion on how young children are able to absorb a huge amount of learning through observation? Your job as a parent is to keep your children safe and loved, and the environment you create has a direct impact on your child's abilities to develop certain skills as well as maintain good mental and physical health. Without the ability to distinguish fact from fiction, the child will store as facts in the subconscious mind everything she hears and observes. These "truths" will therefore impact the child's beliefs about herself and the world, and affect her subsequent behavior. Depending on whether the child *feels* threatened or safe, her cells will be in survival or growth mode, and will either help or hinder her ability to learn and grow. Biology reflects what is happening subconsciously.

So what can you do about this? The magic with behavior is that you can change it at any time in your life. Epigenetics applies here as well—the environment you are in, and which you create, affects the traits and behaviors you develop. Throughout this book, we have suggested that the starting point to changing behavior is with yourself. That includes taking an honest look at your own mistaken beliefs to see what you are potentially projecting onto your kids, including negative self-affirming views (the stories we tell about ourselves that help manifest our view of ourselves). If you believe that life is a constant slog or that you are never perfect enough, you probably aren't instilling a sense of wonder and capability in your child.

You create a healthy environment for your kids by modeling that you are willing to work on yourself. In doing so, you are also training yourself to get better at it. Heard the famous sayings "Fake it till you make it" and "Feel the fear and do it anyway"? By practicing the correct behavior, even if you don't yet feel that confident inside (your own belief system is being challenged but you are overriding your insecurities and doing it anyway), you are growing your behavioral muscles and will, over time, change. Biology works in your favor here too. The neural pathways in your brain will change over time to new preferred pathways, which means the new behavior will soon be second nature.

Changing your behavior is a crucial part of personal growth.

MINDFULNESS

Mindfulness is a mental state achieved by focusing your awareness on the present moment while calmly acknowledging and accepting your feelings, thoughts, and bodily sensations. There is a huge body of evidence that confirms the therapeutic benefits of practicing mindfulness, primarily as it helps you to stay calm and not react to external events without first reflecting on the correct behavior. Put another way, mindfulness helps you to control and manage your fight-flight-or-freeze response. This is a wonderful life skill that can be learned and taught to children. There are two aspects of this definition: awareness and acceptance.

It can be a great sense of comfort to know that by using the body's own abilities for relaxation and self-healing, you can learn to calm down and let go when you feel anxious and angry. Knowing this makes it easier to catch yourself when stress hormones kick in. When you're feeling overwhelmed, focus on your breathing. Illustrate to your child how a simple thing like managing your breath can help anxious feelings subside. The "brain in the palm of the hand" is a great example to use. Teaching kids to be aware of their thoughts and feelings will help them greatly as they create their private logic and learn to interpret the events of their lives.

Learning to accept how you feel in any given moment is really healthy and can help you (and your child) understand the difference between feelings and behavior. It is okay to feel how you feel, but it is not okay to behave in a way that is detrimental to others (and yourself), regardless of those feelings. By addressing the behavior and any mistaken beliefs behind the behavior, we validate someone's emotions while giving him or her the ability to turn a destructive behavior into a productive one. Discussing mindfulness with children can help clarify the difference between feelings and behavior, and help us come up with better solutions to our problems.

Mindfulness also trains you in "mind control," which is very empowering. Do you often feel like you have a monkey chattering nonstop in your head? Do you wish you could just get that monkey to shut up and leave you in peace? Most of us do! Mindfulness, and meditation in particular, can help you to quiet that chatter. The benefit is a relief from the constant worrying, often focused on a future that is uncertain and a past that is gone anyway, leaving you feeling powerless in both instances. Instead you become present in the now, the only part of time and indeed life that is ever under your control—the current moment. This ability to calm the mind and relax helps you to be more observant of what is really going on inside. You can better hear the inner voice that guides you to wise decisions for yourself and your family and helps you stay on course in life.

How can you train in being more mindful? Nonreligious mindfulness meditation training is offered in many places. Many people find nature, exercising, and the arts to be great sources of inspiration and comfort. If you are religious, practices such as prayer or attending sermons might be helpful to you.

Carl Jung, another forebearer of modern psychology, posited the idea that human intelligence is a multifaceted phenomenon. He spoke of physical, emotional, intellectual, and spiritual intelligence. Alfred Adler spoke of social intelligence, or *Gemeinschaftsgefühl*. He also shared a sense of spirituality: "There is a logic from the head. There is also a logic from the heart; and there is an even deeper logic from the whole."

Let's look at these different intelligences. If on a daily, weekly, or at least monthly basis you take time to protect and nurture yourself in all these areas, you are well on your way to a mindful life. If you then teach your children to find their own way to develop these intelligences, you are providing them with a most extraordinary life skill. How might that look?

- *Physical intelligence.* Ensure you engage in and model a healthy lifestyle as much as possible, including exercise, fresh air, sufficient sleep, and a healthy diet. Stress management techniques such as meditation and yoga are also great tools. Often the body can help us release frustration through exercise, and it is important to express anger verbally in a constructive way so it doesn't get stored up in the body.

- *Emotional intelligence.* Practice being in tune with your feelings, naming them and expressing them in a healthy way. Positive Discipline helps if you remember to delve into your own "belief behind the behavior" and seek out encouragement and appreciation.

- *Intellectual intelligence.* This involves being intellectually stimulated in what you do on a regular basis, as well as seeking out new ideas and learning to stretch yourself. It may involve healthy debate and discussion with colleagues, family, and friends. If you feel like the majority of your time is spent driving your child back and forth, and if you're craving discussion that isn't about the practicalities of everyday life, professional engagements, reading, movies, lectures, and further education all help to stimulate the mind.

- *Spiritual intelligence.* At the outset, this involves seeking out and developing curiosity about the greater mysteries of life. Why are we here, how did it all begin, and where is it going? Religion, philosophy, arts, and science all strive to answer these questions. One great privilege in our time is that we don't have to choose just one way to seek truth. We can choose many. The key is to not shy away from these questions and conversations with your children.

- *Social intelligence.* This is the fundamental Adlerian principle upon which rests our need to belong and feel significant, for we are essentially social beings. Social intelligence includes active family and community engagement and respect; participation in humanitarian and religious organizations, charitable causes, and volunteering; and artistic expression and sharing.

Mindfulness takes time to develop. What is important to remember is that the end goal is not important; it is the act of pursuing mindfulness that matters most. It is worth spending some time investigating how well you nurture yourself in all of the above areas, and get a practice or a system in place for maintaining this healthy nurturing.

If the subconscious mind stores your interpretation of your experiences, the conscious mind is what chooses behavior in a mindful way—it is your free will. By being present in the moment, you can override subconsciously stored negative beliefs that lead to destructive behaviors, and instead choose better options. By being present and aware, you can catch yourself before you react and do something you'll later regret. This way you can start to really take control over your life and create your own reality.

LIVING LIFE FULLY

We have described mindfulness as being focused and relaxed in the present moment. An added benefit of this practice is that it helps you work through your fears and insecurities, instead of hiding them behind a mask or fake persona. By taking on different roles instead of being your real self, you give in to the mistaken beliefs you may have about who you "should be" and what kind of behavior is required to be accepted and successful. The risk is that you are playing at life rather than fully experiencing it.

Have you noticed how your children seem to have a knack for sniffing out when you are being real and when you are faking it? As a professional woman heard from her seven-year-old daughter who had observed her mom running into her boss on the weekend, "Mom, why did you laugh so loudly when you met that man? It sounded silly and he wasn't very funny." This ability can be rather unnerving. Let their honesty inform your behavior, and you'll find that it's much easier to make authentic decisions and stand by them, becoming a more mindful parent and human being.

Some people take comfort from the roles they assign themselves. Be cautious of letting one role become your sole purpose in life. The function of being a parent does not require that you alter who you are. Just try to be present in the moment to make sure you do not overreact to unexpected behaviors, and try to monitor your feelings and alter your behavior to model a positive and fruitful solution to the issue or situation at hand.

PARTING THOUGHTS

Between the event and your reaction there is a space, a moment to pause, in which you can catch yourself, become aware of what is happening, and choose a constructive response rather than a destructive one. In the Introduction, we highlighted a number of challenges the modern parent faces. Understandably, many feel totally overwhelmed—they understand what to do but not *how* to do it. Maybe looking for more theories, say, or gurus to find your way isn't the answer; that just gives you more "what." Perhaps it is more about looking within to find that space and work on your reactivity. Stop, listen mindfully, and give yourself a chance to hear that proverbial inner voice. Realize how utterly powerful you are as a person to affect your environment. This space is where wisdom lives, and wisdom leads to proactive behaviors, peace, and equanimity. Every human being has the power to claim this space, and as a parent, you have the opportunity to help shape our future by wise parenting of the next generation. How exciting is that?

You undoubtedly want so much for your children. It can be hard sometimes to stop yourself from setting unrealistic expectations, both for yourself as a parent and for your children, or from falling into fear and worry. Maybe you want them to have the "dream childhood." The dream childhood is one that has a balance of security, challenges, adventures, and setbacks. What is important is that your child's childhood be healthy and sound, with many happy memories, and that it sets him or her on the path to becoming a thriving adult. You can't control everything that is going to happen to your child, but you can hugely impact it.

So let's dream for a moment about all the things we had or would have liked to have had in our childhood. What does that ideal childhood look like? How did you feel? What did you do? Now go and create that for you child. Model physical and emotional health. Stretch yourself and them intellectually by learning, discovering culture, and having adventures. Get involved in your community. Don't be afraid to talk about the bigger and deeper ideas: why suffering exists, what love is, and what happens after all this. Listen to their ideas and you will be amazed! Children are born with a hunger to know, to learn, to experience. By guiding them, you are also reigniting your own life flame.

As you reach the end of this book, our hope is that you feel empowered and excited—empowered by all the tools and exercises, and excited to get on with creating positive change in your life. Remember that perfection is not required! What *is* required is effort—long-term effort that will give long-term rewards. Don't expect overnight miracles. They are not likely to last anyway. Don't lose hope when something that worked previously seems to fail; try again, in a new and creative way. It is a journey, not a final destination, as the saying goes. If you take away just one tool from this book, let it be encouragement. It is truly universal, benefiting yourself, your family, your friends, and your colleagues. So much of life may feel seemingly out of your hands, but you do have some control over your inner state. Let that space be a positive one. Live life to the fullest, and your children will do the same.

TOP TWENTY CHALLENGES AND TOOLS TO CORRECT THEM

In this section, we will list the top twenty challenges (in no particular order of importance) parents have with their children that most consistently come up in our work with parents across the world. If you don't see your challenge listed here, look for a similar one, or go back and review the five criteria for Positive Discipline in Chapter 2 and think about how you can apply them in your parenting. The Mistaken Goal Chart, reproduced in Appendix 2, is also a very good all-encompassing tool to regularly go back to in order to review both challenges and progress. It is important to remember that there isn't one tool that works for every child in every situation. That is why we offer so many Positive Discipline tools.

All Positive Discipline tools fulfill the five criteria for Positive Discipline. In addition, there are also a few core principles that underpin these criteria. Before you engage in any kind of corrective action, ask yourself if your intended behavior is based on these principles: "Am I being kind and firm? Remember to connect before I correct. Will this solution invite cooperation? Am I going for a short-term solution or one that requires training that ensures long-term benefits? Have

I fully understood my child's belief behind the behavior?" There are many possibilities to help children feel better so they'll do better. Positive Discipline Tools are *not* techniques; rather, they are tools based on principles. Techniques are very narrow and often don't work in the long term. A principle is wider and deeper and there are many ways to apply it.

Some parents think these methods take too much time, but if you think about it, it is more a matter of new skills and habits than time. It takes just as much time to lecture, scold, punish, or be angry. Changing habits and learning new skills isn't easy until it becomes easy! In the meantime, be kind to yourself. All parents go through times when they feel overwhelmed. Keep remembering that mistakes are wonderful opportunities to learn. Also try to use these tools mindfully—the feeling behind what you do is as important as what you do.

1. ATTENTION SEEKING

All children crave their parents' attention, but if you're feeling annoyed, irritated, worried, or guilty, then it may be an indication that the child is engaged in the mistaken belief of undue attention. For undue attention, the belief is "I belong only when you pay constant attention to me and/or give me special service." The coded message that provides clues for encouragement is "Notice me. Involve me usefully."

TOOL: Redirect

Instead of saying "don't," redirect to "do." Involve the child in a task to give useful attention. For example, if you are having a conversation with someone and your child keeps interrupting, explain that you need three minutes to finish your conversation. Give your child a timer so he or she can tell you when it is time for you to finish your conversation and give him or her your undivided attention.

TOOL: Special Time

Schedule special time that is different from regular time. Take turns choosing an activity you both enjoy from a list you have brainstormed together (remember to put your cellphone away so you won't be distracted). Age guidelines:

- Two to six years old: ten minutes a day
- Seven to twelve years old: at least thirty minutes a week
- Thirteen and older: once a month (and make the activity something your teen can't resist)

TOOL: Nonverbal Signals

Parents often talk too much. A silent signal can speak louder than words. Set up nonverbal signals in advance so you can communicate with your child as a reminder of manners. It is also helpful to ignore the behavior and touch without using words. When you feel annoyed and/or irritated, try putting your hand on your heart to signal "I love you." You'll both feel better.

TOOL: Show Faith

Avoid special service. Have faith in the child's ability to deal with his or her feelings (don't fix the problem or rescue the child). When we show faith in our children they develop courage and faith in themselves.

2. BACK-TALK, BEING RUDE OR DISRESPECTFUL, AND SWEARING

When our children are rude to us or to other people, we may feel hurt, disappointed, disbelieving, or disgusted. We can feel as if we are failing as parents. Sometimes our feelings of embarrassment, shame, or pain may even cause us to hurt back. It's important to remember that for the mistaken goal of revenge, the belief is "I don't belong, and that hurts, so I'll get even by hurting others." It is often caused by the child having been hurt by something previously, which may need to be recognized (if it is you, you may need to ask forgiveness). The coded message that provides clues for encouragement is "I'm hurting. Validate my feelings."

TOOL: Validate Feelings

Allow children to have their feelings so they can learn they are capable of dealing with them. Don't try to fix, rescue, or talk children out of their feelings. Validate the child's hurt feelings (you might have to guess what they are): "You seem really [angry, upset, sad]."

TOOL: Take a Time-Out

People *do* better when they *feel* better. Positive time-out helps us cool off and feel better. Suggest a positive time-out for both of you. Step out of the revenge cycle by avoiding punishment and retaliation; then focus on solutions in a time of calm.

TOOL: Use "I" Messages

Share your feelings using an "I" message: "I feel hurt by the tone that you used and I wish that you would speak to me in a voice that is respectful so I can hear you better." When you communicate using "I" messages, it takes the person off the defensive, provides him with the opportunity to practice empathy toward you, and creates connection before correction.

TOOL: Don't Back-Talk Back

Do not rise to the challenge and find yourself being rude, loud, or disrespectful back. This creates a power struggle or a revenge cycle. Once you have both taken some time to calm down until you can be respectful, take responsibility for your part: "I realize I talked disrespectfully to you by sounding bossy or critical."

3. BEDTIME HASSLES

Bedtime hassles can be avoided if new skills are taught in a fun way. During a calm time with small children, you can make it a game to brush their teeth. They can try to "beat the clock," or just simply feel good about their accomplishment as you say, "See, you can do it." Once children have the skills, their cooperation will increase tremendously if they are involved in the process of creating routine charts during a no-conflict time.

TOOL: Set Up Routines

Create a routine *with* your child and then stick to it. Brainstorm tasks that need to be done (bedtime, morning, homework, etc.) and take pictures of your child doing each task. Display the chart in a place that's easy to see. Do not take away from feelings of capability by adding rewards.

TOOL: Show Faith

We tend to underestimate what our children can do. When we show faith in our children, they develop courage and faith in themselves. Instead of lecturing, fixing, or doing it for them, say, "I have faith in you. I know you can handle this."

TOOL: One Word

Just as with nonverbal signals, sometimes using one word is enough to communicate your expectations. Don't fall into the trap of being drawn into their drama. Avoid lecturing and nagging. Use one word as a kind reminder: "Bedtime." "Clothes" (as a reminder to lay out their clothes the night before). When agreements are made together in advance, one word is often all that needs to be said.

TOOL: Family Meetings

Children learn social and life skills during weekly family meetings. For a detailed description of family meetings, see Chapter 10.

4. CHORES

Training is an important part of teaching children life skills. Don't expect children to know what to do without step-by-step training. It's also helpful to remember that their standards of cleanliness differ wildly from yours, so you can't simply tell your child to clean his room and expect him to clean it to your satisfaction. When it comes to chores or other tasks around the home it's important to remember not to use bribery or rewards. Rewards cover up the inner good feeling of accomplishment that helps children develop a strong sense of capability.

TOOL: Take Time for Training

Explain the task in a kind way as you perform it while your child watches. Do the task together. Have your child do it by herself while you supervise. When she feels ready, let her perform the task on her own. Don't step in and correct it or do it for her—let her own it.

TOOL: Practice

Practice is an important part of "taking time for training." For example, let children take a turn setting the timer to see how long it takes for them to do all the tasks on their chore chart (or anything else you want to teach). Ask your children what ideas they have to improve their time. Keep solving problems together and keep practicing.

TOOL: Letting Go

Letting go does not mean abandoning your child. It means allowing your child to learn responsibility and to feel capable. Take small steps in letting go. Take time for training and then step back. Have faith in your child to learn from his or her mistakes. And remember, your way is not always the best way.

TOOL: Winning Cooperation

This involves including children in the decision-making process. Just like adults, kids are much more likely to be cooperative if they feel heard and part of creating the solution. Focus on solutions to problems instead of blame: "What should we do about getting the chores done?" instead of "Did you do your chores?" During a family meeting, you can make a list of chores that need to be done each week and rotate assignments.

5. ENTITLEMENT

Many parents will confess that they have been known to overindulge their children with material things or to give in to demands from their children. Working parents may be especially prone to this mistake if they feel guilty about being gone during the day, and try to make up for it by purchasing material items for their children or doing things for them. But then their children are robbed of the opportunity to develop many important life skills, such as resilience, patience, concern for others, and problem-solving. They don't develop the courage and self-confidence that come from finding they can survive disappointment and recover from mistakes on their own. An unhealthy sense of entitlement often ensues.

TOOL: Avoid Pampering

It is not your job to *make* your children suffer; it is your job to *allow* them to suffer. Pampering creates weakness because children develop the belief that others should do everything for them. One of the greatest gifts you can give your children is to allow them to develop the belief "I am capable." Never do for a child what he can do for himself.

TOOL: Encouragement

Use encouraging statements instead of praise. For example, "You worked really hard on that—you must be so proud of yourself."

Encouragement is different from praise, which sounds like this: "You got an A, I'm so proud of you." Can you hear the difference in language between encouragement and praise? Encouragement focuses on an internal locus of control and leads to resiliency and to the child feeling empowered, whereas praise focuses on an external locus of control and builds dependency. It is okay to use a little praise. Every child wants to hear that his or her parent is proud of him or her. Just notice that too much praise can invite your child to depend on the opinions of others.

TOOL: Ask for Help

Telling children they are capable is not effective. They must have opportunities to experience feeling capable. This comes from them being able to contribute. It helps to let go of things needing to be done your way, which may lead to criticism. Look for every opportunity to say "I need your help" and allow them to do it their way. Be sure to let them know how much you appreciate their effort and help.

TOOL: Jobs

Children learn life skills, develop social interest, and feel capable by helping out at home. Brainstorm a family job list together. Create fun ways to rotate jobs, such as a job wheel with a spinner, job charts, or a job jar from which everyone draws two chores for the week. Take time for job training: do chores with them the first six years. Discuss all problems at a family meeting and focus on solutions.

6. FEELING INSECURE OR LACKING CONFIDENCE

The child who believes he or she is not capable may not cause you many problems during the day but may haunt you at night, when you have time to think about how he or she seems to have given up.

Unlike the child who says "I can't" just to get you to pay attention, the child operating from assumed inadequacy really believes it. It is tempting to do more things for this child; however, that may increase his or her feelings of inadequacy.

TOOL: Break the Code

For assumed inadequacy, the belief is "I give up. Leave me alone." The coded message that provides clues for encouragement is "Don't give up on me. Show me a small step."

TOOL: Small Steps

Break tasks down to allow children to experience success. An example is to say "I'll draw one half of the circle, and you can draw the other half" or "I will do the first two steps of this algebra problem, and then you can do the next two." Children give up the belief that they can't when they achieve small steps.

TOOL: Set Up Opportunities for Success

To set up opportunities for success, encourage improvement, not perfection, and build on interests. Then when things don't go according to plan, continue to be encouraging by making comments such as "It's okay to make mistakes. That's how we learn" and "Remember how hard it was when you first tried? Now you have mastered it."

TOOL: Show Faith

If you don't have faith in your children, how else will they learn to have faith in themselves? The foundation actions to show faith in your children are avoidance actions, such as avoiding overparenting, avoiding rescuing, avoiding fixing, and avoiding reminding (lecturing).

TOOL: Take Time for Training

Teach a skill but don't do the work for him or her. As Rudolf Dreikurs said, "A mother who constantly reminds and does things for a child unnecessarily not only takes a child's responsibility away from him but also becomes dependent on him for her feeling of importance as a mother."

7. HOMEWORK HASSLES

The more you make homework your job, the less your children make it theirs. Kids who think homework is more important to their parents than it is to them don't take the responsibility on themselves. Remind yourself that your child isn't lacking ability; he or she is just not interested, or feels discouraged and hopeless. This child probably never needs a reminder to do what she loves or is good at.

TOOL: Connection Before Correction

Create closeness and trust instead of distance and hostility by making sure the message of love gets through: "You are more important to me than your grades. What do your grades mean to you?" Begin by validating feelings and showing understanding: "Your homework is not your priority, and it needs to get done now." Then give choices: "Would you like me to help you or do you want to try it on your own first?" Finish by agreeing on a time for completion and check in. "How long do you think it will take you to complete this assignment? I will give you a ten-minute reminder before I come and check on you." An alternative is to ask curiosity questions: "What will happen if you don't get your homework done? Are you willing to experience those consequences? If not, what do you need to do?"

TOOL: Logical Consequences

Too often logical consequences are poorly disguised punishments. It is important to follow the 3 R's and an H of Logical Consequences.

If any of these characteristics are missing, it is not a logical consequence.

The consequence must be:

- *Related.* Clearly explain how the child's action related to the consequence.

- *Respectful.* Make sure the consequence is not punishing and disrespectful to the child.

- *Reasonable.* The consequence should be reasonable given the event in question.

- *Helpful.* Ensure that the consequence will help the child understand the connection between cause and effect and how she can avoid a similar consequence in the future.

Whenever possible, forget about consequences and focus on solutions *with* your child. Or ask curiosity questions to help your child explore the consequences of his or her choices, and never impose consequences.

TOOL: Limited Choices

Children may not have a choice about many things, such as whether or not to do their homework. Homework needs to be done, but children can be offered a choice as to when they would like to do it, such as right after school, just before dinner, or after dinner.

TOOL: Kind and Firm

Children do better when they feel better. Limits are most effective when they are set with kindness and respect. Follow through on agreements by being kind and firm at the same time. If the child does not want to finish his homework before dinner and that is what was agreed, instead of scolding, threatening, or nagging, be kind *and* firm: "I know you don't want to do your homework, *and* what was our agreement about when it would be done?" Kindly and quietly wait for the answer.

8. IGNORING/NOT LISTENING

When parents say, "My child doesn't listen," what they sometimes really mean is "My child doesn't obey." Most kids don't listen to parents because parents talk too much and don't give children a good model of what listening is about. Children learn what they live. How can they learn to listen if parents don't model what listening looks like? Children will listen to you *after* they feel listened to. Most kids find ways to tune out when the lectures start.

TOOL: Listen

Notice how often you interrupt, explain, defend your position, lecture, or give a command when your child tries to talk to you. It's important to stop and just listen. It is okay to ask questions such as "Can you give me an example? Is there anything else?" Only when your child is finished should you ask if he or she is willing to hear you. After sharing, focus on a solution that works for both of you.

TOOL: Validate Feelings

Learn to validate your child's feelings instead of lecturing him or her about his or her behavior. You may be surprised at how much more effective this is to encourage change.

TOOL: Curiosity Questions

Parents do too much telling instead of asking and then listening. They tell their children what happened, and then tell them what caused it to happen, and then tell them how they should feel about what happened, and then tell them what they should do about what happened.

It is much more effective to ask a child what happened, what caused it to happen, how she feels about it, and what she can do about it. When you feel a lecture coming, switch to curiosity questions.

TOOL: Eye to Eye

Stop whatever you are doing. Get up and get close enough to your child to see his or her eyes. With toddlers, an important way to connect with them is to kneel down to their level so that you are eye to eye. Then you can engage in whatever correction is required. You'll notice that you speak more softly when you make the respectful effort to see your child's eyes. It also helps to model eye to eye in your adult relationships.

TOOL: Closet Listening

During the week take time to sit quietly near your children. If they ask what you want, say "I just wanted to hang out with you for a few minutes." If they talk, just listen without judging, defending, or explaining. We have heard many parents share that this tool is successful to use when children are getting ready for bed at night, in the car, or when teenagers are getting ready to go out.

9. LYING OR FABRICATING THE TRUTH

We need to deal with the reasons children lie before we can help them give up their need to lie. Usually children lie for the same reasons adults do: they feel trapped, are scared of punishment or rejection, feel threatened, or just think lying will make things easier for everyone. Often, lying is a sign of low self-esteem. People think they need to make themselves look better because they don't know they are good enough as they are. Most of us would lie to protect ourselves from punishment or disapproval. Parents who punish, judge, or lecture increase the chances that their children will lie as a defense mechanism. All of the suggestions are designed to create a nonthreatening environment where children can feel safe telling the truth.

TOOL: Curiosity Questions

Stop asking setup questions that invite lying. A setup question is one to which you already know the answer. "Did you clean your room?" Instead say, "I notice you didn't clean your room. Would you like to work on a plan for cleaning it?"

TOOL: Modeling

Set an example in telling the truth. Share with your children times when it was difficult for you to tell the truth but you decided it was more important to experience the consequences and keep your self-respect and integrity. Be sure this is honest sharing instead of a lecture.

TOOL: Appreciation

"Thank you for telling me the truth. I know that was difficult. I admire the way you are willing to face the consequences, and I know you can handle them and learn from them." Children can learn that it is safe to tell the truth in their family. Even when they forget that, they are reminded with gentleness and love.

TOOL: Mistakes Are Opportunities

Help children believe that mistakes are opportunities to learn so they won't believe they are bad and need to cover up their mistakes.

10. LACK OF MOTIVATION

Break the code and explore your child's lack of motivation through the four mistaken goals of behavior. (Refer to Chapter 8 for more information.) Find productive ways for the child to get attention, to feel like he or she's in charge, to deal with hurt feelings, or to get help when he or she feels like giving up. The challenge is to stop doing things that don't work and take time to find ways to encourage both yourself and your child.

TOOL: Encouragement

"A misbehaving child is a discouraged child," as Rudolf Dreikurs said. When children feel encouraged, misbehavior disappears. Encourage by creating connection before correction. Build on strengths. Discuss all the things that are going well for the child, giving him or her a chance to speak first. Once the child feels encouraged in his or her area of strength, you can teach him or her to manage weaknesses.

TOOL: Curiosity Questions

Ask "what" and "how" questions: "How could this be useful to you?" "What are the benefits to you now or in the future if you do this?" "How will you be affected if you choose not to do this?" "How would you be contributing to others if you did this?"

TOOL: Natural Consequences

Let the consequences be the teacher. If a child is doing nothing, this will be reflected in poor grades and in missed opportunities. Show empathy for the child when he or she experiences the consequences of inactivity. Don't display an I-told-you-so attitude. Follow up with "what" and "how" questions to help him or her understand cause and effect, and use this information to form a plan for success.

TOOL: Show Faith

Assure the child that you know he or she is capable of doing a fine job on a particular assignment and/or task. The two of you can determine together that he or she has all the necessary materials and information; then you should confidently count on him or her to do the work.

11. MORNING HASSLES

Most morning hassles are created because parents try to do everything, including dressing their children. During our parenting workshops we often ask parents, "At what age are children capable of dressing themselves?" It is amazing how many parents believe children can't do this task until they are four or five. We happen to know, from our own experience and the experience of many other parents, that children are quite capable of dressing themselves from the time they are two years old if parents take time for training, if they establish a consistent routine, and if they buy the kind of clothing that is easy to pull over or slip on.

TOOL: Problem-Solving

When children are involved in solutions, they have ownership and motivation to follow the plans they have helped create. Sit down with your children during a family meeting or a more informal session. Present the problem and ask for suggestions: "We are having a lot of morning hassles. What ideas do you have on how we could solve this problem?" Your attitude and tone of voice in presenting the problem are crucial. Humiliation invites resistance and defensiveness. Respect invites cooperation. Write down every suggestion. You can make suggestions too, but only after allowing plenty of time for theirs first. Select the suggestion that everyone can agree upon and discuss exactly how it will be implemented. Willing agreement by everyone involved is essential so that everyone feels the desire to cooperate.

TOOL: Routines

Involve children in the creation of routines. One of the best ways to avoid morning hassles is by starting the night before with a routine that helps avoid bedtime hassles. After your child makes a list (either writing him- or herself or with you transcribing) of everything he or she can think of to include as part of his or her bedtime routine, ask, "What about getting your things ready for the next morning?"

During this time, let him or her choose the clothes to wear the next morning. Next, help your children create their own morning routine chart. Let your children decide what time they need to get up, how much time they need to get ready, what part they will play in the breakfast routine, and rules about the television not being turned on until everything is done and there is time left over.

TOOL: Limited Choices

Offering limited choices instead of making demands can be very effective. Children often respond to choices when they will not respond to demands, especially when you follow the choice with "You decide." Choices should be respectful and should focus attention on the needs of the situation. Choices are also directly related to respect for, and the convenience of, others. When getting ready for school, younger children might be given the choice of putting on their shoes before the family leaves in five minutes or putting them on in the car. Older children might be given the choice of being ready in five minutes or riding their bike. Either way, Mom has to leave in five minutes.

TOOL: Natural Consequences

Natural consequences are what happen naturally, without adult interference. When you stand in the rain, you get wet; when you don't eat, you get hungry; when you forget your coat, you get cold. Are you willing to allow your child to go to school without eating breakfast, to arrive at school still wearing pajamas, or to be late without giving him or her an excuse? If you are, your child will learn from his or her mistakes. However, it is important that you don't say "I told you so"; show empathy instead.

12. NEGATIVE ATTITUDE

Negative kids often develop their attitudes and behaviors as a way of finding a unique spot in the family, rebelling against controlling parents, emulating negative parents or siblings, or reacting to parents who are always trying to make them happy. Let's not forget that the more you do for children, the more they expect, and the less capable and confident they become. Does it surprise you that instead of feeling gratitude, children just want more?

TOOL: Pay Attention

Are your children getting the impression that they are not important? Put down whatever you are doing and focus on your child as though he or she is more important than anything else you could do. Don't forget to schedule special time.

TOOL: Kind and Firm

It is important to remain centered and stop oscillating between being too firm (punishing) and too kind (permissive). It includes getting rid of "but" statements and instead using "and." For example: "I know you want some time to relax after a full day at school *and* we both know that you also have to finish your homework, so let's talk about when you can do that." Using "but" negates what was said in the first half of the sentence; consequently, it is highly ineffective and undermines your credibility. Using "and" also means you consistently decide and communicate what you will do and then stick to it.

TOOL: Connection Before Correction

Connecting with the child before you engage in a correction to change the behavior is essential to communicate belonging and significance. Sometimes the best way is nonverbal, using touch. For younger children that means physically getting down on their level and using eye contact. Connecting ensures you have the child's attention; it communicates respect and that you are open and willing to look for a win-win situation. It also helps you to manage your own emotions and stay connected to wise parenting decisions, especially in times of conflict.

TOOL: Encouragement

Instead of basing the interaction that you have with your child on negative comments and criticism, use encouragement.

13. POWER STRUGGLES

It takes two to have a power struggle. And if you're feeling angry, challenged, threatened, or defeated, you might just be involved in a power struggle. It's helpful to remember that for misguided power, the belief is "I belong only when I'm the boss, or at least when I don't let you boss me around." The coded message that provides clues for encouragement is "Let me help. Give me choices." Children will constantly test to see how much power they have. This is normal. It is wise to take these opportunities to teach them to use their power in constructive ways. A good strategy for avoiding power struggles is to look for areas where children can have positive power.

TOOL: Ask for Help

Acknowledge that you can't make the child do something, and redirect to positive power by asking for help. You can also involve the child in finding solutions during your family meetings.

TOOL: Limited Choices

Replacing commands with choices is a great way to reduce power struggles, as it fulfills the child's need for autonomy. "It's time for bed. Do you want to read me the story tonight or do you want me to read to you?"

TOOL: Control Your Behavior

Example is the best teacher. Do you expect your children to control their behavior when you don't control your own? Withdraw from the conflict and calm down. Create your own special time-out area and let your children know when you need to use it. If you can't leave the scene, count to ten or take deep breaths. If you do make a mistake and lose it, apologize to your children.

TOOL: Be Kind and Firm

Firmness and kindness should always go hand in hand, to avoid extremes of either. This is a great way to develop mutual respect. For example: "I can see that you really want to continue playing your video games, *and* it is time for dinner. What was our agreement about video games during mealtime?" Respect invites respect. When you show respect to your children, they are more likely to respect your reasonable wishes.

TOOL: Decide What You Will Do

This is one way to take a small step in letting go of the power struggles you create when trying to make children do something. Let your children know in advance what you plan to do. Decide what you will do instead of what you will make your child do: "I will only wash clothes that have been put in the hamper." Make sure to follow through.

14. REFUSING TO COOPERATE

How can you teach cooperation to your children if you do everything for them? Perhaps you are a parent who nags or pleads with your children to help and cooperate, but then gives in because it is easier to just do it yourself. What have you taught your children? Most likely they have learned to simply wait you out (ignore the nagging and pleading) until you give in. Experience and practice are the keys to effective learning. It is essential to take a close look at the experiences you are providing for your children. Are your children practicing cooperation or manipulation?

TOOL: Winning Cooperation

Good parenting means constantly looking for win-win solutions—never to win at the child's expense. Cooperation is the best way to avoid power struggles and feelings of inadequacy in children. It also models problem-solving and flexibility, both of which are essential life skills. Sticking to agreements and valuing commitments are key. Children feel encouraged when you understand and respect their point of view. This can be done in a number of ways: express understanding for the child's thoughts and feelings, show empathy without condoning challenging behavior, share a time when you have felt or behaved similarly, and share your thoughts and feelings. Children listen to you after they feel listened to. Focus on solutions together.

TOOL: Limited Choices

It helps to offer choice whenever possible to build autonomy. "I know you don't want to wash the dishes, and we can do it together. Do you want to wash or dry?"

TOOL: Act Without Words

At times the most effective thing to do is to keep your mouth shut and act. When children test your new plan, the fewer words you use the better. Keep your mouth shut and follow through on agreed-upon consequences. Make clear to them first what you are going to do. Check that they understand by asking: "What is your understanding of what I am going to do?" Follow through by acting kindly and firmly without saying a word. For example, pull over if kids fight while you are driving, and read a book until they let you know they are ready for you to start driving again.

TOOL: Set Up Routines

Create a routine *with* your child and then stick to it. Allow the routine to be the boss!

TOOL: Family Meetings

It is important to engage children in experiences where they can use their power for problem-solving. Family meetings are great for this process. Children are much more likely to cooperate and stick to agreements that they were involved in creating.

15. SHARING/SELFISHNESS

Sharing is not an inborn trait; it is learned (many adults still don't like to share). Sometimes parents expect sharing before it is developmentally appropriate. Don't expect children to share before the age of three without lots of help. It is also important to teach children when it is appropriate to share and when it's okay not to share.

TOOL: Agreements

It is easier for children to share some things if they don't have to share everything. Discuss which toys they are willing to share and make an agreement that you will ask first before taking someone's toy. Suggest that they put away the things they don't want to share when friends come over to play. With older children, it is okay to ask them to put a toy they are fighting over on a shelf until they can figure out a plan that works for both of them and they can share without fighting.

TOOL: Modeling

Share something of yours with the child, saying, "I'd like to share this with you." You may be pleasantly surprised that from time to time your child may reciprocate and share something with you without being asked. When that happens, make sure you say, "Thank you so much for sharing. You're really getting good at that."

TOOL: Distraction

Small children will not really understand sharing their toy with another child. Instead, use distraction to get small children interested in something else. It usually helps to offer them a new toy to play with, or to sing a song, tickle them, et cetera.

16. SIBLING RIVALRY

Sibling rivalry is normal and happens in just about every family that has two or more children. When it comes to your children's fights, do not take sides or try to decide who is at fault. Chances are you won't be right, because you never see everything that goes on. Right is always a matter of opinion. What seems right to you will surely seem unfair from at least one child's point of view.

TOOL: Put in the Same Boat

If you feel you must get involved to stop fights, don't become judge, jury, and executioner. Instead, put children in the same boat and treat them the same. Instead of focusing on one child as the instigator, say something like "Kids, which one of you would like to put this problem on the agenda?" or "Kids, do you need to go to your feel-good places for a while, or can you find a solution now?" or "Kids, do you want to go to separate rooms until you can find a solution?"

TOOL: Show Faith

When adults refuse to get involved in children's fights, or when they put the children in the same boat by treating them the same for fighting, the biggest motive (to get your attention) for fighting is eliminated. Have faith that they can work things out themselves. Just imagine all the life skills they are learning as a result. You can encourage them by saying something like "Let me know when you two have brainstormed ideas and have a solution you both feel good about trying."

TOOL: Special Time

Make sure that you have one-on-one special time with each child at some point during the day. If a child is jealous of another, let him know that it is okay to feel jealous, and that you want to be with each child, and that you look forward to their special time later in the day.

TOOL: Family Meetings

Have regular family meetings where children learn to verbalize compliments about the strengths of others and to brainstorm for solutions to problems. Plan fun activities after the meetings that stress cooperation and teamwork. Help the kids discover that things are more fun when they include people who have different strengths.

TOOL: Make Sure the Message of Love Gets Through

Make sure each child is loved for being the unique human he or she is. Don't compare the kids in a misguided attempt to motivate them to be like another child. This is very discouraging.

17. TANTRUMS

Many parents went without the things they wanted or needed when they were growing up, and they just honestly want their children to have more than they had. So they give in. Others just hate dealing with tantrums and public disapproval in the toy store or supermarket. So they give in. The biggest mistake is thinking that giving children everything they want is the best way to let them know they are loved. Tantrums are a form of communication. *A misbehaving child is a discouraged child.* It can be difficult to remember this when faced with annoying, challenging, or hurtful behavior. For this reason, it helps to have a plan for behavior that is a pattern.

TOOL: Hugs

A primary principle of Positive Discipline is connection before correction. A hug is a great way to make a connection. Because children have an innate desire to contribute (contribution provides feelings of belonging, significance, and capability), it is important to ask for a hug: "I need a hug" instead of "You need a hug."

TOOL: Validate Feelings

It's okay to say no to your child, and it's okay for your child to be angry. Simply validate your child's feelings: "You are feeling really upset right now, and that's okay. You wish you could have what you want." Then step back and give support while your child works through it.

TOOL: Do the Unexpected

Instead of reacting to the challenging behavior, ask your child, "Do you know I really love you?" This sometimes stops the misbehavior because your child is so surprised by your question/statement, and may feel enough belonging and significance from that simple statement to "feel better and do better." With young children, distractions work really well. Instead of fighting or getting caught up in the energy of the tantrum, make funny noises, sing a song, or say, "Let's go see what's over there."

TOOL: Act Without Words

Sometimes it is best to shut your mouth and act. If you're in a store, take your child outside and get in the car. Let him or her know that it's okay to be upset, and that you both can try again when she or he calms down.

18. TECHNOLOGY ADDICTION

The key lies in finding a balance. Yes, kids are keeping up with technology and learning new skills that will help them in their lives. And yes, too much media use does prevent them from becoming proficient in person-to-person communication skills. What you can do to help your kids find a balance between screen time and "real life" is to work together to set limits around daily media use, including your own. Try these Positive Discipline tools to help manage your family's screen time so it doesn't manage you.

TOOL: Family Meetings

Get the whole family involved in a plan for reducing screen time. Part of the solutions should include things to do in place of screen time. It is more difficult to give something up when you don't have plans for what else to do.

TOOL: Agreements

Start with one time of the day to be screen free (such as dinner), and periodically add on other times of day.

TOOL: Create a "Parking Lot" for Electronics

Have a basket or charging station in a central location in the house at which family members park their electronics during certain times of day (especially at night).

TOOL: Hold Limits with Kindness and Firmness

Changing a screen-time habit is hard; be ready for disappointment, anger, and sad feelings. Hold your limits by empathizing with a child's feelings and sticking with the limit you've set.

19. VIOLENCE, BULLYING, TEASING

If you feel hurt or find yourself saying "I can't believe he just did that," this is your clue that the child's mistaken goal of the misbehavior is revenge. When people feel hurt, they hurt back (often without even realizing what they are doing). It can be difficult to understand the mistaken goal of revenge because too often we have no idea where hurt feelings come from.

TOOL: Break the Code

For the mistaken goal of revenge, the child's belief is "I don't belong, and that hurts, so I'll get even by hurting others." The coded message that provides clues for encouragement is "I'm hurting. Validate my feelings." Even when understanding the mistaken goal of revenge, it is difficult to avoid reacting with a little revenge of our own.

TOOL: Validate Feelings

Validating a vengeful child's feelings is an important (but sometimes difficult) first step. The basic need to belong must be addressed, but it is also important to follow up by finding solutions to the problem. Examples: "I'm guessing you feel hurt by something and want to hurt back." "No wonder you feel upset when it seems you always get in trouble while others don't get caught." "Looks like you are having a bad day. Want to talk about it?" "I love you. Why don't we take a break and try again later?"

TOOL: Focus on Solutions

You can first help the child explore the consequences, or you can just go straight to focusing on solutions. Helping him or her explore the consequences of his or her choice could go something like this: "What happened? How did you feel about what happened? How do you think others felt? What did you learn from this? What ideas do you have to solve this problem now?" Asking the child "What would help you?" is the key. Focusing on solutions might sound something like this: "Would you like to brainstorm solutions with me, or would you like to put this on the family meeting agenda and get the whole family to help brainstorm solutions?"

TOOL: Act Without Words

Too often the words you use are based on reacting to the behavior. Acting without words requires that you stop and think about how to respond proactively. It requires you to get into the child's world and understand the belief behind the behavior so that you can encourage new beliefs that motivate new behavior. Using nonverbal signals is one way to act without words. Another Positive Discipline tool related to acting without words is the one-word tool. In that case, the signal is replaced by one word.

TOOL: Be Supportive

If your child is being bullied, be supportive. Watch for signs of bullying—if your child "loses" too many lunch boxes (or other items), he or she may be afraid to tell you for fear of increased bullying. If your child is afraid to go to school, it could be because of bullying. Don't hesitate to go to the principal to find solutions. Encourage teachers to have daily class meetings, which have proven to greatly reduce (if not eliminate) bullying. Because children are feeling a sense of belonging during the process, they listen to how others feel, and they are learning the benefits of focusing on solutions.

20. WHINING

Children do what works. If your child is whining, he or she is getting a response from you. Oddly enough, children seem to prefer punishment and anger to no response at all. Whining is usually based on the goal of seeking undue attention. This child believes "I belong only if you pay constant attention to me, one way or the other." For some children, whining is the only method they know to get their needs met. Other children go through a whiny time and then the whining disappears as quickly as it started. It's fun to give children the things they want and see their faces light up with joy. It's the whining and coaxing part that isn't fun.

TOOL: Silent Signal

During a happy time, work out a signal with your child about what you will do when you hear whining. Perhaps you will put your fingers in your ears and smile. Another possibility is to pat your hand over your heart as a reminder that "I love you."

TOOL: Decide What You Will Do

Tell your child what you are going to do: "When you whine, I will leave the room. Please let me know when you are willing to talk in a respectful voice so I will enjoy listening to you." Still another possibility is to explain, "It's not that I don't hear you. I just don't want to have a discussion with you until you use your regular voice. I don't answer whiny voices." When your child stops whining, say something like, "Oh, I'm so glad I can hear you now. I really want to hear what you have to say." Another possibility is to let your child know in advance that when she is whining, you will sit next to her and stroke her arm for as long as she needs to feel her feeling and until she is ready to stop.

TOOL: Hugs

Every time your child whines, take him on your lap and say, "I bet you need a big hug." Do not say anything about the whining or what the child is whining about; just hug until you both feel better.

TOOL: Encouragement

Whining could be a sign of discouragement that will stop when a child feels enough belonging and significance. Ignore the whining and find lots of ways to encourage your child.

THE CHILD'S GOAL IS:	IF THE PARENT FEELS:	AND TENDS TO REACT BY:	AND IF THE CHILD'S RESPONSE IS:	THE BELIEF BEHIND THE CHILD'S BEHAVIOR IS:
Undue attention (to keep others busy or get special service)	Annoyed Irritated Worried Guilty	Reminding Coaxing Doing things for the child he could do for himself	Stops temporarily, but later resumes same or another disturbing behavior Stops when given one-on-one attention	I count (belong) only when I'm being noticed or getting special service. I'm only important when I'm keeping you busy with me.
Misguided power (to be boss)	Angry Challenged Threatened Defeated	Fighting Giving in Thinking "You can't get away with it" or "I'll make you" Wanting to be right	Intensifies behavior Defiant compliance Feels he/she's won when parent is upset Passive power	I belong only when I'm boss, in control, or proving no one can boss me. You can't make me.
Revenge (to get even)	Hurt Disappointed Disbelieving Disgusted	Retaliating Getting even Thinking "How could you do this to me?" Taking behavior personally	Retaliates Hurts others Damages property Gets even Intensifies Escalates the same behavior or chooses another weapon	I don't think I belong, so I'll hurt others as I feel hurt. I can't be liked or loved.
Assumed inadequacy (to give up and be left alone)	Despair Hopeless Helpless Inadequate	Giving up Doing for them Overhelping Showing a lack of faith	Retreats further Passive No improvement No response Avoids trying	I don't believe I can belong, so I'll convince others not to expect anything of me. I am helpless and unable. It's no use trying because I won't do it right.

HOW ADULTS MAY CONTRIBUTE:	CODED MESSAGES:	PARENT'S PROACTIVE AND EMPOWERING RESPONSES INCLUDE:
"I don't have faith in you to deal with disappointment." "I feel guilty if you aren't happy."	Notice me. Involve me usefully.	Redirect by involving child in a useful task to gain useful attention. • Say what you will do: "I love you and ____" (Example: "I care about you and will spend time with you later"). • Avoid special services. • Say it only once and then act. • Have faith in child to deal with feelings (don't fix or rescue). • Plan special time. • Set up routines. • Engage child in problem-solving. • Use family meetings. • Ignore (touch without words). • Set up nonverbal signals.
"I'm in control and you must do what I say." "I believe that telling you what to do, and lecturing or punishing you when you don't do it, is the best way to motivate you to do better."	Let me help. Give me choices.	Acknowledge that you can't make him/her do something and redirect to positive power by asking for help. • Offer a limited choice. • Don't fight and don't give in. • Withdraw from conflict and calm down. • Be firm and kind. • Act, don't talk. • Decide what you will do. • Let routines be the boss. • Develop mutual respect. • Get help from child to set reasonable and few limits. • Practice follow-through. • Use family meetings.
"I give advice (without listening to you) because I think I'm helping." "I worry more about what the neighbors think than about what you need."	I'm hurting. Validate my feelings.	Validate child's hurt feelings (you might have to guess what they are). • Don't take behavior personally. • Step out of revenge cycle by avoiding punishment and retaliation. • Suggest positive time-out for both of you; then focus on solutions. • Use reflective listening. • Share your feelings using an "I" message. • Apologize and make amends. • Encourage strengths. • Put kids in same boat. • Use family meetings.
"I expect you to live up to my high expectations." "I thought it was my job to do things for you."	Don't give up on me. Show me a small step.	Break task down into small steps. • Make task easier until child experiences success. • Set up opportunities for success. • Take time for training. • Teach skills/show how, but don't do for. • Stop all criticism. • Encourage any positive attempt, no matter how small. • Show faith in child's abilities. • Focus on asset. • Don't pity. • Don't give up. • Enjoy the child. • Build on his/her interests. • Use family meetings.

NOTES

1. John Chancellor, "Why Emotional Intelligence (EQ) Is More Important than IQ," Owlcation, September 2, 2017.

2. Ira Wolfe, "65 Percent of Today's Students Will Be Employed in Jobs That Don't Exist Yet," Success Performance Solutions, August 26, 2013.

3. Baumrind, 1967; Furnham and Cheng, 2000; Maccoby and Martin, 1983; Masud, Thurasamy, and Ahmad, 2015; Milevsky, Schlecter, and Netter, 2007; Newman et al., 2015.

4. Baumrind, 1966, 1967, 1991, 1996.

5. Bower, 1989, 117.

6. Gershoff and Larzele, 2002; Gershoff, 2008.

7. Bruce Lipton, *The Biology of Belief* (Hay House, 2016).

8. https://software.rc.fas.harvard.edu/lds/wp-content/uploads/2010/07/Warneken_2013_Social-Research.pdf.

9. Ellen Galinsky, *Ask the Children* (William Morrow, 1999).

10. Melissa Milkie, 2012.

11. Kyle Pruett, *Fatherneed* (Harmony, 2001).

12. Eric Jackson, "The Top 8 Reasons Your Best People Are About to Quit—and How You Can Keep Them," *Forbes*, May 11, 2014.

13. Carol Dweck, *Mindset* (Random House, 2006).

14. Pew Research Center website, www.pewresearch.org.

15. Anne Boysen, "Millennials Embrace 'Resilience Parenting,'" *Shaping Tomorrow*, February 14, 2014.

16. VisionCritical website, visioncritical.com.

17. Jane Nelsen, Mary Tamborski, and Brad Ainge, *Positive Discipline Parenting Tools* (Harmony, 2016).

18. Jane Nelsen and Kelly Bartlett, *Help! My Child Is Addicted to Screens* (Positive Discipline, 2014).

19. Alfie Kohn, *Punished by Rewards* (Mariner Books, 1999).

20. Rudolph Dreikurs and Vicki Soltz, *Children: The Challenge* (Dutton, 1987).

21. Stella Chess, *Know Your Child* (Basic Books, 1989).

22. Bruce Lipton, *The Biology of Belief* (Hay House, 2009).

23. David C. Rettew and Laura McKee, "Temperament and Its Role in Developmental Psychopathology," *Harvard Review of Psychiatry* 13, no. 1 (2005): 14–27.

24. Lea Winerman, "The Mind's Mirror," *Monitor on Psychology*, 36, no. 9 (October 2005): 48.

25. Daniel Siegel, *Parenting from the Inside Out* (TarcherPerigee, 2013).

26. Jane Nelsen, *Jared's Cool-Out Space* (Positive Discipline, 2013).

27. *Sleepless in America*, video, National Geographic Channel, 2014.

28. NHLBI 2003.

29. Kate Vitasek, "Big Business Can Take a Lesson from Child Psychology," *Forbes*, June 30, 2016.

ACKNOWLEDGMENTS

FROM JOY:

"Where did we get the crazy idea that in order to make children do better first we have to make them feel worse?"

—*Jane Nelsen*

When I first came across these words of Jane Nelsen, it was like a lightbulb went off in my brain and a spark was ignited in my heart. It woke me up as an educator and as a person and I was inspired to share this wisdom with my students, colleagues, and parents.

A very special thanks to my friend and mentor Jane Nelsen for believing in us and encouraging us to write this book. I am deeply honored to be a part of your life's work and I will always cherish you as my teacher, colleague, and friend. Thank you for teaching me one of my greatest life lessons, the courage to be imperfect.

To Kristina, my fabulous friend and confidante, thank you for the tireless hours spent writing, sharing stories, and drinking tea. Over the course of the two years it took to complete this book, our lives took many unexpected turns; you were my rock! I could not have written this book without you, so thank you for helping to make this book a reality.

Max, your endless love and support have made this possible for me. Most of all I am grateful for your patience when I was overwhelmed and "flipped my lid." I am grateful for our partnership that continues to grow, for your investment in our growing family and me, and for being open to new perspectives.

To my mom and dad for always believing in me and encouraging me to pursue my dreams no matter how crazy they seemed. Mom, you are a true Positive Discipline parent! You have been and continue to be an incredible role model for me. I can only hope that I am half the mother that you have been to me.

Thank you to all my friends for their continuous support and encouragement. I am so lucky to have such dear friends and extended family in London and beyond. A special thanks to my spiritual midwife John Akayzar, who guided me through my toughest moments of writing this book.

To my baby girl, Chloe, who taught me as many lessons before she was born as she is now that we have been blessed to have her in our lives. You are the reason I wrote this book and I promise to do the very best that I can to live this book each and every day at home, at work, and with all my interactions throughout the days.

FROM KRISTINA:

To my parents, who taught me resilience, grit, and love. To my sister for your boundless love, support, and for allowing me to "parent" your daughter when she came along. To my brother for your inspiring youthfulness and unrivaled good humor.

To Joy for introducing me to Positive Discipline. For all your tireless support and generosity of spirit throughout our challenges.

To Jane for your enormous wisdom, inspiration, and guidance in this process, as well as your belief in us.

FROM ALL OF US:

To our insightful editor, Michele Eniclerico, thank you for your tireless hard work and supporting us through this labor of love. We greatly appreciate your honesty, patience, and thoughtfulness throughout this process.

Our gratitude to the outstanding team at Harmony, who work extremely efficiently and didn't give up until we got it right! To Andy Avery for your attention to detail and thoughtful comments that helped shape this book early on in the process.

Our deep appreciation goes to the many parents throughout the years who so generously shared from their own lives and experiences. To the brave parents who shared their "real stories" and showed us how mistakes are such wonderful opportunities to learn: Alicia Assad, Brad Ainge, Kristen Glosserman, Annabel Zicker, Nadine Gaudin, Karine Quarez, and the few others who remained anonymous. Deep gratitude to all the parents who answered our survey and shared their invaluable knowledge with us.

INDEX

ABOUT THE AUTHORS

JANE NELSEN, ED.D., coauthor of the bestselling Positive Discipline series, is a licensed marriage, family, and child therapist, and an internationally known speaker. Her books have sold more than two million copies worldwide. Not only is Jane an expert in Adlerian psychology, she is a mother of seven, grandmother of twenty-two, and great-grandmother of fourteen. We believe that makes her an expert on parenting. Jane lives with her husband in Sacramento and San Diego.

KRISTINA BILL, B.A., is a multitalent active across business, arts, and personal development. She coauthored the critically acclaimed *101 Days to Make a Change* (Crown House, 2011), which was nominated for the 2012 People's Book Prize in two categories: Best Nonfiction and Best Debut Writer. Kristina holds a business degree and is a certified Life Coach and Positive Discipline Parent Educator. She is a highly sought-after corporate coach specializing in leadership and personal impact. Her creative work spans music, media, and film. Kristina is Swedish by birth and lives with her partner in London.

JOY MARCHESE, M.A., is an educational consultant, a certified Positive Discipline Trainer, and a high school teacher. Joy has worked with thousands of children and families for over twenty years, both in private schools and in public schools. She is the founder of Positive Discipline UK and runs a successful coaching practice, as well as offers seminars and workshops as a Positive Discipline Trainer to various schools and organizations throughout Europe, the Middle East, Asia, and the United States. Before moving from New York City to London, Joy had a private practice as a holistic health counselor and was the program director for an educational nonprofit organization working to build resiliency with at-risk youth. Joy is the mother of a beautiful baby girl and lives with her daughter and husband in London.

JANE, KRISTINA, AND JOY see themselves as entrepreneurs and agents of change. With their combined passion and experience in parenting, education, professional development, wellness, and creativity, they are able to give you a comprehensive look into the modern world of parenting, relationships, and personal and professional development. With this book, not only will you receive the well-researched and evidence-based strategies behind the success of Positive Discipline, you may also go on a personal journey of self-discovery that will help you make concrete changes to achieve peace, happiness, and success both personally and professionally.